To My Dear Son Mark
Happy Birthday &
Merry X mas
Mom 2005

W9-ALT-624

BIRDS & BLOOMS BOOKS

BACKYARD PROJECTS

60 great step-by-step plans for you to build and enjoy
...from readers across the country.

Editor:
Jeff Nowak

Assistant Editor/Lead Woodworker:
Cliff Muehlenberg

Associate Editors:
Deb Mulvey, Jean Steiner, John Schroeder,
Mike Martin, Ken Wysocky, Tom Curl

Editorial Assistants:
Katie Kronenberg, Kris Krueger, Julie Schnittka

Art Director:
Bonnie Ziolecki

Associate Artists:
Claudia Wardius, Maribeth Greinke, Tom Hunt,
Jim Sibilski, Nancy Robjohns, Brian Sienko, Ellen Lloyd

Contributing Editor/Woodworker:
Stanley Badzinski

Woodworkers:
Joe Brenner, Norb Brunhoefer, Ron Disch,
Ted Fennig, Bret Hess, Troy Hildebrant,
Bruce Jacobson, Daniel Kennelly, Andy Rothfelder,
Tito Ruiz, Chad VanderHyden

Painter:
Sally Chadwick

Photography:
Scott Anderson, Glenn Thiesenhusen, Jerry Bojarski

Photo Studio Manager:
Anne Schimmel

Publisher:
Roy Reiman

Safety First!

Throughout this book, we've tried to emphasize safe practices in the workshop and backyard when building and installing these projects. However, caution and good judgment must be used when following the instructions in this book.

Here are some basic guidelines that should be followed when building any backyard project:

• Keep safety foremost in your mind when working in the shop or outdoors.

• All instructions and information should be carefully studied and clearly understood before you build any project.

• Take into consideration your level of skill before attempting any project.

• Study the instructions and understand how to properly operate your hand and power tools. Using hand or power tools improperly, or ignoring standard safety practices, can lead to permanent injury or death.

• Keep all electrical power tools away from water. When working in the yard, attach all electrical cords to a properly installed GFCI outlet.

• Always wear the proper eye and hearing protection.

• Read and follow all label directions when using chemical products.

• Before digging, check with local utilities to ensure that you don't hit buried wire, cable and pipe.

• Make sure projects are in compliance with local building codes.

Reiman Publications, LLC assumes no responsibility for injuries suffered or damages or losses incurred as a result of information in this book.

BIRDS & BLOOMS BOOKS

© 1999 Reiman Publications, LLC
5400 S. 60th St., Greendale WI 53129
International Standard Book Number: 0-89821-264-2
Library of Congress Catalog Card Number: 99-74411
Printed in U.S.A.

Third Printing, July 2004

We Created a Cloud of Sawdust When We 'Built' This Book

"I BUILT IT MYSELF!"

There's such a *satisfying* ring to that phrase. It puts a smile on the face of anyone who enjoys working with wood.

Here at *Birds & Blooms* magazine, we could picture proud smiles on our readers' faces as we reviewed the *hundreds* of photos and plans they sent us for consideration in this *Backyard Projects* book.

You'll find 60 of their best projects between these covers—*practical* projects you're sure to enjoy building, admiring and using in your own backyard for years to come.

Each project is presented simply, in a step-by-step fashion that will guide you smoothly from start to finish—from selecting the right materials to applying the finishing touches. It's like working alongside a wise old craftsman!

We've included projects that offer varying degrees of difficulty, so there's plenty here for everyone…whether you're a first-time birdhouse builder with basic tools, or an experienced woodworker with an elaborate shop who's ready to build an intricate arbor.

But this book is about more than the tools, hardware, measurements and materials it takes to accomplish these fun woodworking projects. It's really about the *people* who designed, built and shared them.

Their projects, their personalities and their excitement about these homecrafted items is what makes this book unique. As you browse the chapters to come, you'll see what we mean.

Meet the People Behind the Projects

The *Birds & Blooms* readers who shared these projects are friendly folks from all across the country. They took time to sit down at their kitchen tables to sketch plans and write down the directions so we could share them with you.

Many of these handymen and women went even further—they shared touching stories about why their project holds special meaning for them. You'll "meet" some interesting folks and feel you know them as you browse through this book.

Some of these home woodworkers went so far as to entrust us with plans that have been passed through generations like a treasured family heirloom. Many explained how—as they worked through the project—it rekindled fond memories of the loved one who originally built it.

PAINTING POINTERS. Mary Johnson of Parsons, Kansas will show you how to custom paint a patriotic birdhouse on page 20.

Sprinkled here and there on the following pages, you'll find some of their helpful tips, common-sense suggestions and valuable bits of "Workshop Wisdom" (we're starting you off with a sample below right).

If you're a beginning woodworker, these hints would likely take you *years* to learn on your own. And even if you're a seasoned "sawdust slinger", you're bound to find a new trick or two in this *Backyard Projects* book.

We Put 'Em to the Test

No matter which project you tackle, we know you'll enjoy some success. That's because members of our staff built every project in this book.

That means each one has been "test-built" at least twice. First, by the reader who shared it; second, by our ambitious crew of woodworkers pictured at right.

Besides generating loads of sawdust, they simplified and modified steps to make sure each plan is clear and concise. Then they helped our talented art staff prepare the "exploded-view" diagrams of each project, as well as additional detail drawings, to clearly illustrate a particular step.

Along the way, these woodworkers offer valuable hints to help you head off any problems they may have encountered.

Our woodworking team includes Reiman Publications staff members, their relatives and an eager group of retired volunteers who work at The Birdhouse Workshop, located next to our company Visitor Center in Greendale, Wisconsin.

We hope you enjoy this book as much as we enjoyed assembling it for you. Rest assured, we sanded off plenty of corners to make your shop experience nothing but smooth.

And remember, before you fire up that trusty table saw, *think safety*. Then keep in mind the woodworker's rule: "Measure Twice, Cut Once."

Ready? Start building!

GATED ARBOR. Ted Stanfield of Sharon, Connecticut was proud to share his personal plans for a beautiful gated arbor. His instructions for building the arbor and gates begin on page 135.

BACKWOODS BIRD FEEDE[R] Harold Neyes of Marshall, Illin[ois] built a special log-cabin b[ird] feeder that keeps the porch ar[ea] filled with fresh seed. He'll sh[ow] you how on page 41.

BUSY BUILDERS. Meet the volunteer woodworkers who built the backyard projects sent to us by readers. It was our way of assuring each project was "buildable", the instructions were clear and the ones you build will be as beautiful as those pictured. Our woodworking staff includes (front row, from left) Sally Chadwick (painter), Ron Disch, Norb Brunhoefer, Troy Hildebrant, Tito Ruiz, (back row, from left) Stanley Badzinski, Daniel Kennelly, Ted Fennig, Tom Curl, Chad VanderHyden, Cliff Muehlenberg, Jim Sibilski and Joe Brenner. Not pictured are Bruce Jacobson, Bret Hess and Andy Rothfelder.

Workshop Wisdom
Less Than Meets the Eye

YOU MAY have noticed that a 2 x 4 doesn't *actually* measure 2 inches x 4 inches. Its true size is 1-1/2 inches x 3-1/2 inches, less than its "nominal" thickness and width. (Length, however, always remains true.)

Keep in mind that's the case for *all* standard board dimensions. We've listed the actual size of many boards used in this book at right to help you better understand their true dimensions.

So, all dimensions on the plans in this book are based on *actual* measurements.

Standard Board Size In Inches	Actual Size In Inches
1 x 2	3/4 x 1-1/2
1 x 3	3/4 x 2-1/2
1 x 4	3/4 x 3-1/2
1 x 6	3/4 x 5-1/2
1 x 8	3/4 x 7-1/4
1 x 10	3/4 x 9-1/4
1 x 12	3/4 x 11-1/4
2 x 2	1-1/2 x 1-1/2
2 x 4	1-1/2 x 3-1/2
2 x 6	1-1/2 x 5-1/2
2 x 8	1-1/2 x 7-1/4
2 x 10	1-1/2 x 9-1/4
2 x 12	1-1/2 x 11-1/4
4 x 4	3-1/2 x 3-1/2

Backyard Projects Contents

Chapter 1
Home Tweet Home

$\mathcal{Y}$ou could say these houses are for the birds—and that's the way it should be!

Each of the birdhouses included on the following pages is well built and functional. We think you'll agree that the readers who shared these plans have a flair for designing creative and innovative birdy architecture.

You're sure to have fun building these birdhouses. Whether you make one or all of them, the feathered friends in your backyard are certain to enjoy a nesting place worthy of being called "home tweet home".

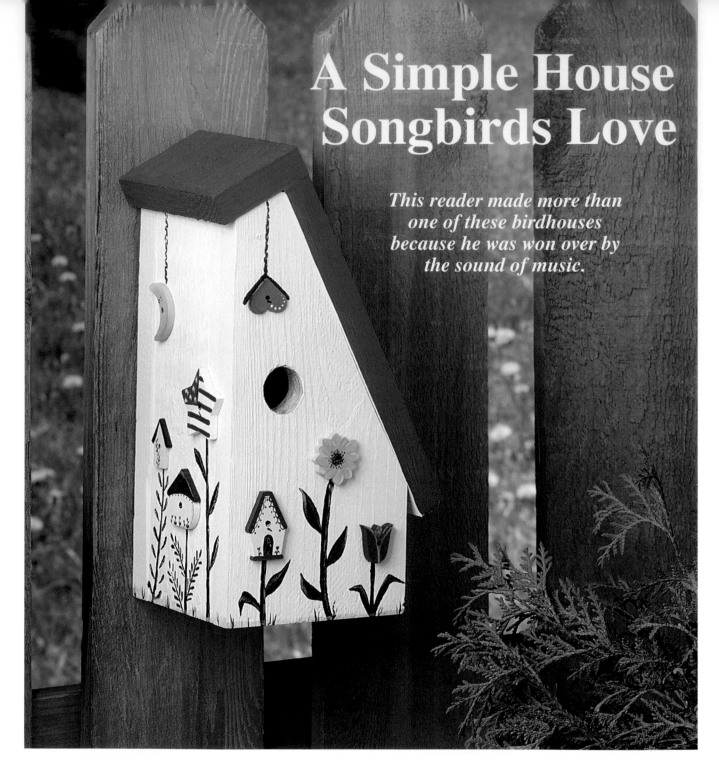

A Simple House Songbirds Love

This reader made more than one of these birdhouses because he was won over by the sound of music.

FOR YEARS, Kevan Judah built birdhouses to welcome whatever birds came along. But that was before a pint-sized vocalist won him over.

"Carolina wrens decided to raise a brood in a birdhouse like this right outside my office window," recalls Kevan, of Broken Arrow, Oklahoma. "The chalet-style birdhouse I'd put out 2 years before suited it just fine.

"I could see the birds up close—and even with the window closed, I could hear them. Man, can they sing! After that season, I put up another house like it, which attracted another pair."

Kevan's design calls for a 1-1/8-inch entrance hole, but you can experiment with other sizes to attract dif-

ferent birds. (We've included a birdhouse-building chart on page 39 to help.) "Chickadees and wrens both like this type of house, so you never know what kind of bird will move in," Kevan says.

We dressed up our version of the house with a few coats of paint (paint only the outside of the house) and added some precut wooden decorations, which are sold at most craft stores. But if you choose to make the birdhouse from cedar, it's fine to just let your creation weather naturally.

"If you're a cedar lover like me, it saves a lot of painting time," Kevan points out. "It takes about 2 years for it to weather to that beautiful silver color." 🔨

Here's What You'll Need...

❏ One 4-foot 1-inch x 6-inch rough cedar board
❏ 2-inch galvanized finishing nails
❏ 1-5/8-inch galvanized deck screws

Recommended Tools...

❏ Table saw   ❏ Power drill

Let's Start Building!

1. Cut the pieces for the birdhouse from a 4-foot 1-inch x 6-inch rough cedar board by following the board layout below left. Cut the roof, front and back pieces first. (The angle between the front and back pieces can be cut on a table saw by setting the miter gauge at 63°, or on a radial arm saw by setting the angle at 27°.) Then cut the rest of the pieces to size.

2. Bore an entrance hole in the front piece using a spade bit. Drill until the tip of the bit comes through the other side, then flip the board and finish the hole.

3. Drill a 1/2-inch hole near the top of the back for ventilation or for hanging. (This house can either be hung from the back or the long side. However, if mounting from the side, you will need a spacer board between the house and the surface it's being mounted to because of the overhanging roof.) If hanging from the back, we recommend adding another vent hole near the top of the long side.

4. Drill four 1/4-inch drainage holes in the floor.

5. Assemble the house with 2-inch finishing nails. Predrill the holes to prevent the wood from splitting. Fasten the sides to the back first, then add the front before attaching the floor.

6. Position the long section of the roof so its top edge is flush with the front and back peaks. Attach it to the front and back pieces with two 1-5/8-inch deck screws (drill pilot holes first). When it's time to clean out the birdhouse after nesting season, just remove the screws and take the roof section off.

7. Attach the short roof piece so it overlaps the long roof piece. Fasten it to the *front and back pieces* (not the long roof section or you will not be able to open the cleanout) with 2-inch finishing nails.

That's it—your birdhouse is ready to decorate or mount, and you're ready to face the music!

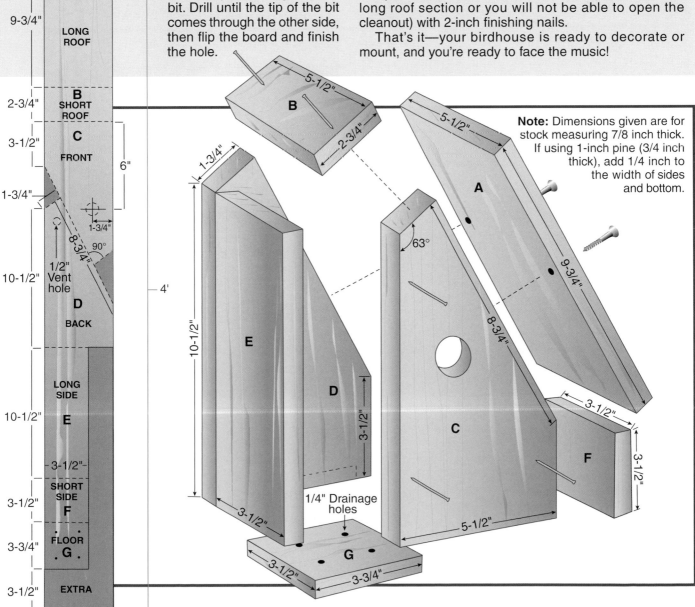

Note: Dimensions given are for stock measuring 7/8 inch thick. If using 1-inch pine (3/4 inch thick), add 1/4 inch to the width of sides and bottom.

This Birdhouse Is a Cozy Abode

The sturdy nest box will provide a refuge for your feathered friends for years to come.

THERE'S a good reason why this birdhouse may look familiar—it's featured on the cover of this book!

We were charmed by its sturdy simplicity as well as its classic good looks. Coincidentally, the man who designed and built it—Bill Dunn of Greendale, Wisconsin—is a "neighbor" who lives near our offices.

Bill started building birdhouses some years back as a high school freshman in a woodworking class. Several years later, while serving with the military in Korea, he built houses for the local birds.

Now he's retired and still building birdhouses. Over the years, Bill estimates that he's constructed about 300 abodes for his feathered friends. "Whenever I want a new one, I go downstairs, find out what kind of wood I have and start building," he says.

This particular house is designed for smaller birds such as chickadees, bluebirds or wrens. The pieces (except for the optional chimney and perch) can be cut from a 6-foot piece of 1-inch x 8-inch pine board.

Time to Talk Shop

1. Cut the pieces for the birdhouse from a 6-foot 1-inch x 8-inch board by following the board layout on the next page.

2. Cut a 45° peak on the front and back pieces. These angles are easy to cut on a table saw using the miter gauge, but they can also be cut with a hand saw. To saw these angles, first draw them by marking the center point at the top edge of the board. Then draw a guideline with a combination square.

3. Cut off each corner of the floor piece at a 45° angle to provide added ventilation and drainage.

4. Bill located the entrance hole 4-3/4 inches up from a center point marked at the bottom of the front board. We recommend checking the birdhouse-building chart on page 39 first. Then use an appropriate-size spade bit to drill a hole that's the right size and in the right position for the type of bird you wish to attract. Drill until the tip of the bit starts to come through the other side, then flip the board over and continue drilling from that side. Finish the hole by smoothing with a piece of sandpaper.

5. Round the bottom of the mounting board by using a 1-quart paint can to draw a guideline at the bottom of the board, then cut along the line with a saber saw. Cut the top of the board to match the peak.

6. Assemble the house. Start by attaching the sides to the back with 1-1/2-inch finishing nails. Then attach the front to the sides.

7. Position the floor so it sits up 3/4 inch from the bottom of the house. Predrill holes through the sides, then attach the floor with 1-5/8-inch deck screws from the

ONE OF MANY. Bill Dunn (at left) has built hundreds of birdhouses in his basement workshop. He shares one of his favorite plans for a house that will attract a variety of backyard birds.

3-5/8"

3-5/8"

45°

A
BACK

7-1/4"

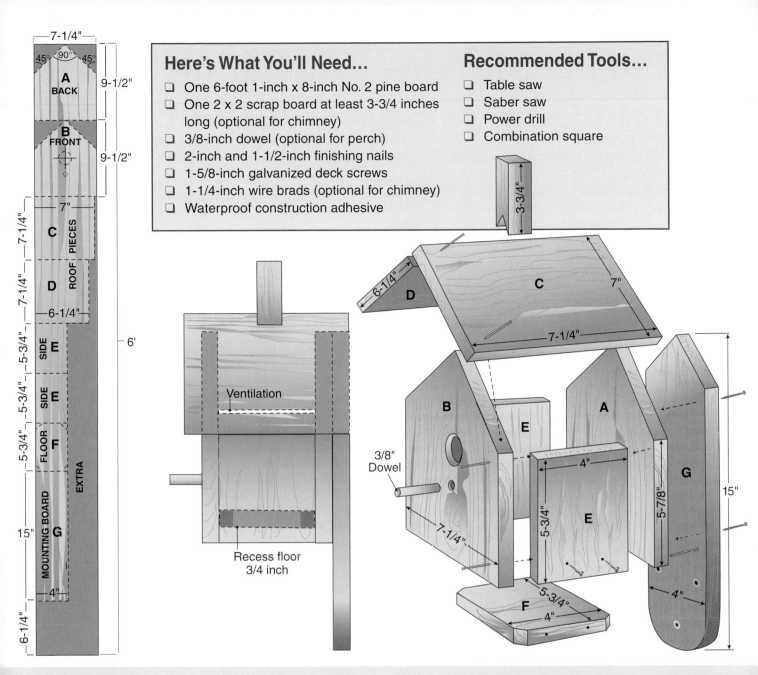

Here's What You'll Need...

❑ One 6-foot 1-inch x 8-inch No. 2 pine board
❑ One 2 x 2 scrap board at least 3-3/4 inches long (optional for chimney)
❑ 3/8-inch dowel (optional for perch)
❑ 2-inch and 1-1/2-inch finishing nails
❑ 1-5/8-inch galvanized deck screws
❑ 1-1/4-inch wire brads (optional for chimney)
❑ Waterproof construction adhesive

Recommended Tools...

❑ Table saw
❑ Saber saw
❑ Power drill
❑ Combination square

sides. Unscrew the floor to clean out the birdhouse after nesting season.

8. Attach the short piece of roof with 1-1/2-inch finishing nails. Allow a 3/4-inch overhang in back to cover the mounting board. Then nail the larger roof piece in place, overlapping the smaller piece. Use construction adhesive where the roof pieces join at the peak to keep water out of the house.

9. Attach the mounting board from the back with 1-5/8-inch deck screws. At the bottom of the mounting board, predrill three holes for screws to mount the birdhouse. Bill recommends using 2-1/2-inch galvanized deck screws.

Here Are Some Options...

• If you want to add a perch (it's not necessary for the birds), measure 2 inches down from the center point of the entrance hole. Drill a 3/8-inch hole through

the board for the perch, which is made from a 3-inch-long piece of 3/8-inch diameter dowel. Squeeze glue into the hole and tap in the dowel.

• Bill gave the birdhouse a "cozy" feel by adding a decorative "chimney" as the finishing touch. He used a leftover piece of handrail, but since flat wood is much easier to work with, we suggest using a scrap piece of 2 x 2 as shown in the plan above.

Cut a 90° notch in the center of a 2 x 2 for the chimney by making a 45° cut on each side. It's safer to cut the notch in a longer 2 x 2, then cut the piece to length. Glue it to the peak. When it dries, predrill holes on both sides of the chimney and fasten with four 1-1/4-inch wire brads.

• For a more finished appearance, round the front edges of the roof with sandpaper or a router with a roundover bit (this needs to be done before assembling). You may want to protect the wood with a coat of paint stain or polyurethane before mounting.

Purple Martins Will Think This House Is Simply *Gourd*-geous

If properly preserved, a homegrown gourd birdhouse will last for decades.

GOURDS make great birdhouses, and the time spent creating one is a worthwhile investment. Cured hard-shell gourds are almost as tough as plywood. And they will last up to 30 years if properly coated with a preservative and handled with a little care.

Gourds have been used to make purple martin houses for centuries. Native Americans used to hang them to attract martins to their settlements. Today, martins depend on people to supply them with houses and gourds. If you live east of the Rocky Mountains, you may want to give the martins a hand.

These basic gourd birdhouses are popular with the birds and purple martin "landlords". The best part is, there's no limit to the number you can produce and hang right in your yard. We've heard of one martin enthusiast who puts up and maintains more than 600 gourd houses every year!

Other birds will nest in a gourd, too. Just customize it with the proper-size entrance hole for the species you're trying to attract and place it in the right habitat. (See "Gourds Will Attract Other Birds, Too" on page 14.)

Because many *Birds & Blooms* readers have expressed an interest in learning how to make gourd houses specifically for purple martins, we've included this project. ⚒

James R. Hill, III

Here's What You'll Need...

- ❑ One hard-shell gourd, also known as a bottle gourd or birdhouse gourd
- ❑ Bleach (for disinfectant)
- ❑ Fine steel wool
- ❑ Wood preservative or copper sulfate
- ❑ Oil-based primer
- ❑ Oil-based white enamel paint
- ❑ Plastic-coated copper wire, 24 inches long
- ❑ Face mask (see "Safety First!" tip at far right)

Recommended Tools...

- ❑ Power drill
- ❑ 2-1/8-inch hole saw or a keyhole saw

Step 2

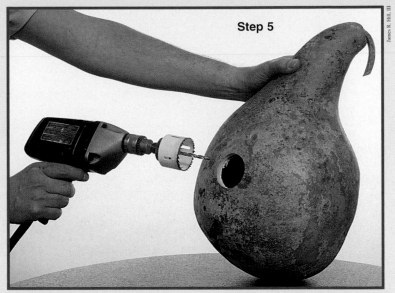

Step 5

HOMEGROWN BIRDHOUSE. Gourd houses are easy to make—but they take a bit of time and patience. It may take 3 to 6 months before a gourd completely dries and you can begin working on it. Mold will form on the gourd as it dries (at left). Don't throw it away like many first-time gourd crafters do. This is just part of the natural drying process. Eventually you'll wash the mold off and drill a 2-1/8-inch entrance hole (above) when it's completely dry. See the illustration below to help locate the entrance.

Let's Get Gourding

1. Harvest a hard-shell gourd when the vine has withered. Be careful to leave the stem attached. It's best to cut the stem with a pruning shears so you don't bruise it.

A good purple martin gourd has a diameter of about 8 to 13 inches. Wash it thoroughly in water, rinse in a solution of 1 part disinfectant (bleach works fine) and 10 parts water, and dry it with a towel.

2. Hang the gourd in a sunny spot or place it on newspaper in a warm dry spot (such as an attic or basement) for 3 to 6 months. If the gourd is lying on a flat surface, be sure to frequently turn it.

The gourd will begin to mold as it dries (see photo above left)—*don't throw it out!* This is a natural part of the curing process. Gourds dried indoors will grow the most mold and should be wiped clean frequently with the same concentration (1 to 10) of disinfectant you used for cleaning. However, discard any gourds that become soft or wrinkled.

3. Check if the gourd is dry by giving it a good shake—if the seeds rattle, you can begin making a birdhouse.

4. Soak the gourd for 15 minutes in hot soapy water, then scrape it with a dull knife to remove the outer skin and mold. Scrub the gourd in the water with fine steel wool. Rinse it well and allow it to thoroughly dry.

5. To locate the entrance hole, hold the gourd by its stem between your index finger and thumb and let it hang. Mark a center point along the outer-

most part of the curve so the hole faces straight out—not towards the sky or the ground (see illustration below).

The hole should measure 2-1/8 inches and can be easily and quickly drilled with the proper-size hole saw as pictured above. (Be sure to wear a face mask.)

You can also use a keyhole saw to cut the entrance by hand. If you do, it's best to cut the hole immediately after washing the gourd, while it's still wet.

6. Make seven drainage holes in the bottom of the gourd about 2 inches apart using a 5/16-inch drill bit.

7. With the same bit, drill two sets of holes about 2 inches from the top of the gourd's neck for hanging and ventilation. One set should be drilled perpendicular to the entrance hole and the other in line with it. (You'll only use one set of holes for hanging. Choose the pair that will allow the entrance hole to face the most open direction.)

(Continued on next page)

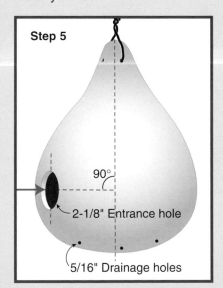

Step 5

90°

2-1/8" Entrance hole

5/16" Drainage holes

Safety First!

Protect Yourself from Harmful Gourd Dust

GOURD dust is a caustic substance. Always wear a tight-fitting dust mask when drilling gourds or scraping out seeds. You should also wear a mask when removing bird nests from the gourds in fall.

8. Remove seeds and membrane through the entrance hole with a long-handled metal spoon, screwdriver or a wire coat hanger (wear a face mask). If this is difficult, soak the gourd in water for several hours. The inside does not have to be completely clean.

9. Dip the gourd in a wood preservative for 15 minutes, weighting it down with a brick. Then remove the gourd and hang it up to dry for several days.

For a cheaper alternative, dissolve 1 pound of copper sulfate (available at garden centers and farm-supply stores) in 5 gallons of warm water and dip the gourd as instructed above. Wear rubber gloves while handling it.

HOUSE PAINTING (WITHOUT A LADDER). Purple martins prefer white houses, so painting the gourds (below) is an important part of the process. Use an oil-based primer and top coat with white exterior enamel paint. Paint only the outside, and be careful not to clog the drainage holes. Gourd houses need to be repainted every few years, but if properly maintained, they'll last for decades to come.

Step 10

Gourds need to be retreated and repainted every few years. So whatever preservative you use, store the solution in a covered plastic bucket for reuse, but keep it away from children and pets.

10. Sand the gourd smooth and paint with an oil-based primer. Allow it to dry.

11. Paint the gourd house with white exterior enamel paint with a nylon brush. (Do not use water-based latex paint because it will peel.) Apply two coats. Be careful not to clog drainage holes.

12. When dry, you can hang your gourd (you'll need at least 4 to 6 gourds to attract martins) from a 24-inch plastic-coated copper wire. Thread the wire through two of the holes directly across from each other and hang it from a support line (see page 12), below a martin house (like the one on page 34) or on a specially made gourd rack. The gourd will swing, making it less attractive to nest competitors, such as starlings.

Hang the gourd 10 to 15 feet high, with the entrance hole facing an open area.

13. In late August or early September, after the martins depart for their winter homes in the tropics, take the gourd house down for cleaning. Break up nests with the handle of a wooden spoon and shake out the contents. Then store until early spring (the martins return as early as February in the deep South) in a spot inaccessible to rodents.

Your gourd house will be ready to use again, but you might want to prepare a few more over winter, because the martins will probably bring along a few more friends!

Editor's Note: *Want to know more about martin gourd houses? A 12-page booklet, "Growing & Preparing Gourd Homes for Martins", is available for $3 from the Purple Martin Conservation Association, Edinboro University of Pennsylvania, Edinboro PA 16444. Gourd seeds and instructions to grow them are also available for $5.*

Gourds Will Attract Other Birds, Too

IF YOU LIVE in an area that's not the most suitable for attracting purple martins, don't despair. Gourds make fine homes for several varieties of cavity nesters, including bluebirds, swallows, chickadees, wrens, woodpeckers, great crested flycatchers, titmice, screech owls, kestrels and nuthatches.

Each bird has its own requirements for habitat, entrance-hole size and cavity dimensions. For instance, house wrens need a 1-inch entrance hole in a gourd 5 to 6 inches in diameter and prefer gourds hung in a shady area close to brush.

Chickadees need a 1-1/4-inch hole and like to nest in wooded areas. Bluebirds and tree swallows require a 1-1/2-inch hole and prefer to nest in open areas. For flycatchers, make the hole 1-3/4 to 2 inches in diameter and hang the gourd in a tree close to a brushy area.

A Birdhouse With Country Charm

Made from scraps of vinyl siding and wood, this birdhouse is economical and as down-home as it gets.

THIS CLEVER "bird barn" is sure to add a touch of the country to your backyard, whether it's in the city or along a rural back road.

Harlan Olson of Manitowoc, Wisconsin has given away dozens of these birdhouses. To his surprise, some of the recipients refuse to hang them outdoors.

"They say they're too nice to put outside," Harlan chuckles. "So they keep them inside for decoration."

Harlan designed the barn-style birdhouse in 1997, when a contractor was putting new vinyl siding on his house. "I asked him to leave the scraps behind, figuring I'd think of some use for them," he recalls. "Eventually, I came up with this birdhouse pattern that worked with the leftover siding.

"I made four or five barns from the stuff and gave them to relatives. Later, my nephew tore down a shed and had a bunch of extra siding. I really got busy building!"

Since then, Harlan has built nearly 50 of these barns and was getting ready to make "another 10 or 20" when we spoke to him.

He painted the first houses he made red, but now Harlan's tinkering with different shapes and designs. "The possibilities are endless," he says.

Your possibilities are endless, too. You can paint the birdhouse barn-red, develop your own color scheme or perhaps find some scraps of real weathered barn wood.

However, we recommend using light-colored siding or painting dark siding a light color before assembling. This will help keep the house cooler for the birds inside when the sun is shining.

When you're finished, go ahead and hang the birdhouse outside—no matter how pretty it is! The birds will love its country decor.

(Step-by-step instructions begin on next page)

Here's What You'll Need...

❏ One 2-foot 1-inch x 10-inch No. 2 pine board
❏ 20 inches of double 4-inch vinyl siding
❏ 1-1/4-inch galvanized deck screws
❏ 1-1/4-inch wire brads
❏ 1/4-inch dowel (optional for perch)
❏ Glue stick
❏ Two screw eyes and chain for hanging the birdhouse

Recommended Tools...

❏ Table saw
❏ Saber saw
❏ Utility knife
❏ Hot-melt glue gun (optional)
❏ Hand saw
❏ Power drill
❏ Router (optional)

Time to Raise the Barn!

1. Begin by making two copies of the full-size pattern shown at right—one for the front of the birdhouse and one for the back. Cut the paper patterns out with a scissors about 1/2 inch outside the guidelines.

2. If you like the optional router cuts pictured on the front of the barn, it's important to make them *before* cutting the front and back pieces from the pine board.

To do this, lay the patterns on a 2-foot-long piece of 1-inch x 10-inch pine, making sure the grain runs horizontally. Lightly trace the pattern onto the wood, then mark where you'd like to route the grooves.

If you don't have a router or just want to keep things simple, move on to the next step.

3. Use a glue stick or spray adhesive to affix the patterns to the 1-inch x 8-inch board, but apply it sparingly so they'll peel off easily later. Again, make sure the grain runs horizontally. (See "Workshop Wisdom" on page 103 for a helpful hint.)

4. Cut out the front and back pieces with a saber saw or band saw. It might be tempting to cut the board in half and stack the two pieces of wood to cut them both at once, but we don't recommend it—most saber saws are made to cut material 1 inch thick or less.

Your cuts must be precise for the vinyl siding to fit properly. Cut carefully along the guideline, then peel off the pattern. If any adhesive remains on the wood, remove it by lightly sanding.

5. On the bottom edge of the front and back pieces, make

a 5/16-inch deep cut with a hand saw, 1/4 inch in from each corner. The bottom edge of the siding will fit into this slot.

6. Drill the entrance hole with a spade bit to a size appropriate for the type of bird you'd like to attract. (See page 39 for recommended hole sizes.) If you'd like an optional perch, drill a 1/4-inch hole 1 inch below the entrance hole. Cut a 3-inch piece of 1/4-inch dowel and glue it into the hole.

7. From the remaining pine board, cut a piece 5-5/8 inches x 6-3/4 inches for the floor. Predrill holes through the front and back pieces and into the floor board and secure it with 1-1/4-inch deck screws. (After nesting season, when it's time to clean out the birdhouse, remove the screws and the floor.) Add 1/4-inch drainage holes in the floor and vent holes under the barn eaves. Also add a 1/2-inch vent hole near the top of the back piece.

8. Rip a 2-foot 3/4-inch x 1/2-inch strip from the pine board. Cut two pieces from it—one 6-3/4 inches long (the inside roof beam) and another 10 inches long (the outside roof beam). Glue the inside roof beam to the front and back pieces and attach with 1-1/4-inch wire brads nailed through the front and back to hold it in place. Lay the outside roof beam aside.

9. Cut two pieces of double 4-inch vinyl siding into 10-inch lengths. (It's really 8 inches from top to bottom, but has two 4-inch sections molded into it.) Trim only the bottom 4-inch section with a utility knife to "indent" it 7/8 inch on each end. (The fin-

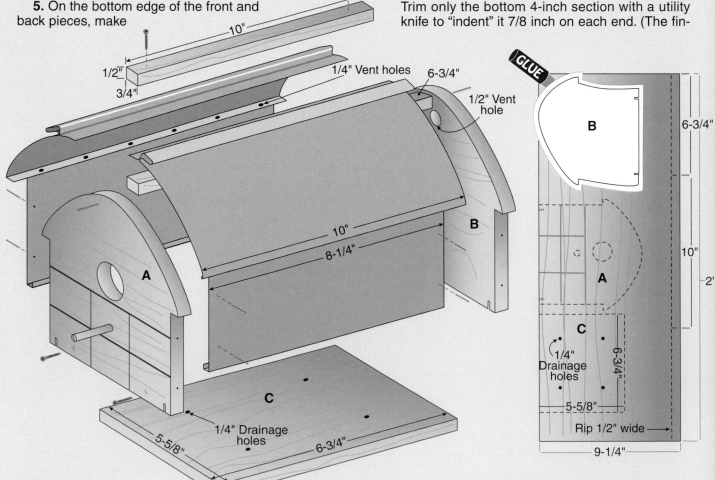

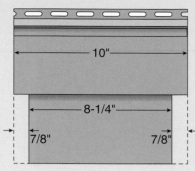

ished width of the bottom section should be 8-1/4 inches.) The wider top section provides an overhang.

10. Slip the bottom lip of the siding into the slots, then fasten the bottom sections of the siding to the front and back pieces with wire brads.

11. Roll the siding so each piece meets and overlaps at the peak of the roof. To help hold them in place, tack with hot-melt glue. Then place the outside roof beam into the channel formed by the siding as it meets at the peak. Predrill two holes to fasten the beam to the front and back pieces. Attach with two 1-1/4-inch deck screws. Be careful not to tighten the screws too much, or the wood may split.

12. You can use just about any type of strong chain or wire to hang this birdhouse. (We don't recommend rope or twine because it can break or be chewed by predators.) If you want to use two screw eyes and a chain like we did in the photo on page 15, use two small pliers to twist open the screw eyes.

Before adding the chain, screw the eyes into the outside roof beam between the galvanized screws. Then insert the ends of the chain into the screw eyes and close them with a pliers. Your barn is ready for some feathered "livestock"!

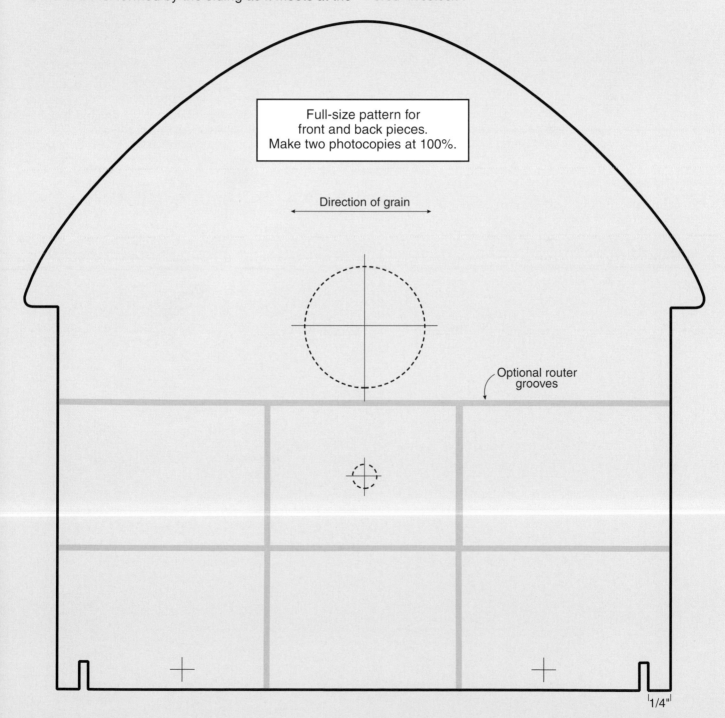

Full-size pattern for front and back pieces. Make two photocopies at 100%.

Direction of grain

Optional router grooves

1/4"

For 'Wrent'...
To a Bird with a Lot of Spirit!

You'll flip your lid over this inventive birdhouse.
It will even give you a chance to "sneak a peek" at baby birds.

IF YOU'VE longed for a birdhouse that actually allows a glimpse at what's going on inside, this one's for you.

Mary Johnson of Parsons, Kansas developed this design several years ago using two basic pieces of hardware to make it possible—a small hinge and a simple hook and eye.

Ever since Mary first heard the song of wrens near her patio, she's been building houses to encourage them to stay around. After experimenting with several different designs, Mary developed this hinged-roof house that lets her get a close look at the nesting process. She painted it in bright colors, let it sit for several days to air out any odors and mounted it on a shed as soon as she saw a wren in her yard. (If you like Mary's festive decorating, see "A Patriotic Paint Job" on page 20 so you can paint your birdhouse the same way.)

"The house hadn't been in place more than 30 minutes when the wren took it over," Mary says. "If people tell you wrens won't nest in bright-colored houses, they're wrong!"

If you want to look in on the nestlings, Mary offers this advice. "Remember to only peek for a moment, so you don't worry Mom or Dad," she says. "They already have their 'wings full'." (It's best not to disturb the nestlings after about 10 days or they may try to leave the nest too soon.)

The hinged roof is also handy for cleaning out the house after nesting season. However, with wrens, it's not necessary to remove all the contents from the previous season—they'll often take care of spring cleaning themselves.

Give this easy-to-make house a try. We think you'll soon be hooked on its clever design.

Here's What You'll Need...

- ❑ 5-foot 1-inch x 6-inch No. 2 pine board
- ❑ 1-1/2-inch hinge
- ❑ 2-inch and 1-5/8-inch galvanized deck screws
- ❑ 5/16-inch dowel, 3 inches long (optional for perch)
- ❑ Hook-and-eye assembly
- ❑ Waterproof glue

Recommended Tools...

- ❑ Table saw
- ❑ Power drill
- ❑ Combination square

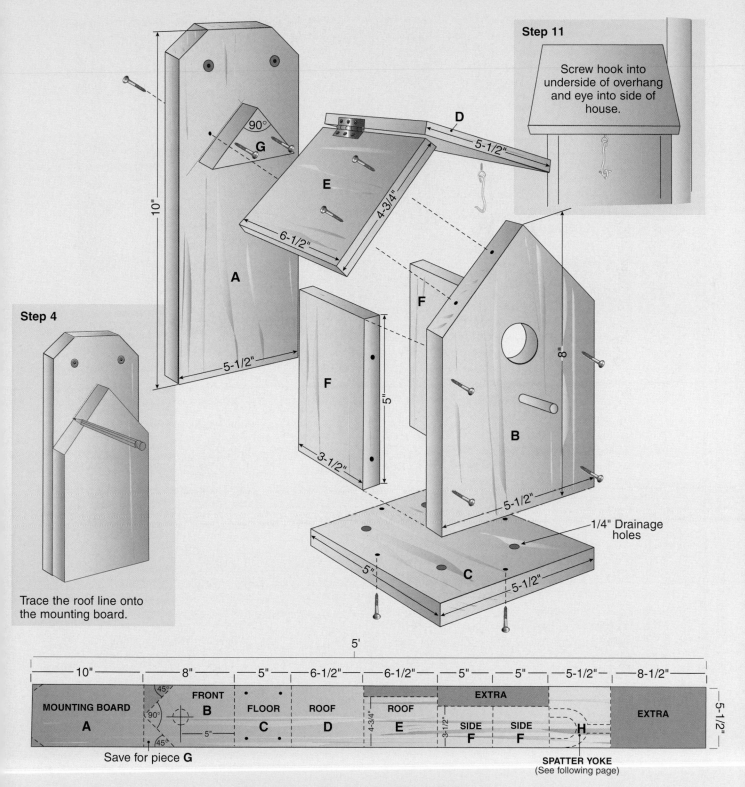

Step 11
Screw hook into underside of overhang and eye into side of house.

10"

90°

G

D

5-1/2"

E

6-1/2"

4-3/4"

A

5-1/2"

F

5"

3-1/2"

F

8"

B

5-1/2"

1/4" Drainage holes

5"

C

5-1/2"

Step 4

Trace the roof line onto the mounting board.

5'

10"	8"	5"	6-1/2"	6-1/2"	5"	5"	5-1/2"	8-1/2"
	45°	**FRONT**	**FLOOR**	**ROOF**	**ROOF**	**EXTRA**		
MOUNTING BOARD	90°	**B**	**C**	**D**	4-3/4" **E**	3-1/2" **SIDE F**	**SIDE F**	**EXTRA**
A	45°	5"					**H**	

Save for piece **G**

SPATTER YOKE
(See following page)

5-1/2"

Let's Start Building

1. Cut the birdhouse pieces from a 5-foot 1-inch x 6-inch pine board as pictured in the board layout above.

2. On the front piece, make two 45° angle cuts to form a centered peak.

3. Save a triangular piece from the front board for the rear support or make one from the corner of a scrap board.

4. Place the front of the birdhouse on top of the mount-ing board, lining them up so the bottom and sides are flush (see illustration above left). Hold the pieces firmly in place and, with a pencil, draw the roof line onto the mounting board. Fasten the triangular roof support on the mounting board so the right angle (90°) aligns with the peak you just drew. Predrill the holes, then attach with 1-5/8-inch deck screws.

(Continued on next page)

A Patriotic Paint Job

DRESSING UP this birdhouse is a simple task, with the right equipment, says Mary Johnson of Parsons, Kansas, who built and painted this clever patriotic wren house.

Mary (that's her pictured at right) decorates her birdhouses with folk-art paints, available at Wal-Mart and most hobby and craft stores.

"I usually use antique white as a base coat, with a contrasting color for the perch, roof edges and outer edges of the floor," Mary says. "Then I just stencil on different designs."

For the patriotic house, Mary stenciled on red and blue hearts, stars and birds. The rooftop flags are painted by hand. To ensure straight stripes, Mary used strips of masking tape to help.

The last step is the most fun. Mary lightly "spatters" the whole birdhouse with a contrasting color of paint.

She does this with a homemade "spatter yoke" (below), which is very simple to make. Just form a "Y" shape out of scrap pine, stretch a bit of wire window screen across the opening and staple it in place.

Here's the trick to "spattering":

1. Put a small amount of paint on a piece of aluminum foil and thin it with a drop or two of water.

2. Rub the bristles of a toothbrush in the paint.

3. While holding the spatter yoke over the birdhouse, press the toothbrush onto the screen and brush with an outward stroke, flinging the paint toward the house.

"This technique does a great job of spattering and saves your fingers from getting covered with paint," Mary says.

5. "Dog-ear" the top corners of the mounting board by cutting 1 inch off each corner at a 45° angle.

6. On the front piece, measure 5 inches from the bottom and drill a centered 1-inch entrance hole with a spade bit. Drill a 5/16-inch hole about 1 inch below the entrance if you'd like to add an optional perch, however, it's not necessary for the birds' sake.

7. Attach the front piece to the sides, then the sides to the mounting board using 1-5/8-inch deck screws (drill pilot holes first). The bottom edges of all four pieces should be flush. There will be a small gap at the top of each side for ventilation.

8. Drill four 1/4-inch drainage holes in the floor approximately 1-1/2 inches from the edge. Set the house on top of the floor board so it's flush on all sides. Then, holding the floor in place, turn it over and drill pilot holes from the bottom for 1-5/8-inch deck screws.

9. Put the smaller roof piece in place and attach it to the front piece and through the mounting board with 1-5/8-inch deck screws. Drill pilot holes.

10. Position the larger roof piece (this will be the door) so it overlaps the smaller piece at the peak. Allow 1/16-inch clearance next to the mounting board so it doesn't rub when you open it. Attach the longer roof piece to the smaller one with a 1-1/2-inch hinge.

11. Screw the hook into the underside of the right overhang and the eye into the right side of the house (as pictured on the previous page) to keep the door closed. Make sure the hook and eye are on the snug side so the house is safe from predators.

12. Glue the optional perch in place. If you're leaving the house unfinished, your work is done—just mount it with 2-1/2-inch deck screws (drill pilot holes for the screws first) and wait for the wrens to move in. If you want to give it a patriotic paint job similar to Mary's, see the story at left for instructions.

Workshop Wisdom
Leave the Inside Natural

BIRDHOUSES may be painted or stained on the outside, but the interiors should never be finished—just leave them natural.

Exterior stain and paints work well and will hold up to the elements. However, never use any lead-based alkyd paints or creosote.

The easiest way to preserve a birdhouse is to build it from cedar. It may cost a little more, but it's basically weatherproof and will turn a beautiful natural silver color in just a few years.

H

Give Bluebirds a Helping Hand

Thanks to man-made nest boxes, the population of these beautiful birds is on its way up!

SIMPLE SOLUTION. Man-made nest boxes have made a difference for bluebirds. They provide the nesting cavities these birds need to raise their young. The side door (above) is great for monitoring the activity in these birdhouses.

WANT TO DO something that's good for bluebirds—*and* fun for you? Build them a nesting box!

You'll be charmed by the brilliant birds' beauty and their cheerful singing. Since their diet consists primarily of insects and grubs, your garden may benefit, too.

In the past, bluebirds relied on woodpeckers and other cavity-dwellers to provide the majority of their nesting places. They'd select abandoned cavities in dead trees or rotten fence posts to raise their families. As development wiped out many of these natural nesting sites, the bluebird population declined dramatically.

But man-made nesting boxes like the one above have played a vital role in reviving the beloved bluebird.

Bluebirds prefer to nest in open areas with low or sparse ground cover. The North American Bluebird Society, which provided the plans, says rural areas, cemeteries, golf courses and parkways with minimal human traffic are good places to mount these nesting boxes.

The bluebird box above has a couple of interesting fea-

(Continued on next page)

tures worth pointing out. It's assembled with the rough side of the wood facing *out* so it more closely resembles the birds' natural nesting sites. And there's no perch. Notches beneath the entrance hole provide footing for bluebirds, but discourage visits from competing house sparrows and wrens.

The swing-open side is convenient, also. You can check for nests of unwanted birds (since house sparrows and European starlings are not protected by law, simply remove their nests) and have easy access for cleaning out the bluebird's nesting materials after the young have fledged. You'll want to do this immediately, since bluebirds often raise as many as three broods in one nesting season.

Best of all, the swing-open side will give you a chance to peek in on the nestlings for whom you've provided a sturdy and safe home.

Step 9

A RELIABLE MOUNT. Mounting these nest boxes is easy. Simply drive a 3/4-inch piece of electrical conduit into the ground and attach the house 5 feet above the ground with conduit straps as shown above. Attach a predator guard and coat the pipe with grease to deter nest raiders.

Here's What You'll Need...

❑ One 4-foot 1-inch x 6-inch rough cedar board
❑ One 10-1/2-inch 1-inch x 10-inch rough cedar board
❑ 2-inch finishing nails
❑ 1-5/8-inch galvanized deck screws
❑ 8 feet of 3/4-inch conduit and two straps

Recommended Tools...

❑ Table saw   ❑ Power drill

Editor's Note: *For more information on bluebirds, send a self-addressed stamped envelope to the North American Bluebird Society, Dept. G, P.O. Box 74, Darlington WI 53530-0074 or visit their Web site at www.cobleskill. edu/nabs/.*

Attract the Bluebird Of Happiness

1. Using the full width of a 4-foot 1-inch x 6-inch rough cedar board, cut the pieces as pictured in the board layout at far right. When making the angled cuts, keep in mind that all the pieces will be assembled rough side out.

2. Drill a 1-1/2-inch entrance hole in the front piece with a spade bit for eastern and western bluebirds. In areas where mountain bluebirds reside, drill the entrance hole 1-9/16 inches. Center the hole about 1-1/2 inches from the top of the board.

3. Starting about 1/2 inch below the entrance hole, make three shallow cuts about 1/4 inch apart on both sides of the front board. On a table saw, set the blade at 1/8 inch deep and use the saw's miter gauge to cut the notches. Flip the piece over and make identical cuts on the other side. If you want the front board to fit flush with the roof, cut an optional angle along the top edge by tilting the table saw blade 12°.

4. Position the sides flush with the top of the front board. Fasten the *right* side to the front with two 2-inch finishing nails. Fasten the *left* side to the front with a 1-5/8-inch deck screw near the top (drill a pilot hole first). Be careful not to over-tighten this screw because it will serve as a hinge for the side door.

5. Cut an optional 12° angle along the top edge of the back piece if you want it to meet flush with the roof. Then place the assembled front and sides on top of the back piece, leaving the top of the back board 1/4 inch higher than the sides. The space provides ventilation.

Turn the box over and attach the back to the left side of the box (the one with the "hinge") with a 1-5/8-inch deck screw. Drill a pilot hole first *directly opposite* the screw on the front (this ensures proper hinge action) and fasten with a screw. Again, don't make it too tight. Secure the

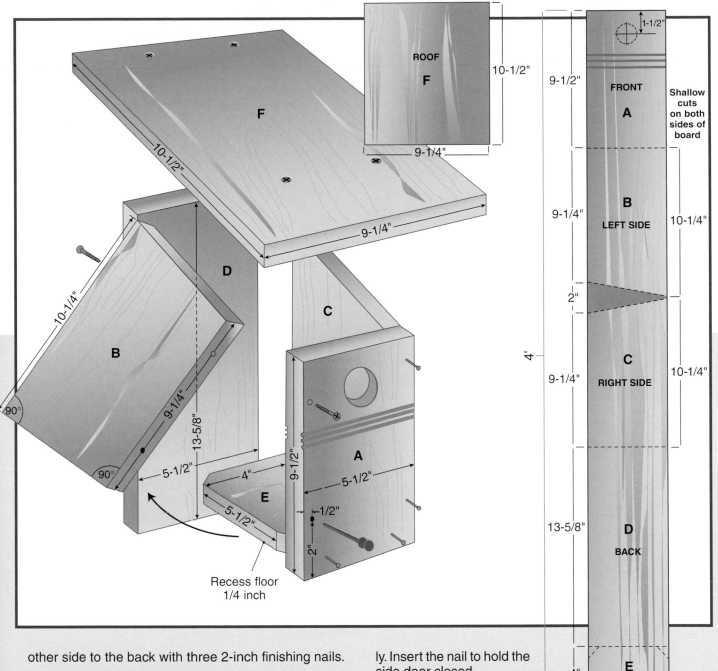

ROOF
F
10-1/2"
9-1/4"

10-1/2"
9-1/4"

F

10-1/4"
9-1/4"
13-5/8"

B
90°
90°
D
C
A
E

5-1/2"
4"
9-1/2"
5-1/2"
1/2"
2"

Recess floor
1/4 inch

1-1/2"
9-1/2"
FRONT
A

Shallow
cuts
on both
sides of
board

9-1/4"
B
LEFT SIDE
10-1/4"

2"

9-1/4"
C
RIGHT SIDE
10-1/4"

13-5/8"
D
BACK

4'

4"
E
FLOOR
5-1/2"
3/8"

other side to the back with three 2-inch finishing nails.

6. Cut about 1/2 inch off each corner of the floor to provide drainage. Position the floor 1/4 inch up from the bottom of the nest box. (Recessing the floor helps keep the box dry.) Attach the floor with 2-inch finishing nails on the front, back and right side. *Do not use nails through the "hinged" left side or you won't be able to open it.*

Step 7

7. Drill a hole on the hinged side 2 inches up from the bottom and 1/2 inch in from the side. Drill at a slight downward angle, going through the front of the house and into the side. Make the hole large enough for a double-headed nail to slip in and out easi-ly. Insert the nail to hold the side door closed.

8. Align the roof flush with the back and attach with 1-5/8-inch deck screws (drill pilot holes first).

9. The nest box is ready to mount. Keep the entrance hole about 5 feet above ground.

The Bluebird Society recommends attaching it to a smooth round pipe, such as a 3/4-inch electrical conduit, rather than on a tree or fence. Conduit straps (pictured at far left) attached to the back work well for mounting. For extra protection from predators, coat the pipe with grease and put hardware cloth under the box to deter snakes.

Face the box away from prevailing winds and towards a tree or shrub no more than 100 feet away. This will provide a landing spot for young birds when they first leave the box—a sight that'll show you why these feathered friends are called the "bluebird of happiness".

Fun's Brewing With This Coffee-Can Birdhouse

Sit down, relax and have another cup of coffee. You'll need to empty the can first to make this simple birdhouse.

HERE'S a terrific birdhouse that's as enjoyable as the aroma of the morning's first pot of coffee.

And it has a lot more going for it, too. The house is simple to build, costs pennies to make and is a great way to recycle coffee cans and scrap wood. As a bonus, it's a breeze to clean out after nesting season—just slip out the dowel and empty the can.

You don't have to paint it, but if you're like reader Jean Walters of Fort Worth, Texas who shared this plan, you might want to dress it up.

"These are great projects for children's groups, and they cost about $2 to make," Jean says. "Have your friends and neighbors save their coffee cans and precut the wood yourself. Then let the kids paint and assemble them. (If you plan to decorate your birdhouse, Jean suggests sanding and painting the pieces before assembly.) They're easy as store-bought pie to make, and sell faster than a cup of coffee in a doughnut shop.

Here's What You'll Need...

❏ Two scraps of 3/4-inch-thick pine board, measuring at least 4-1/2 inches square
❏ Two 1/4-inch-thick plywood or paneling scraps, measuring at least 6 inches x 9 inches each
❏ 1/4-inch dowel, 8-1/2 inches long
❏ 1-1/4-inch finishing nails
❏ One 11-ounce coffee can
❏ Hooks, wire or a chain for hanging the birdhouse

Recommended Tools...

❏ Table saw   ❏ Power drill

Start Building...We'll Keep the Coffee Warm!

1. Cut the ends of the birdhouse 4-1/2 inches square from scrap pine boards.

2. Locate the entrance hole in one board by measuring 3-7/16 inches from one corner. (When measuring, place your ruler diagonally from corner to corner and draw a light pencil line.) Be sure to mark the corner from which you're measuring—you'll need to measure from it again in step 4.

3. Drill a 1-inch entrance hole for wrens or the appropriate-size hole for other small birds you'd like to attract. (See the birdhouse-building guidelines on page 39.)

4. Hold the front and back pieces together in a vise or clamp them together. Locate the perch by measuring 1-1/4 inches from the same corner used in step 2 and mark this spot on the pencil line. Then drill a 1/4-inch hole through the front piece (with the entrance hole) and most of the way through the back. (See "Workshop Wisdom" at right for a helpful hint.)

5. Cut the roof pieces from 1/4-inch plywood or paneling scraps. Cut one piece to measure 5-3/4 inches x 9 inches, and the other 6 inches x 9 inches.

6. Nail the roof pieces to the front and back boards with 1-1/4-inch finishing nails. The large roof piece should overlap the smaller at the peak. (If you're using paneling, the back side should face out.) Leave enough room between the front and back pieces so you can easily insert the coffee can.

7. Clean and dry the coffee can (watch out for sharp edges). Drill two 1/4-inch holes in one side of the can for drainage. Drill two more 1/4-inch holes on the opposite side of the can for ventilation.

8. Place the coffee can between the front and back boards. Cut a 1/4-inch dowel to 8-1/2 inches long and insert it through the perch holes. If the fit is too snug, lightly sand the dowel, which holds the can in place.

9. Attach a chain, hooks or wire for hanging the birdhouse. With any luck, you won't have to wait long for your feathered friends to discover the new home you've provided. Just sit back, have another cup of coffee and enjoy the show.

Workshop Wisdom
Drilling Holes Partially Through a Board

IF YOU NEED to drill a hole only partway through a board, here's an easy method to make sure you don't drill too deep.

1. Lay the drill bit against the outside edge of the board to determine the proper depth you need to drill.

2. Mark the depth on the bit with a piece of masking tape, making sure the bottom edge lines up at the depth you should stop drilling. Wrap the piece of tape around the drill bit.

3. Drill the hole into the board, stopping when you reach the bottom edge of the tape.

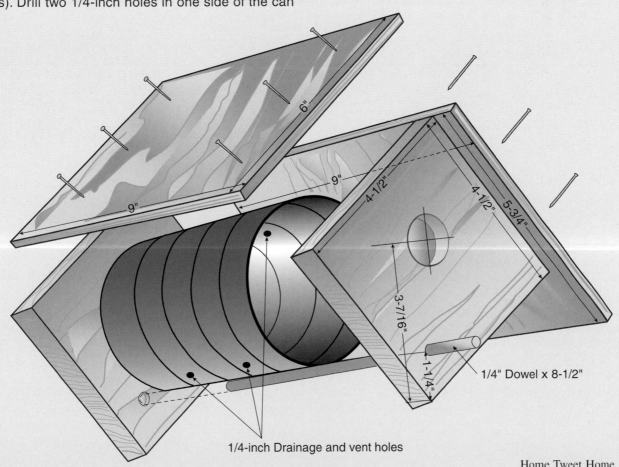

6"   9"   9"   4-1/2"   4-1/2"   5-3/4"   3-7/16"   1-1/4"   1/4" Dowel x 8-1/2"

1/4-inch Drainage and vent holes

Double Your Enjoyment with Birds *and* Blooms

This nest box duplex is joined by a handy flower box. The combination lets you reap the benefits of two projects for the price and effort of one.

IF YOU LOVE both birds and blooms but only have time to build one outdoor project, here's one that pays double dividends.

The design comes from Edward Wilson of Sheridan, Oregon, who found a clever way to combine both of his hobbies—backyard birding and flower gardening. He sent us this design of a birdhouse/flower box that has been a rousing success at his place.

"It hangs on my front porch all summer long for my family and neighbors to enjoy," Edward relates. "It's very entertaining because birds will use one of the nest boxes every year. Plus, the double pentunias I plant in the flower box give me extended color long after the nesting season."

While there are two birdhouses on this planter, it's most likely only one of them will be used at a time. That's because nesting birds are very territorial and will chase other birds from their breeding territory while raising young.

When hanging this project, be sure to find a sturdy support. It's fairly heavy on its own and will weigh even more when the plants are watered.

But we think you'll agree, this one project will give you a chance to have twice as much fun. 🔨

Building This One's Twice as Nice!

1. Cut the pieces for the birdhouse/flower box from 1-inch x 6-inch rough cedar boards by following the board layouts at far right.

2. Nail the sides of the box to the floor with 2-inch finishing nails. It's best to predrill these holes first. Drill and nail straight.

3. Cut the peaks on the front and back pieces of the birdhouses at a 45° angle.

4. Drill an entrance hole in each piece with a spade bit. Be sure to stop when the bit point goes through the board. Then flip it over and finish the hole. (To determine hole size, see the chart on page 39.)

5. Nail the fronts of each birdhouse to the sides with 2-inch finishing nails. Predrill the holes first.

6. Trim the back pieces to a width of 4 inches below the roof line using a hand, saber or jig saw. These pieces should fit snugly against the sides and floor. Before trimming these pieces, it's best to measure the

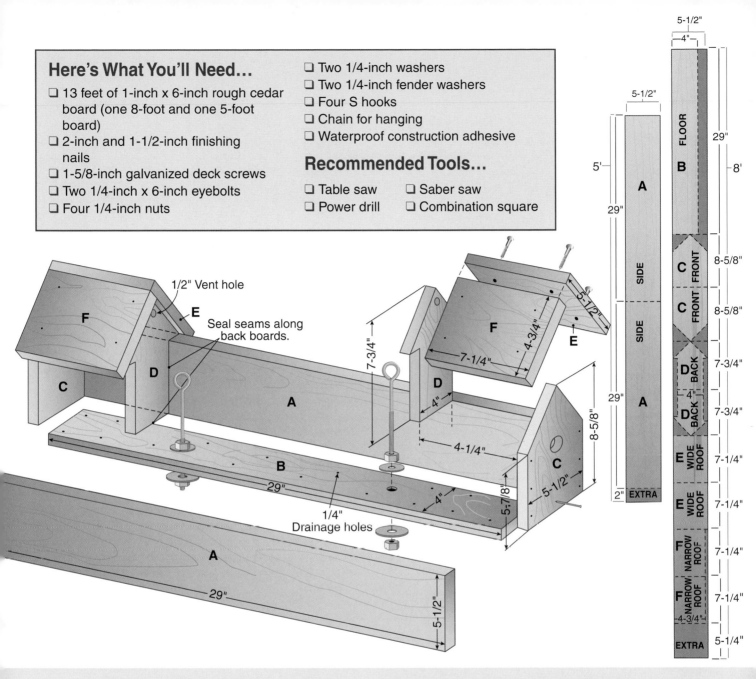

Here's What You'll Need...

❏ 13 feet of 1-inch x 6-inch rough cedar board (one 8-foot and one 5-foot board)
❏ 2-inch and 1-1/2-inch finishing nails
❏ 1-5/8-inch galvanized deck screws
❏ Two 1/4-inch x 6-inch eyebolts
❏ Four 1/4-inch nuts

❏ Two 1/4-inch washers
❏ Two 1/4-inch fender washers
❏ Four S hooks
❏ Chain for hanging
❏ Waterproof construction adhesive

Recommended Tools...

❏ Table saw   ❏ Saber saw
❏ Power drill   ❏ Combination square

---

inside width of your flower box since it may be slightly different. Then adjust accordingly.

7. Position the back pieces 4-1/4 inches from the front pieces (inside measurement). Carefully nail them in place from the outside of the box. Check the position with a combination square as you go, making sure it is straight both vertically and from side to side. (*Don't drive the nails home until you're satisfied each piece is square.*)

8. When both back pieces are nailed in place, lay a bead of waterproof construction adhesive along the bottom and side seams to keep water from the flower box from seeping into the houses. Smooth the adhesive into the seam with your finger to ensure a good seal.

9. Attach a narrow roof section to each birdhouse with 1-1/2-inch finishing nails. Set the nails so they're below the surface.

10. Fasten the wide roof sections to the birdhouses with four 1-5/8-inch deck screws. Predrill the holes first to

keep the wood from splitting. Remove the screws to clean out the birdhouses after nesting season.

11. Center and drill a 1/4-inch hole near each end of the flower box floor to hold a 1/4-inch x 6-inch eyebolt. Secure the bolts with nuts and 1/4-inch washers on the inside, and nuts and 1/4-inch fender washers on the outside. Position the outside nuts close to the ends of the bolts so the eyes will sit above the potting soil line.

12. Attach a strong chain to the bolts with sturdy S hooks. Crimp the hooks closed with pliers to secure.

13. Drill 1/4-inch drainage holes in the floor flower box and each birdhouse. Add a 1/2-inch vent hole in the back piece of each birdhouse. Locate it near the peak, just below the roof as shown in the plan.

14. Hang the planter from something secure and plant some flowers in a potting mix that drains well. Just add water; the birds will do the *nest*...oops, we mean *rest*.

STORYBOOK BIRDHOUSE. Ron Pavelka adds a whimsical touch to his cleverly built nest boxes with sweeping roof lines, rounded edges and colorful paints.

No Fairy Tale—This Birdhouse Really Is Cute

This lovely laminated lair for feathered friends is straight out of a children's storybook.

ONCE UPON A TIME, there was a birdhouse builder who found a way to use scrap wood that otherwise would have been thrown into the fireplace.

The craftsman's name was Ron Pavelka, and he constructed storybook bird abodes like the one pictured above in his little workshop located in Orange, California.

"I've built many of these storybook birdhouses for friends and family," Ron shares. "They use them to decorate their gardens and yards…the style is different, and I get lots of compliments on them."

This is one of the more challenging and time-consuming birdhouse designs in this book. But we've given you a head start by providing the patterns on page 31 to duplicate its sweeping and whimsical curves. All you'll need to add to this house is a colorful paint job.

"You can easily alter the plan to suit your own taste," Ron adds. "You'd be surprised how a difference in color or choice changes its appearance."

One word of caution—because there's a lot of wood and glue in this project, the birdhouse weighs about 8 pounds when finished. So we suggest mounting it in a sturdy place, such as on a post or on a deck rail. That way, you can be sure the feathered family that moves in will live happily ever after.

🐦 *Once Upon a Project...* 🐦

1. Enlarge the birdhouse pattern so it measures 11-1/4 inches from roof peak to floor. This can be done on a photocopy machine by increasing it 200%. Or you can make a grid of 1-inch squares and draw the pattern square by square. Also, enlarge the patterns for the roof eaves and chimney by using one of the same methods.

2. With a scissors, cut out the paper patterns (see "Workshop Wisdom" on page 103 for a helpful hint). Trace or glue the birdhouse, roof and chimney patterns onto 1-inch x 12-inch board. (Don't forget the inside area,

too. When cut out, this will become the nesting cavity.)

3. Cut out the nesting cavity area from this board using a saber saw or scroll saw. Drill a hole inside the nest cavity area for a place to insert the saw's blade.

(Continued on next page)

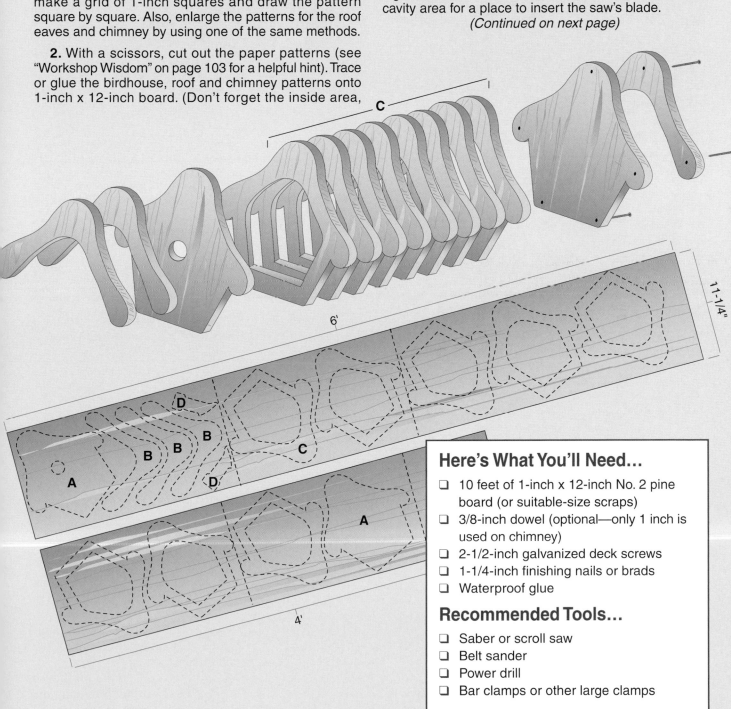

Here's What You'll Need...

- ❑ 10 feet of 1-inch x 12-inch No. 2 pine board (or suitable-size scraps)
- ❑ 3/8-inch dowel (optional—only 1 inch is used on chimney)
- ❑ 2-1/2-inch galvanized deck screws
- ❑ 1-1/4-inch finishing nails or brads
- ❑ Waterproof glue

Recommended Tools...

- ❑ Saber or scroll saw
- ❑ Belt sander
- ❑ Power drill
- ❑ Bar clamps or other large clamps

4. Cut out the outside of the birdhouse from the board, being careful to support it on your workbench so it does not break. Also cut out the roof eaves and chimney.

When finished, these pieces will serve as patterns, so sand the edges smooth. Hang on to these pieces because once your friends and family see this house, they'll want you to make one for them, too.

5. Trace the wooden birdhouse pattern (both inside and out) eight times onto the boards. Then trace only the outside of the birdhouse pattern two more times. You will not cut out a nest cavity from these two pieces because they're the front and back of the house.

Trace the roof-eaves pattern three times and the chimney twice.

6. Cut out all pieces, carefully following the guidelines you drew. (The neater you cut, the less sanding you'll have to do later.) Remember to cut the nesting cavity of each birdhouse piece first.

7. Drill an entrance hole (see chart on page 39 to help determine the size and location) into the front board with a spade bit. (See step 4 on page 26 for a helpful hint.)

8. Now it's time to glue the birdhouse pieces together (except for the back, which will be removable). Glue them in sets of two or three pieces at a time and clamp them together until dry. This will help keep the pieces from sliding out of position.

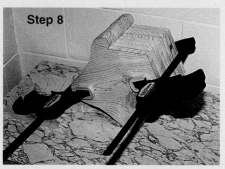
Step 8

The trick to this step is to apply an even coat of glue to each piece, line it up with the next piece and carefully tack them together with two 1-1/4-inch finishing nails or brads. This will keep the pieces from sliding as you clamp them together. Work quickly so you can clamp the pieces together before the glue sets.

If you don't have clamps large enough to hold the pieces together, place something heavy on top of each set.

After each set dries, begin gluing the sets together to form the birdhouse (see photo above). Again, clamp the sections together until the glue dries.

At the end of this step, the front of the birdhouse should be attached to eight pieces with nesting cavities.

9. Glue two roof eaves onto the front piece, using the same method as in the previous step.

10. Glue the last eave to the back piece. When dry, line up the back piece with the rest of the birdhouse and drill pilot holes for attaching it with five 2-1/2-inch deck screws. (At the end of the nesting season, remove these screws. The back of the birdhouse will open for easy cleaning.)

11. Belt sand the roof and body of the birdhouse for a smooth, one-piece appearance. This could take some time (it took us 1-1/2 hours, which included some hand sanding), so be patient.

You may also want to sand the edges round, or use a

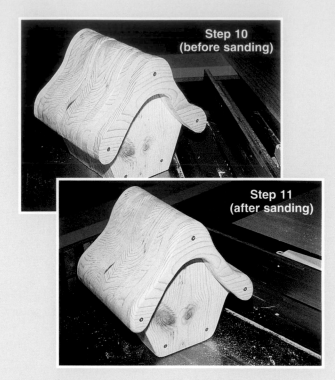
Step 10
(before sanding)

Step 11
(after sanding)

router with a round-over bit to give the birdhouse a smoother finish.

12. Drill four 1/4-inch drainage holes in the floor.

13. Glue the two chimney pieces together with waterproof glue (see below). When they're dry, sand the edges round, except at the base. This is where you'll attach the chimney to the roof.

14. Attach the chimney to the roof with waterproof glue and wire brads.

15. To add even more character to the chimney, cut two 1/2-inch pieces from a 3/8-inch-diameter dowel and glue them to the top of the chimney to resemble flues.

3/8" Dowel

You're now ready to paint, stain or decorate your storybook birdhouse. Just use your imagination…it may attract elves, gnomes, fairies or, hopefully, feathered friends.

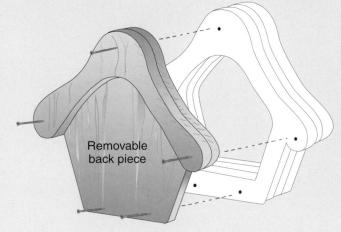
Removable
back piece

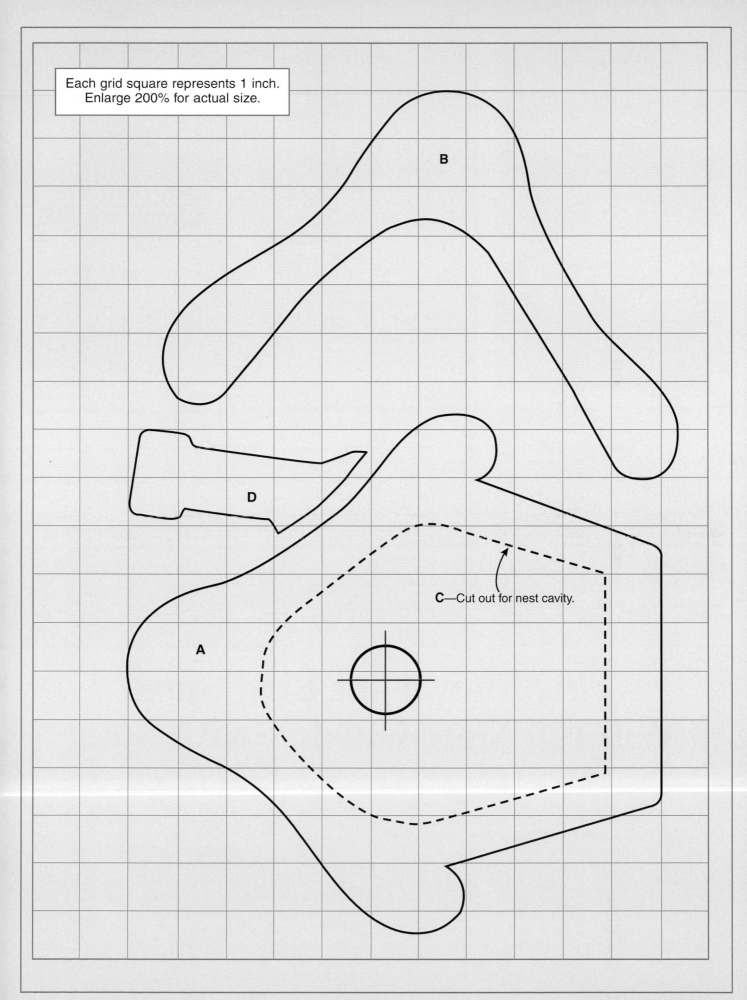

Each grid square represents 1 inch.
Enlarge 200% for actual size.

B

D

C—Cut out for nest cavity.

A

This Flowerpot Birdhouse Will Fill Your Garden with Song

With a few modifications, this clay pot will "grow" generations of wrens.

HERE'S a rather interesting twist—a flowerpot project that has nothing to do with plants and everything to do with birds.

With a little bit of remodeling, you can put out the welcome mat for wrens with this easy-to-build birdhouse, which requires a minimum of tools and effort.

Susan Vater created this birdhouse for her garden in Middleton, Wisconsin. Because the house is small, she says it's perfect for hanging in the thick vegetation that wrens prefer.

The only difficult part of this project is making the entrance hole in the flowerpot. The hole should be 1 inch in diameter, or as veteran wren house builders say, "large enough for a quarter to pass through".

Glass drill bits work best for drilling into the clay, but masonry bits work almost as well. If you don't have either, don't worry—regular drill bits will do the job, too. They'll just need sharpening after you're finished. But if you think you can take a shortcut by using a spade bit, don't try it. You'll end up with a broken pot. 🔨

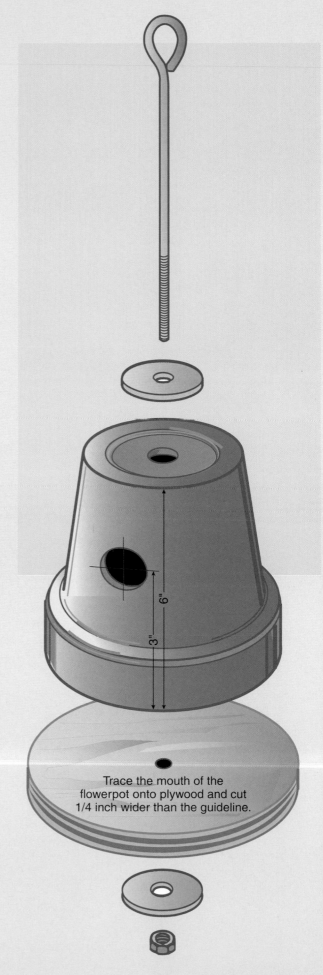

Here's What You'll Need...

❑ 8-inch clay flowerpot
❑ 10-inch x 10-inch piece of plywood at least
   1/4 inch thick
❑ One 8-inch eyebolt and nut
❑ Two fender washers
❑ Hook or chain for hanging birdhouse

Recommended Tools...

❑ Rat-tail file   ❑ Power drill
❑ Half-round file   ❑ Saber saw

A Little at a Time

1. Locate the entrance hole and use a small drill bit (1/8 inch or less) to start a hole at its center. Then work your way up to larger bits, gradually enlarging the hole. Here are some suggestions that may help:
• Use a slow speed while drilling.
• Wipe the bit often with a damp rag to clean it. (Keep electric drills away from water!)
• Do not use force as you drill.

2. Once you've used your largest drill bit, it's time to test your patience—the rest of the hole will be enlarged by hand with a rat-tail file and finished with a half-round file. This may take up to 30 minutes.

There's a secret to making steady progress—keep your file clean. Tapping or brushing out the dust won't be enough; you'll need to rinse the file in a bucket of water before continuing.

Once the entrance is just large enough to pass a quarter through, the most difficult work is finished. But be careful...this is no time to accidentally drop the flowerpot!

3. Trace the open end of the pot on a piece of 1/4-inch or thicker plywood to make the floor to the house. (Be sure to use plywood and not particle board, which soaks up water like a sponge.) Cut the circular base with a saber saw about 1/4 inch wider than the guideline.

4. In the center of the plywood base, drill a hole large enough for the eyebolt to pass through. Then set the flowerpot upside down on top of the plywood base.

5. Slip a fender washer onto the eyebolt and pass it through the pot's drainage hole and through the plywood base. Slip another washer over the end of the eyebolt and secure it with a nut. (Be careful not to over-tighten the nut—you might break the pot.)

Now your wren house is ready to hang. Using a hook or chain, suspend the house from a sturdy support 5 to 10 feet above the ground, preferably in an area with plenty of low growth. Then wait for your tenants to arrive.

There'll be no doubt when the wrens do move in—they're especially robust singers, with a distinctive trill at the end of each song.

Because the wrens' diet consists primarily of insects, you'll not only be grateful for their beautiful serenade. They'll police your garden, eating many uninvited pests.

6"

3"

Trace the mouth of the
flowerpot onto plywood and cut
1/4 inch wider than the guideline.

The Martins Will Love It!

Purple martins are one of the trickiest birds to attract to your backyard. But with this deluxe apartment, the birds may be knockin' on your door.

FOR MANY BIRD LOVERS, purple martins are a passion. After all, attracting a colony of these fabulous fliers that devour insects by the thousands poses the ultimate challenge.

We've looked at many designs for purple martin houses, attempting to find ones that can be built with basic tools by beginning woodworkers.

Thanks to the Pennsylvania Game Commission and the Purple Martin Conservation Association (they jointly developed this plan), we think we've found the ideal home-built purple martin house. It's a perfect starter house and takes only basic woodworking skills to build.

The house can also be expanded by four rooms—simply hang a purple martin gourd from a hook at each bottom corner. (See page 12 to make your own purple martin gourds.)

Just as important as good design is mounting and placing purple martin houses in the right location. Remember, to get these acrobatic fliers to nest in your backyard, the martin house will need to be mounted 10 to 15 feet high in an open area. That means it will need to be at least 40 feet from your house and any shrubs and trees (see illustration at left).

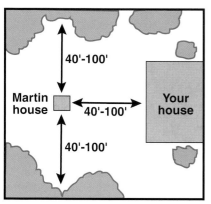

LOCATION, LOCATION. Purple martin houses should be mounted 10 to 15 feet high in an area with plenty of open space—at least 40-feet from shrubs, trees and houses in all directions.

The Pennsylvania Game Commission recommends mounting this purple martin house on top of a 14-foot pressure-treated four-by-four (see step 11 on page 38 for detailed instructions on mounting). This will keep the house low enough to the ground that you can safely monitor the nest compartments from a household ladder.

If European starlings are a nuisance, consider using the starling-resistant entrance hole pictured on the upper door of the house at bottom left (see "Starlings a Problem?" article on page 36).

Turn the page to see the plan for this purple martin house and the board layouts for cutting the pieces.

Yes, it will take a bit of work to make this purple martin house. But when a colony moves in, we think you'll agree your efforts in the workshop were well worthwhile.

Editor's Note: *This plan was reproduced from the book "Woodcrafting for Wildlife: Homes for Birds and Mammals", produced by the Pennsylvania Wild Resource Conservation Fund and the Pennsylvania Game Commission. Copies of this book are available for $5.66 by sending a check or money order to Pennsylvania Game Commission, Dept. MS, 2001 Elmerton Ave., Harrisburg PA 17110-9797 or by calling 1-888/888-3459. (Pennsylvania residents must add 6% sales tax.)*

Here's What You'll Need...

❑ One 4 x 8 sheet of untreated 3/4-inch-thick plywood (1/2-inch plywood may be substituted for the second-level floor and the roof)
❑ One 2-foot 2-inch x 6-inch pine board
❑ One 6-foot 1-inch x 8-inch pine board
❑ One 10-foot 1-inch x 6-inch pine board
❑ One 14-foot pressure-treated 4 x 4
❑ Four 3/8-inch x 3-inch lag bolts with washers
❑ 2-1/2-inch and 1-5/8-inch galvanized deck screws
❑ Twelve small brass hinges
❑ Six brass hook-and-eye assemblies
❑ White exterior stain or paint
❑ Waterproof construction adhesive
❑ Quick-setting post cement (2 to 3 bags)

Recommended Tools...

❑ Table saw
❑ Circular saw
❑ Saber saw
❑ Power drill
❑ Post-hole digger
❑ Carpenter's or post level

Let's Start Building a Martin House

1. Cut all pieces from the plywood and boards as pictured in board layouts on page 37.

2. Assemble mounting box with 2-1/2-inch deck screws. Make certain the assembled box fits over the end of the mounting post.

Step 3

3. Center and attach mounting box to the underside of the base of the house using 2-1/2-inch deck screws. Screw through the floor of the house into the mounting box. Drill pilot holes first.

4. Assemble the lower level of the house first. We recommend drawing where the walls will be located on the floor of the house. Then drill pilot holes (using the guidelines you drew) for the 1-5/8-inch deck screws that will hold the walls in place.

Install the interior walls first by driving the screws up through the floor and into the walls. Then attach the exterior walls (see photos on page 38).

5. Assemble the top level using the same method as in the previous step. We recommend also taking time to draw guidelines for the lower-level walls on top of the floor. This will help locate the pilot holes for the screws that will hold the two levels together (see step 8).

(Instructions continued on page 38)

Starlings a Problem? Lock Them Out With This Half-a-Hole

IF YOU'VE BEEN TRYING to attract purple martins to your backyard, but pesky European starlings are keeping them from moving into the neighborhood, you may want to give this starling-resistant entrance a try.

The half-a-hole has been tested throughout North America for several years and has proven to be successful on both purple martin houses and gourds. They work because starlings are too large to fit their bodies into the narrow entrance.

The height of the hole (1-3/16 inches) is extremely critical to making the entrance work. A hair too big and starlings will get in. A hair too small and the martins will be locked out.

To make the entrance hole easier to cut with a saber saw, we recommend locating it flush with the porch floor as pictured in the bottom photo on page 34.

If you're attempting to attract purple martins to your yard for the first time, the Purple Martin Conservation Association recommends using these holes *only* in the upper compartments (as pictured). If they work, simply switch the doors to the lower compartments to match before the martins return from their winter grounds the next spring.

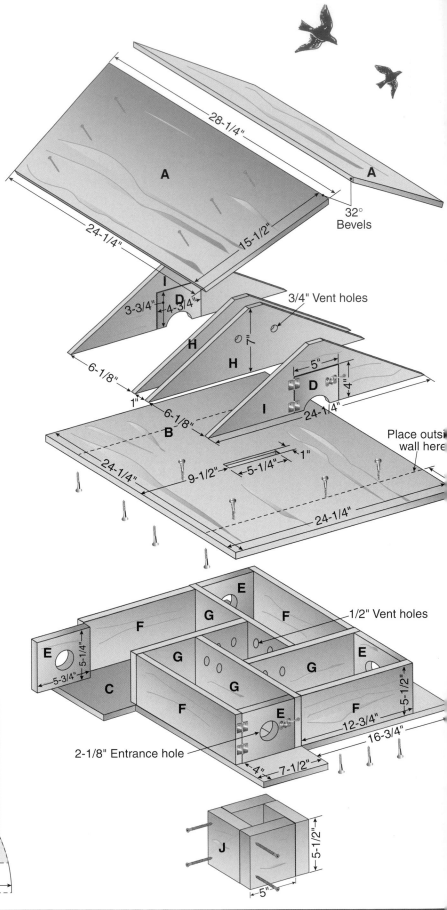

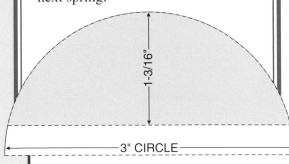

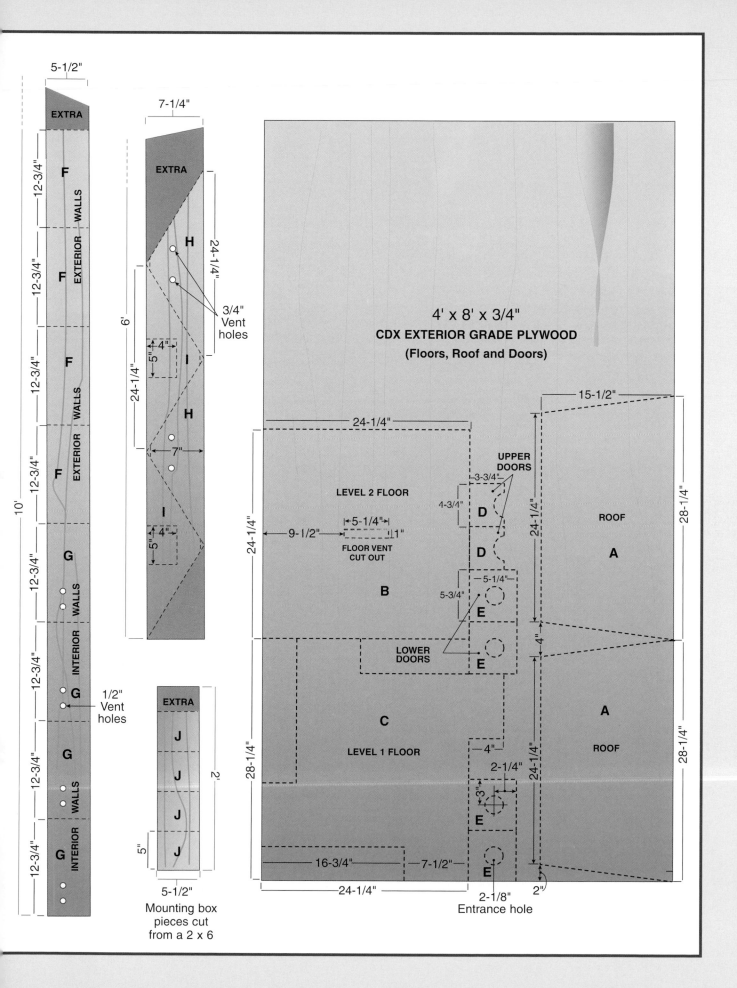

5-1/2"

EXTRA

12-3/4"

F

EXTERIOR WALLS

12-3/4"

F

EXTERIOR WALLS

12-3/4"

F

12-3/4"

F

EXTERIOR WALLS

12-3/4"

F

10'

12-3/4"

G

INTERIOR WALLS

12-3/4"

G

1/2" Vent holes

12-3/4"

G

INTERIOR WALLS

12-3/4"

G

INTERIOR WALLS

7-1/4"

EXTRA

H

3/4" Vent holes

24-1/4"

6'

24-1/4"

4"

5"

I

H

7"

I

5"

4"

EXTRA

J

J

2'

J

5"

J

5-1/2"

Mounting box
pieces cut
from a 2 x 6

4' x 8' x 3/4"
CDX EXTERIOR GRADE PLYWOOD
(Floors, Roof and Doors)

15-1/2"

24-1/4"

LEVEL 2 FLOOR

UPPER DOORS

3-3/4"

4-3/4"

D

D

ROOF

A

24-1/4"

28-1/4"

9-1/2"

5-1/4"

1"

FLOOR VENT CUT OUT

B

5-1/4"

5-3/4"

E

24-1/4"

LOWER DOORS

E

4"

C

LEVEL 1 FLOOR

A

ROOF

28-1/4"

4"

2-1/4"

3"

E

24-1/4"

16-3/4"

7-1/2"

E

24-1/4"

2-1/8"

2"

Entrance hole

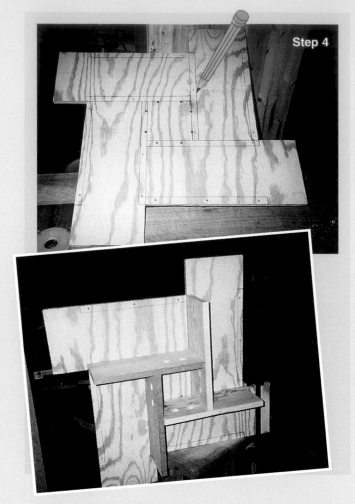

Step 4

Step 9

6. Cut an entrance hole in each door (see "Starlings a Problem?" on page 36). Before installing the doors, stain or paint all exterior surfaces. White houses are preferred by purple martins.

7. Install upper- and lower-level doors at each opening with small hinges and a hook-and-eye to keep the doors closed.

8. Join the top and lower levels using 1-5/8-inch deck screws. (If you haven't already, drill pilot holes using the guidelines drawn in step 5 to help locate them.) Screw through the floor of the top level into the lower-level walls. Be sure not to screw into the doors.

9. Using a table saw, cut a 32° bevel along the top of both roof pieces where they meet to form the peak. On top of each roof piece, draw the layout of the second story walls to help locate where to drill pilot holes. Then attach the roof pieces using 1-5/8-inch deck screws. Use waterproof construction adhesive at the peak to keep water from seeping into the house (see top right photo).

10. Mount the house on top of the 14-foot post with a 3/8-inch x 3-inch lag bolt and washer through each side of the mounting box. Now's a good time to touch up the paint if necessary and fill each compartment with 1 cup of cedar pet shavings.

(Before placing the house on top of the post, the Purple Martin Conservation Association recommends installing a predator guard, which will help keep raccoons, snakes and other nest raiders from climbing the post.)

11. Install the mounting post and house in an open area 40 to 100 feet from your house, trees or shrubs (see illustration on page 35).

With a post-hole digger, dig 3 to 4 feet into the ground. Place the base of the post against the mouth of the hole. Then, with the help of 2 or 3 people and a rope on both sides (one to pull the house up and the other to steady it), gently pull the house upright. As the post becomes near vertical, it will drop into the hole.

Anchor the post with quick-setting cement. Use a carpenter's level to straighten the post before the cement sets. (A post level, available at most hardware stores for less than $7, comes in handy here.)

Then keep your fingers crossed and wait. If you've placed your house in a proper location, you may soon be the "landlord" of the most active purple martin apartment in the neighborhood.

A Word To Martin Landlords

The Purple Martin Conservation Association urges landlords to monitor their houses for European starlings and house sparrows—non-native species that often drive martins from their homes and destroy their eggs and nests.

Since these birds are not native, they are not protected by law. So remove their nesting materials from the house as soon as they appear, reserving the compartments for the purple martins as intended.

The PMCA also recommends mounting a predator guard below purple martin houses to protect the birds from raccoons, snakes and other nest raiders.

For More Information about purple martins and attracting them to your backyard, send a self-addressed stamped envelope to: The Purple Martin Conservation Association, Edinboro University of Pennsylvania, Edinboro PA 16444; or visit their Web site at *www.purplemartin.org*.

Build a Better Birdhouse!

Here are some basic guidelines you'll find helpful when building birdhouses for specific species.

Species	Dimensions	Hole	Placement	Color	Notes
Eastern bluebird	5" x 5" x 8"h.	1-1/2" centered 6" above floor	5-10' high in the open; sunny area	light earth tones	likes open areas, especially facing a field
Tree swallow	5" x 5" x 6"h.	1-1/2" centered 4" above floor	5-8' high in the open; 50-100% sun	light earth tones or gray	within 2 miles of pond or lake
Purple martin	multiple apts. 6" x 6" x 6" ea. (minimum)	2-1/8" hole 2-1/4" above floor	15-20' high in the open	white	open yard without tall trees; near water
Tufted titmouse	4" x 4" x 8"h.	1-1/4"	4-10' high	light earth tones	prefers to live in or near woods
Chickadee	4" x 4" x 8"h. or 5" x 5" base	1-1/8" centered 6" above floor	4-8' high	light earth tones	small tree thicket
Nuthatch	4" x 4" x 10"h.	1-1/4" centered 7-1/2" above floor	12-25' high on tree trunk	bark-covered or natural	prefers to live in or near woods
House wren	4" x 4" x 8"h. or 4" x 6" base	1" centered 6" above floor	5-10' high on post or hung in tree	light earth tones or white	prefers lower branches of backyard trees
Northern flicker	7" x 7" x 18"h.	2-1/2" centered 14" above floor	8-20' high	light earth tones	put 4" sawdust inside for nesting
Downy woodpecker	4" x 4" x 10"h.	1-1/4" centered 7-1/2" above floor	12-25' high on tree trunk	simulate natural cavity	prefers own excavation; provide sawdust
Red-headed woodpecker	6" x 6" x 15"h.	2" centered 6-8" above floor	8-20' high on post or tree trunk	simulate natural cavity	needs sawdust for nesting
Wood duck	10" x 10" x 24"h.	4" x 3" elliptical 20" above floor	2-5' high on post over water, or 12-40' high on tree facing water	light earth tones or natural	needs 3-4" of sawdust or shavings for nesting
American kestrel	10" x 10" x 24"h.	4" x 3" elliptical 20" above floor	12-40' high on post or tree trunk	light earth tones or natural	needs open approach on edge of woodlot or in isolated tree
Screech owl	10" x 10" x 24"h.	4" x 3" elliptical 20" above floor	12-40' high on tree	light earth tones or natural	prefers open woods or edge of woodlot
Nesting Shelves					
American robin	6" x 6" x 8"h.	none—needs roof for rain protection	on side of building or arbor or in tree	light earth tones or wood	use is irregular
Barn swallow	6" x 6" x 8"h.	none—does not need roof	under eaves of building	light earth tones or wood	prefers barns or outbuildings
Phoebe	6" x 6" x 8"h.	none—does not need roof	under eaves of building	light earth tones or wood	prefers water nearby

Note: With the exception of wrens and purple martins, birds do not tolerate swaying birdhouses. Birdhouses should be firmly anchored to a post, a tree or the side of a building.

Source: *Garden Birds of America* by George H. Harrison. Willow Creek Press, 1996.

Chapter 2
Fantastic Feeders

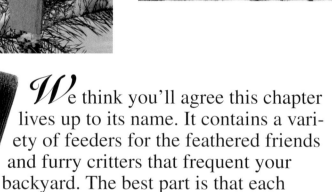

*W*e think you'll agree this chapter lives up to its name. It contains a variety of feeders for the feathered friends and furry critters that frequent your backyard. The best part is that each feeder is as practical as it is unique.

These feeders offer four seasons of fun as well. So if you're looking for a neat way to provide fresh water in winter or seeds in summer, you're sure to find it on the following pages. Before you know it, word will spread that your backyard is the best restaurant in the neighborhood.

A Backwoods Bird Feeder

This log cabin feeder looks great and works like a charm. Birds won't be able to resist stopping in for some down-home cookin'.

IF THE BIRDS have any say, Harold Neyes of Marshall, Illinois assures his log cabin feeder is a sure winner.

"They seem to love this bird feeder," Harold writes. "It might be its good looks, but my guess is they like the protection offered by the covered porch and the constant supply of food."

Once your backyard birds discover this feeder, it's sure to become one of the most popular in the neighborhood. Its clever design includes a metal slide inside, which keeps the feeding area filled with a fresh seed. And, because the porch roof overhangs the feeding area, it keeps the food dry and prevents larger birds, such as pigeons, from taking over.

Harold has included other special features, too. Each log is individually cut and stacked with crossed corners, giving this log cabin feeder a true rustic feel. The base is removable for easy cleaning, and the hinged roof-

BUILT BY A WOODSMAN. Harold Neyes (that's him above) of Marshall, Illinois shares his plan for this rustic bird feeder. The cabin's logs are individually cut and stacked, giving the feeder an authentic backwoods look. It includes a flip-open top for easy filling and a slide on the inside, which keeps fresh birdseed coming.

top pops wide open for quick and spill-proof filling.

Harold writes that this plan is also versatile. "I've used the same plan to make birdhouses. Just leave out the metal slide and complete the front wall from top to bottom. Then add an entrance hole in one of the sides."

When you're finished, Harold advises giving the project a coat of cedar preservative. After all, it'll take a bit of work to make this feeder. You, and the birds, will want to enjoy it for years to come.

(Step-by-step instructions begin on next page)

Log a Few Hours in the Shop

1. Cut an 8-inch x 12-inch base from a piece of 1-inch x 10-inch cedar board. You can also make the base from a sheet of 3/4-inch plywood.

2. Rip four 6-foot lengths of 3/4-inch-square strips from the 1-inch x 8-inch board. (Remember to use a push stick for safety!) These long strips will be used to make the individual logs for the feeder.

3. Before cutting the logs to size, use a block plane to create a 45° bevel on two adjacent edges of the 3/4-inch-square pieces (see illustration below). Each bevel should be about 1/4 inch, but it doesn't need to be exact—a little variation enhances the rustic appearance.

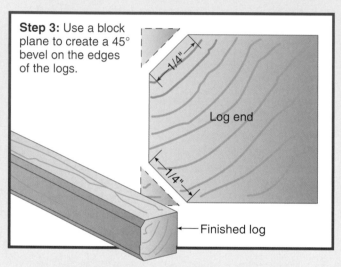

Step 3: Use a block plane to create a 45° bevel on the edges of the logs.

1/4"

Log end

1/4"

Finished log

4. Cut the logs to size from the 3/4-inch-square strips. Here's a cutting list to help:

- Four pieces 10-3/4 inches long (for gables)
- Two pieces 10 inches long
- Six pieces 8-1/2 inches long
- Four pieces 7-1/2 inches long
- Six pieces 6-1/4 inches long
- Six pieces 5-1/4 inches long

Also, rip one strip 1/2-inch square and at least 16 inches long for the porch supports.

5. Glue the four 10-3/4-inch-long pieces together and clamp them until the glue dries. Then cut 45° angles as shown in the diagram below.

6. From the bottom, screw (don't glue) the 10-inch-long log pieces to the base so they're flush with the front edge and sides of the base. This will square up the walls of the feeder. (When you want to clean the feeder, remove these screws and the base will come off.)

7. Glue two 6-1/4-inch log pieces between the 10-inch logs—one in the front and one in the back. Do not glue to the base. Tack in place to the 10-inch logs with 1-1/4-inch brads.

8. Log by log, begin building the walls of the feeder. Notice that the front wall will be built 3 inches back from the front log of the feeder. Do not place a log at the bottom of the front wall. This should remain open for the seed to flow out.

Use a bead of waterproof glue between each log and tack them in place using 1-1/4-inch brads at the ends of each log. Alternate where the brads are placed with each log to avoid hitting the nail used to secure the previously laid log (see illustration at right).

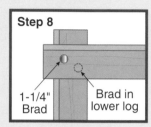

Step 8

1-1/4" Brad

Brad in lower log

9. When the walls are complete, add the piece of aluminum flashing to the inside of the feeder. Bend a 1/4-inch lip on each side so it measures 6-1/4 inches wide. (This can be done by hammering the flashing on the edge of a workbench or by bending it in a vise.) This will give you a small lip to attach the slide to the inside of the feeder.

To attach, simply punch one small hole at the top of each lip with a wire brad. Lay the flashing in the feeder at an angle so birdseed can slide down to the front feeding area. Insert a 5/8-inch brad in the hole punched earlier and push in with a pliers.

10. Attach each gable to the sides. Drill pilot holes, glue and nail at the ends using 1-1/2-inch finishing nails.

11. Notch the 2 x 2 chimney with a saber or hand saw. The notch should measure 1 inch x 4-3/4 inches (see plan at right).

12. Cut two pieces of cedar siding for the roof pieces. The front roof measures 5-3/4 inches x 8-3/4 inches. The back roof measures 5-1/4 inches x 8-3/4 inches. *Cut away the thinnest part of the siding.*

13. Cut the porch roof 3-1/2 inches x 8-3/4 inches from another piece of cedar siding. *This time cut away the thickest part of the siding.*

14. Attach the chimney to the back wall with two 1-1/4-inch deck screws. Using a saber saw, cut out the back roof as pictured in plan so that it fits around the chimney. Note that the thinner part of the roof will be at the peak.

(Continued on page 44)

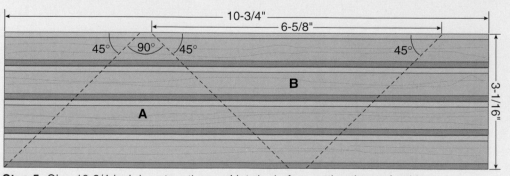

10-3/4"

6-5/8"

45° 90° 45° 45°

B

A

3-1/16"

Step 5: Glue 10-3/4-inch logs together and let dry before cutting the roof gables.

Here's What You'll Need...

- ❑ One 1-inch x 10-inch cedar board, at least 12 inches long (or 3/4-inch plywood)
- ❑ One 6-foot 1-inch x 8-inch cedar board
- ❑ One scrap 2 x 2, at least 9-1/2 inches long (for chimney)
- ❑ Three pieces of 8-inch cedar siding, at least 8-3/4 inches long
- ❑ 6-inch x 6-3/4-inch piece of aluminum flashing
- ❑ 1-5/8-inch and 1-1/4-inch deck screws
- ❑ 1-1/2-inch finishing nails
- ❑ 1-1/4-inch, 7/8-inch and 5/8-inch brads
- ❑ Two 1-inch brass hinges
- ❑ One magnetic catch
- ❑ Landscape stone or pea gravel
- ❑ Polyurethane concrete sealant (for mortar)
- ❑ 12 or 14 gauge copper wire (optional, for window and door-frames, see next page)
- ❑ One large soup can (optional, for windows and door)
- ❑ Waterproof carpenter's glue

Recommended Tools...

- ❑ Table saw
- ❑ Saber saw
- ❑ Block plane
- ❑ Clamps
- ❑ Propane torch (optional, to solder window frames)
- ❑ Solder and flux (optional)

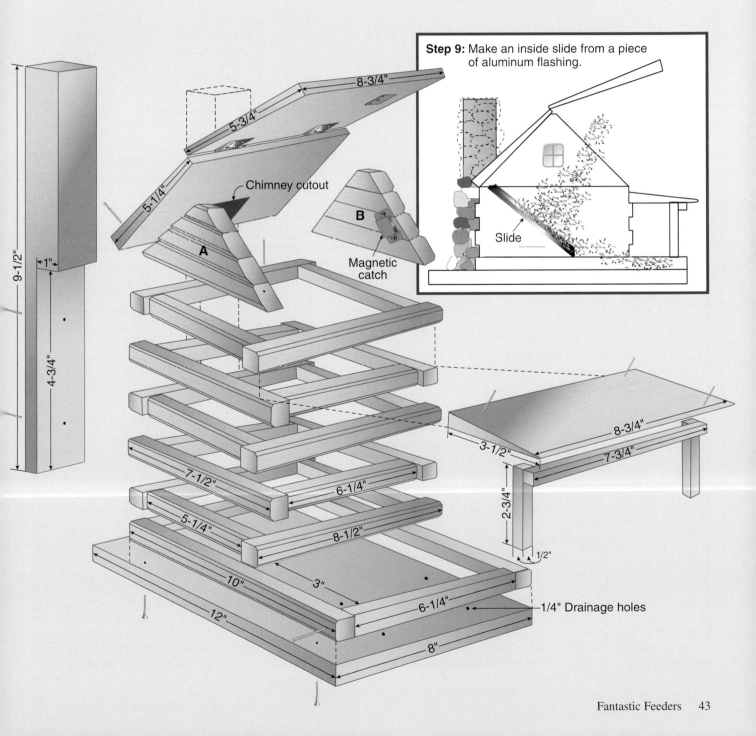

Step 9: Make an inside slide from a piece of aluminum flashing.

Chimney cutout

Magnetic catch

Slide

9-1/2"

1"

4-3/4"

8-3/4"

5-3/4"

5-1/4"

A

B

7-1/2"

6-1/4"

5-1/4"

8-1/2"

10"

3"

6-1/4"

12"

8"

8-3/4"

3-1/2"

7-3/4"

2-3/4"

1/2"

1/4" Drainage holes

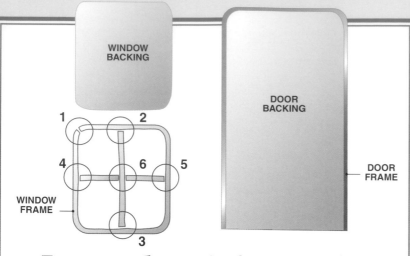

WINDOW BACKING

DOOR BACKING

DOOR FRAME

1 2

4 6 5

WINDOW FRAME

3

Leave the Lights on for Feathered Friends

PART OF THE BEAUTY of this bird feeder is that the golden windows give it a realistic look, as if a crackling fire is burning inside the cozy log cabin.

One of our staffers, Troy Hildebrandt (that's him pictured below), built this feeder from Harold Neyes' plan. Troy came up with a clever way to create these shimmering windows using scrap material you probably already have laying around the house. You may want to try his method (below), or simply paint the windows onto thin scraps of wood and glue them in place.

Golden-Glow Windows

1. Bend copper wire with needle-nose pliers to create the window and door frames. Cut off the excess wire and cut smaller pieces to size for the inside window panes (see diagram at top).

2. Use a grip-type pliers to hold the pieces you're soldering. Heat and solder each joint in the order they are numbered in the illustration above. Troy used a propane torch to quickly heat each joint. Then he removed the window frame from the heat and touched the hot area with solder to secure the joint.

Each corner has to be heated quickly—if the entire window becomes too hot, the solder at the previously finished joints will melt and loosen.

3. Using a tin snips, cut the window and door backings to size from a large soup can. These cans have plenty of smooth area (free of ridges) to work with.

Flatten the backings and glue the copper window and door frames onto them.

4. Before gluing the completed windows onto the bird feeder with construction adhesive, clean them with mineral spirits. This will remove any flux used in soldering, which would eventually turn the metal black.

15. Attach the back roof using waterproof glue and 1-1/4-inch wire brads. Be sure to drill pilot holes in the siding so it does not split.

16. Attach the front roof to the back roof piece with 1-inch brass hinges. The hinges should be attached to the *underside* of the front roof piece and the *outside* of the back roof. You may need to file down the screws a bit if they're longer than the thickness of the siding.

17. Attach the magnetic catch to the inside of the feeder.

18. Cut three pieces from the 1/2-inch-square stock—one piece measuring 7-3/4 inches long and two pieces measuring 2-3/4 inches long.

Glue and nail the porch supports together using 7/8-inch brads as shown in the plan on page 43. Then glue the assembly in place at the front of the feeder.

With 7/8-inch brads, nail the porch roof to the supports and the logs that the back edge of the roof rests on. Again, drill pilot holes to prevent the siding from splitting.

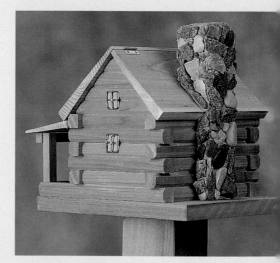

19. Decorate the chimney with landscaping stone or pea gravel (see photo above). This gives the log cabin an authentic look. Polyurethane concrete sealant works well for the mortar because it dries very slowly, but the stones will not move after placing them on the chimney.

20. Drill four 1/4-inch drainage holes in the porch floor area where the birds feed. Mount the feeder on a post—we do not recommend hanging it because of its weight. Then fill it with seed (see the "Birds and Their Favorite Foods" chart on page 60 for recommended feed) so your feathered friends can log some time feeding!

Here's a No-Wobble Tray Feeder

Creatures great and small will enjoy dining at this sturdy portable feeder.

IF YOU ENJOY seeing a variety of animals feeding in your backyard, this easy-to-build triangular feeder is all you'll need to attract a crowd.

Cardinals and other "tray feeders" will love it…and the low platform will attract birds that feed close to the ground like dark-eyed juncos and mourning doves.

You'll also see plenty of squirrels and chipmunks, so keep the tray well stocked with cracked corn. (If these furry critters can count on a reliable food supply here, they'll be less likely to disturb other feeders set up only for birds.)

One of our *Birds & Blooms* editors came up with the idea for this unique triangular feeder. The three legs prevent wobbling no matter where you put it in your yard. Plus, it's lightweight enough to move with ease.

Here's What You'll Need...

❏ One 8-foot 2 x 2
❏ One 3-foot 1-inch x 8-inch board (or 4-foot 2 x 4)
❏ One 2-foot-square piece of metal window screen
❏ 2-1/2-inch and 2-inch galvanized deck screws
❏ Waterproof carpenter's glue
❏ Masking tape

Recommended Tools...

❏ Table or miter saw   ❏ Heavy-duty stapler

Start with the Tray

1. To make the seed tray, cut three 24-inch lengths from an 8-foot 2 x 2 with 60° opposing angles on each end (remove 30° on each cut).

2. On a flat surface, fit the pieces together with the edges overlapping and temporarily fasten them with carpenter's glue. Hold the joints tight with masking tape. When the glue is dry, drill a pilot hole in each corner and secure with 2-1/2-inch deck screws.

3. From a 2-foot-square piece of screen, cut out a triangle that fits the frame, extending about halfway between the inner and outer edge of the frame. Staple the screen to the wood securely, leaving about 1 inch between staples.

4. For the legs, rip three 2-1/2-inch widths from a 3-foot 1-inch x 8-inch board. Cut each piece to 16 inches. If you want a more finished appearance, bevel the tops of the legs 15°. The legs can also be made from 2 x 4's to reduce warping.

5. Position a leg so it bridges the joint of the frame (see plan and photo at right). Then predrill two holes for the screws, being careful not to hit the screws holding the seed tray together.

6. Use 2-inch deck screws to attach each leg to the frame. (To make the tray a little sturdier for chunky wildlife, you can glue the leg joints with carpenter's glue before driving the screws.)

Now fill the tray with seed and cracked corn—it shouldn't take long for the neighborhood critters to discover the banquet you've set out for them!

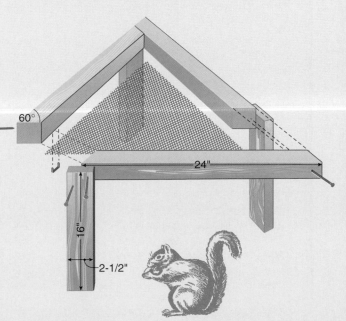

Birds Flock To This No-Muss, No-Fuss Feeder

Spilled birdseed leaving a mess on your patio or deck? This suet feeder offers a tidy alternative.

THE SPIRIT of holiday gift-giving inspired Robyn MacDuff of Sandy, Utah to develop this easy-to-use suet feeder.

"I wanted to make Christmas gifts for friends and family to share my enjoyment of feeding birds," Robyn recalls. "Some people on my gift list didn't like spilled birdseed on their patios, so I decided on suet feeders—they're perfect for attracting winter birds and don't spill seeds on the ground."

Searching for an attractive design, Robyn perused back issues of *Birds & Blooms* and found some great ideas. "Then I set up my drafting table and got to work," she says.

Robyn's feeder is designed to hold the pre-made suet cakes that can be purchased at bird-supply stores, hardware stores and garden centers. Before making this feeder to the dimensions shown, we recommend finding out the standard size of the suet cakes available in your area and adjust the measurements if needed.

Here's What You'll Need...

❑ One 3-foot 1-inch x 6-inch No. 2 pine board
❑ One scrap piece of 1/4-inch plywood (4 x 4 inches minimum)
❑ One piece of hardware cloth with 1/2-inch or 1/4-inch squares
❑ 1-1/4-inch and 3/4-inch wire brads
❑ Netting staples
❑ Three double-headed (duplex) nails
❑ Waterproof carpenter's glue
❑ Two screw eyes
❑ Chain for hanging the feeder

Recommended Tools...

❑ Table saw   ❑ Tin snips   ❑ Pliers

Time for Tools

1. Begin with a 3-foot 1-inch x 6-inch pine board. Rip the board on a table saw so one piece measures 1-1/4 inches wide. From that board, cut:
  • Two side pieces 6 inches long
  • One bottom piece 6-1/4 inches long
  • One top piece 4-3/4 inches long

2. Adjust the blade in your table saw so it is low enough to make a groove, called a "dado", 1/4 inch deep. (Check the depth of the dado on a scrap board. For safety, be sure to use push sticks when cutting—see photo next page.) Cut the dado lengthwise in the center of the 6-1/4-inch long piece. This will accommodate the tail support. You'll need to make a few passes over the saw blade until the dado is 1/4 inch wide.

Cutting the dado will require you to adjust your saw's fence—the guide used for ripping a board—a few times. It may be tempting to leave the saw running during these adjustments, but don't! *Always* shut off the saw when adjusting the fence.

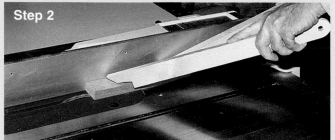

Step 2

SAFETY FIRST! When cutting small wood pieces and making "dado" cuts on a table saw, use push sticks to guide the wood (as pictured above). This keeps your hands and fingers a safe distance away from the dangerous saw blade.

3. For the tail support, you'll need a scrap piece of 1/4-inch plywood at least 4 inches square. Cut this piece 3-1/2 inches wide at the top and taper it to a width of 2-3/4 inches at the bottom. The angle is 85°...or you can just measure in 3/8 inch from each bottom corner, draw a pencil line to the top corner and then cut off the waste.

4. Rip the remaining 3-foot-long pine board 2-1/4 inches wide (remember to use a push stick!). Then cut a 7-3/4-inch-long piece from it for the top of the feeder.

5. Using 1-1/4-inch wire brads, nail the framework together following the plan at right. The 4-3/4-inch piece should be centered under the top piece and fastened with 1-1/4-inch brads from below. *Make sure the groove in the bottom piece is facing down.*

6. To hold the suet cake in the feeder, you'll need enough 1/2-inch-square or 1/4-inch-square screening to cut two pieces measuring about 5-1/2 inches x 6 inches. Trim the wire nubs with a tin snips as closely to a full square as possible. This will give the feeder a finished look and keep you and the birds from being poked by sharp ends.

7. Attach one piece of screening on one side of the feeder with netting staples on all four sides.

8. On the front side, staple the screening *only at the bottom edge*, fastening with three or four staples. These staples act as a hinge, allowing you to swing open the screen to fill the feeder. If the screen doesn't swing open easily, loosen the staples a bit.

9. To hold the "screen door" closed, drill three holes 3/8 inches from the edge of the top board for double-headed (duplex) nails. These will protrude through the top and extend past the screening to keep the door tightly shut (see photo at top left).

(*Hint:* We suggest drilling the center hole first and testing the fit with one of the nails. Then adjust the end holes if needed so the screen is held tightly in place.)

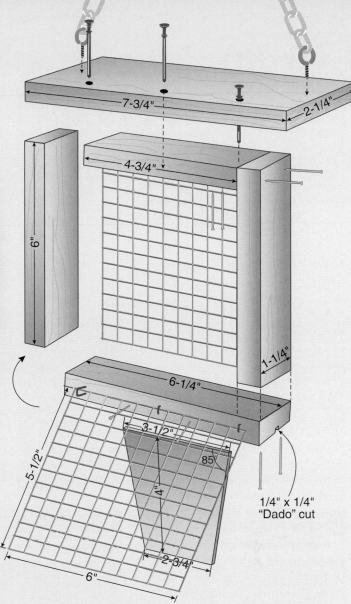

1/4" x 1/4" "Dado" cut

Choose a drill bit slightly larger than the nails, since they will be removed each time you fill the feeder. Don't make them too loose, or this feeder will be an easy target for a crafty squirrel.

For a finished look, cut the nails with a hacksaw so they're about 1-3/4 inches long.

10. Center the tail support into the dado and fasten with waterproof glue and 3/4-inch wire brads from both sides.

Step 7: Staple back hardware cloth on all four sides.

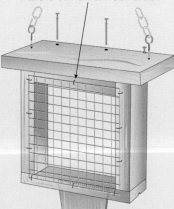

11. Before adding the chain, open and screw the eyes into the top board. Then insert the ends of the chain into the screw eyes and squeeze them shut with a pliers.

Fill the feeder with a fresh suet cake and hang from a tree or feeding station, or attach to a tree trunk. Soon the birds in your neighborhood will be in "fat city".

In Spring, Orioles and Oranges Are a Perfect Combination

It doesn't get any easier than this one. And the colorful birds it attracts will amaze you!

NO NEED to break the budget when it comes to feeding orioles. With this simple orange feeder, you're sure to bring these beautiful birds to your backyard—after all, they can't resist citrus in the spring.

The best part is this project may not even cost a dime, because there's a good chance you probably already have enough scrap lumber and hardware around the house to build several of these surefire feeders.

This feeder was inspired by one designed by Daniel Medbury of Plymouth, Michigan. We've simplified it a bit so anyone can build it—even a child with a little adult supervision. In less than an hour, you'll be hanging your own exclusive oriole feeding station.

Here's What You'll Need...

- ❑ One scrap 2 x 4, at least 13 inches long
- ❑ One 1-inch x 8-inch board, about 12 inches long
- ❑ One 1/4-inch dowel, at least 18 inches long
- ❑ Four 2-1/2-inch galvanized finishing nails
- ❑ Four common nails
- ❑ Waterproof carpenter's glue
- ❑ One screw eye for hanging the feeder

Recommended Tools...

- ❑ Table saw
- ❑ Power drill
- ❑ Combination square

BALTIMORE ORIOLES can't resist citrus in the spring.

Easy as Orange Pie

1. Cut a scrap 2 x 4 at least 13 inches long.

2. Cut two 45° angles to form a centered peak on one end (this will become the top). Use a combination square or tri-square to help draw the cutting angles.

3. "Dog-ear" the corners at the bottom end of the 2 x 4 by sawing about 3/4 inch off each corner at a 45° angle.

4. Drill two 1/4-inch holes through the 2 x 4. Center one hole 1-1/4 inches from bottom of the board and the other 6-1/2 inches from bottom. Make sure you drill the holes perpendicular to the 2 x 4. This will ensure that your perches will be straight. (See "Workshop Wisdom" at bottom right for a helpful hint.)

5. Cut two roof pieces from the 1-inch x 8-inch board. One section should measure approximately 6 inches x 7-1/4 inches and the other 5-1/4 inches x 7-1/4 inches. If you'd like, dog-ear the outside corners of the roof pieces by cutting off about 1 inch from each corner at a 45° angle.

6. Nail the roof pieces to the 2 x 4 peak with two common nails. The longer piece overlaps the shorter.

7. The oranges are held onto the feeder by spearing them onto 2-1/2-inch finishing nails. Center these nails on each side of the 2 x 4 about 3 inches above each perch hole. Drive the nails about 1 inch into the 2 x 4 at a downward angle so they hold the oranges better.

8. Cut the 18-inch dowel in half for perches. Insert the dowels into the holes and center them. A little waterproof carpenter's glue in the holes will hold the perches firmly in place.

9. File or cut a flat spot in the center of the roof peak for a screw eye, which is used to hang the feeder. Drill a pilot hole first—this will prevent the wood from splitting.

A coat of deck stain is optional, but it'll help protect the wood from weather. Be sure the stain is dry before using the feeder.

Then cut two oranges in half, spear them onto the nails and wait for the orioles to show up while you enjoy a glass of iced tea.

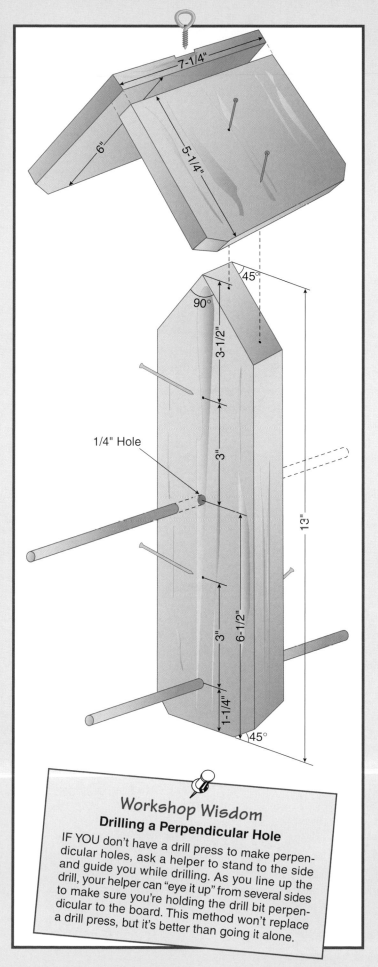

Workshop Wisdom
Drilling a Perpendicular Hole

IF YOU don't have a drill press to make perpendicular holes, ask a helper to stand to the side and guide you while drilling. As you line up the drill, your helper can "eye it up" from several sides to make sure you're holding the drill bit perpendicular to the board. This method won't replace a drill press, but it's better than going it alone.

Birds Go Nuts Over This Feeder

Sorry, squirrels…this easy-to-make peanut feeder is reserved for feathered friends only.

IF YOU WANT A PARADE of new birds coming to your backyard, try offering them something new…peanuts!

One of our editors added a simple peanut feeder like the one pictured at left to his backyard. Birds he's never seen near his place—woodpeckers (both hairy and downy), nuthatches and blue jays—came out of their shell to sample the peanuts.

We've received a lot of interest in this type of peanut feeder ever since we pictured one like it on the cover of *Birds & Blooms* (October/November '98 issue). The wire feeder caught the eye of Alice Schultz of Gasport, New York.

"I'd sure like to make one for myself," Alice writes. "I figure it must be made for squirrels since it's filled with peanuts."

Actually, the wire hardware cloth keeps those furry critters from getting to the goobers. Squirrels can be persistent and destructive though (some even chewed through the wire when we filled it with peanuts out of the shell), so we recommend filling the feeder with peanuts *in the shell*.

This makes it even more difficult for squirrels to get to the feed, while woodpeckers, nuthatches and other birds have little trouble breaking the shells and finding the hidden treasures inside.

Here's What You'll Need...

- ❑ One 2-foot 1-inch x 6-inch board
- ❑ Approximately 12 inches x 18 inches of hardware cloth with 1/4-inch squares
- ❑ 36-inch-long light-duty chain
- ❑ One screw eye
- ❑ Netting staples
- ❑ Waterproof carpenter's glue (or 1-5/8-inch deck screws)

Recommended Tools...

- ❑ Band, saber or scroll saw
- ❑ Wire cutter
- ❑ Needle-nose pliers
- ❑ Soldering iron (optional)

Let's Start Building

1. Cut out four disks—two should measure about 4-3/4 inches across and two should measure about 3 inches across—with a band, saber or scroll saw. Make the circles with a compass, or simply trace the rims of quart and 1/2-pint paint cans (or other cans similar to the dimensions above).

Cut the smaller disks carefully—they should be as close to identical as possible.

2. Center and glue (or predrill and fasten with three 1-5/8-inch deck screws) each small disk to a larger disk. Clamp these pieces together until the glue dries. This will form the top and base of the feeder.

3. Fasten one end of the chain to a screw eye. Open the eye with two small pliers. (With the pliers parallel to the screw, twist in opposite directions until the eye opens just enough for the chain to be inserted.) Close the eye with a pliers.

Drill a pilot hole in the center of one of the small disks and turn in the screw eye. This will become the feeder's base.

4. Wrap hardware cloth around the completed base. (If using a 1/2-pint paint can to determine the size of the smaller disks, wrap the hardware cloth around the base and the can, which should be positioned about 10 inches higher than the base. Wrap heavy-duty rubber bands around the base and can to form a cylinder.)

Cut the hardware cloth about 1/4 inch beyond the last complete square where it comes together. This will leave small wire tabs on one end (see illustration at lower left). Remove the rubber bands and paint can.

5. Bend hardware cloth into a cylinder and attach to the feeder's base with netting staples (with the chain inside).

6. Join the two ends of hardware cloth to form a cylinder. Secure by wrapping the tabs around the other end using needle-nose pliers. Make sure the cylinder isn't too tight at the feeder's top, otherwise it will be difficult to lift up and close when filling with peanuts.

We recommend spot soldering the wire at the seam about every 2 inches for a better hold. If there is excess wire at the tabs, trim with a wire cutter.

7. Drill a hole in the center of the feeder's top large enough for the chain to easily slide through. Thread the chain through it and place the top of the feeder onto the cylinder.

The chain can be looped for hanging or attached to a S hook.

8. Slide the top up along the chain and fill the cylinder with peanuts. We think you'll enjoy watching the parade of feathered friends from the "peanut gallery".

18"

3"

4-3/4"

Dimensions can vary as indicated in step 1.

Step 4: When cutting hardware cloth, leave wire tabs on one 18-inch side. Roll the cloth into a cylinder and bend the wire tabs around the other end to hold them together.

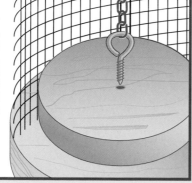

This Recycling Project Is *Really* for the Birds!

A juice bottle and a few scraps of wood are all you need to make this surprisingly handsome feeder.

HOMEMADE bird feeders don't have to be homely. This one is made mostly from recycled materials, yet looks as attractive as an expensive store-bought product.

Kenneth Higgins designed this feeder for his yard, which overlooks Lake Buchanan in Burnet, Texas. Filled with sunflower seed, it is a favorite of the tufted titmice in his area.

It's a great project for builders on a budget or those who would like to try something new. Kenneth points out that he made three feeders like this one from a leftover piece of cedar fencing.

"That's pretty cheap," he observes. "One board is all it takes, and you feel good about it because you're recycling, too."

Since wide boards tends to warp, we recommend making the roof and feeding tray from plywood, which stands up to weather well (it won't warp). Although plywood isn't as attractive, we've disguised it a bit by edging the tray with cedar.

Here's What You'll Need...

- ❏ One 1-gallon plastic juice bottle with cap
- ❏ Plywood scraps, at least 1/2 inch thick
- ❏ Cedar or pine scraps
- ❏ 1-1/4-inch galvanized deck screws
- ❏ 1-1/2-inch wire brads
- ❏ Small sheet-metal screws
- ❏ 18-inch-long light-duty rustproof chain
- ❏ Two S hooks

Recommended Tools...

- ❏ Table saw
- ❏ Utility knife
- ❏ Power drill
- ❏ Saber saw
- ❏ Compass

Finish Your Juice, It's Time to Start Building!

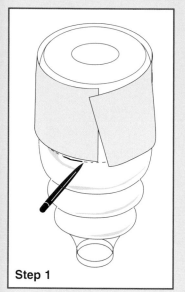

Step 1

1. Wash and dry a 1-gallon plastic juice bottle (we used an Ocean Spray juice bottle). Mark at least 3/4 inches below the point where the bottle straightens out.

Wrap a piece of paper around the bottom of the bottle, lining up the edge of the paper with the point you've marked. Make sure the paper is straight as it wraps around the bottle. Then trace around the edge of the paper with a permanent marker to make a cutting line (at left).

Carefully cut (away from yourself) along the line with a utility knife or scissors. Take your time with this step because the plastic will become flimsy as you cut.

2. Cut or drill three 1/2-inch holes in the narrowest part of the bottle's neck. Don't worry too much about the size of the holes—you can always enlarge them later if necessary. Start by using a smaller bit.

3. Cut a scrap of plywood 6-1/2 inches square for the seed tray.

4. Rip trim pieces that will make a tray 1 inch deep (thickness of plywood plus 1 inch).

They'll overlap at the corners, so the four bottom trim pieces should measure 6-1/2 inches *plus* the thickness of the wood you're using. Attach them to the tray with 1-1/2-inch wire brads. Drill a 1/4-inch drainage hole in each corner of the seed tray.

5. Cut a scrap of plywood 10-inches square for the roof. The larger roof will protect seed in the feeding tray from rain and snow. Trim the roof edging in the same manner as the seed tray in step 4.

6. From another scrap of plywood, cut a disk to fit the diameter of the wide part of the bottle. Measure the diameter of the wide opening and use a compass to draw the circle, or trace around the bottle. Cut the piece with a saber saw right on the cutting line. This will allow the piece to slip in and out of the bottle easily when you fill the feeder.

Center and attach the disk to the underside of the roof with four 1-1/4-inch deck screws.

7. Drill a hole through the center of the roof pieces. Connect opposite corners with straight pencil lines. They'll meet in the center of the board. (It's important that this hole be centered or the feeder will not hang straight.) Make the hole just large enough to accommodate the chain you'll use to hang the feeder.

8. Remove the cap from the bottle and carefully drill two holes near its outside edge. Start with a small drill bit and

gradually increase the size until the small sheet-metal screws fit through it easily. *Do not apply pressure while drilling.* Going slow and sure like this will help prevent the plastic cap from cracking.

Attach the cap centered in the feeding tray with the small screws, but don't tighten them too much or the cap may crack.

9. Drill a hole through the center of the bottle cap and tray. Again, increase the drill bit size gradually. Be very careful when starting the hole—drill slowly so the cap doesn't break.

10. String the chain through the roof, bottle and tray. Loop the top of the chain or use an S hook for hanging. Attach another S hook at the bottom to keep the chain from slipping up through the feeder. Close the hook with pliers.

Hang it, fill it and let the wild birds come and get it!

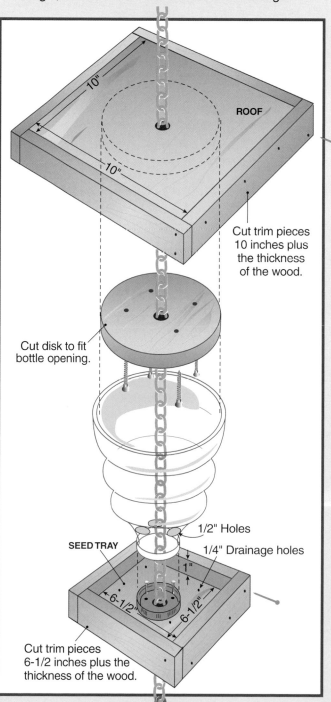

10"

ROOF

10"

Cut trim pieces 10 inches plus the thickness of the wood.

Cut disk to fit bottle opening.

1/2" Holes

1/4" Drainage holes

SEED TRAY

1"

6-1/2"

6-1/2"

Cut trim pieces 6-1/2 inches plus the thickness of the wood.

Hold the Ice, Please

Even in the winter, backyard birds need water. You can supply it with this easy-to-make heated water hole.

"NORTH DAKOTA winters are long and cold," says Erlys Haerter, of Williston. "I thought if we could provide some water for the birds, it would make their life a bit easier.

"So my father came up with a great idea for a heated water hole," Erlys continues. "He gave the directions to my husband, Paul, who built it."

We gave this project a try in our own workshop and placed it out on a deck in the dead of winter. It worked surprisingly well, and took a very low-wattage standard light bulb to keep the water from freezing.

We recommend using the lowest wattage bulb possible that keeps the water ice-free. The birds will be happy, and so will you since it will have little impact on your electric bill.

Here's What You'll Need...

- ❏ One 2-foot x 4-foot plywood board, 1/2 inch thick
- ❏ One piece of 5-foot 1-inch x 14-1/2-inch foam insulation
- ❏ Round metal cake pan, 8-1/2-inch diameter
- ❏ Waterproof outdoor spotlight fixture
- ❏ One 15- to 40-watt standard light bulb
- ❏ 1-1/4-inch finishing nails
- ❏ 5/8-inch sheet-metal screws
- ❏ Waterproof construction adhesive
- ❏ Waterproof carpenter's glue
- ❏ Four chair skids
- ❏ Properly installed GFI outlet

Recommended Tools...

- ❏ Table saw
- ❏ Saber saw
- ❏ Utility knife
- ❏ Compass
- ❏ Rat-tail file

Time to Start Building

1. Cut the side, top and bottom pieces from plywood using the board layout at top right. On one of the side pieces, cut a small notch in the center along the bottom edge. This will be for the outdoor light fixture's cord.

2. Determine the size hole to make in the top piece of the plywood for the cake pan. (We recommend practicing this step with a piece of cardboard or scrap board before cutting the actual hole.)

To quickly find the center of the top piece, draw diagonal lines from corner to corner. Draw a circle with a compass the diameter of the cake pan just below the rim.

3. Cut the hole for the pan with a saber saw, cutting right along the guideline. (To start this hole, see "Workshop Wisdom" at far right for a handy tip.) This will allow the pan to sit down into the hole. Make adjustments if necessary. The pan is sitting properly when the top lip rests on top of the board, and the rest is below the surface.

4. Overlap the sides of the box to form a square. Drill pilot holes and fasten the sections together with 1-1/4-inch finishing nails. Use waterproof carpenter's glue between the joints.

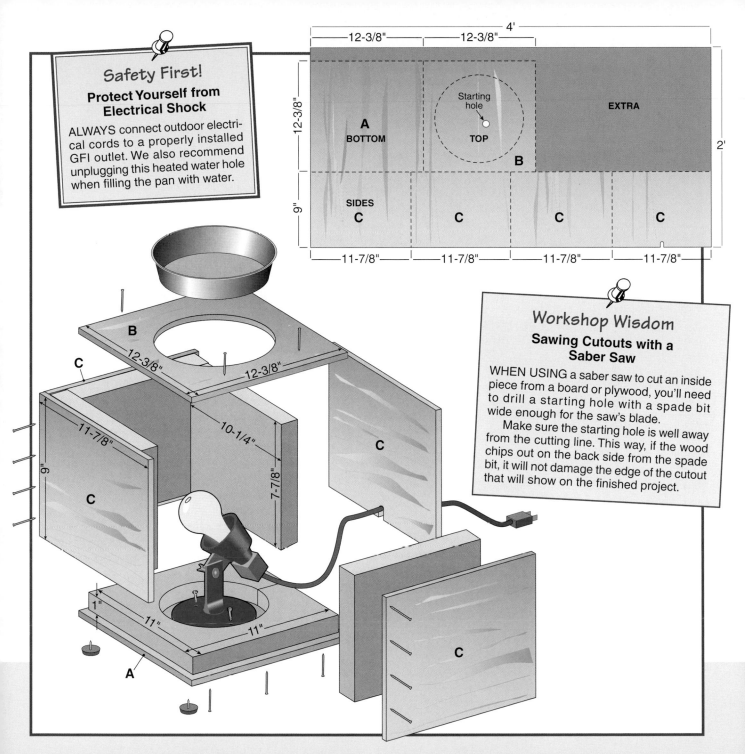

Safety First!
Protect Yourself from Electrical Shock
ALWAYS connect outdoor electrical cords to a properly installed GFI outlet. We also recommend unplugging this heated water hole when filling the pan with water.

Workshop Wisdom
Sawing Cutouts with a Saber Saw
WHEN USING a saber saw to cut an inside piece from a board or plywood, you'll need to drill a starting hole with a spade bit wide enough for the saw's blade.
Make sure the starting hole is well away from the cutting line. This way, if the wood chips out on the back side from the spade bit, it will not damage the edge of the cutout that will show on the finished project.

5. Center and mount the light fixture to the bottom with 5/8-inch sheet-metal screws. Align the fixture so that the cord is centered on one side, as pictured in the plan above.

6. Tuck the cord into the notch before gluing and nailing the bottom board to the sides (drill pilot holes first).

7. Cut a piece of insulation 11-inches square with a utility knife (be careful when cutting) to fit in the bottom of the box. Cut a hole in the center of it to fit over the mounted light fixture. Also slice one side of the insulation so that it can be placed over the cord. Glue the insulation to the bottom of the box using waterproof construction adhesive.

8. For the sides, cut the insulation 10-1/4 inches x 7-7/8 inches. Glue insulation to the sides of the box.

9. Glue, then nail the top to the sides with 1-1/4-inch finishing nails. Turn the box over and attach one chair skid to each bottom corner.

10. Screw a standard light bulb ranging from 15 to 40 watts into the outdoor fixture. Choose the lowest wattage that will keep the water from freezing. In our test, a 25-watt bulb kept the water from freezing, down to about 18° Fahrenheit.

11. With the fixture unplugged, set the pan in the hole and fill it with fresh water. Then plug it into a properly installed GFI outlet (see "Safety First!" at the top of the page) and watch the birds enjoy this unexpected winter watering hole.

A Squirrel Feeder That's Sure to Get Some Chuckles

Most people enjoy the antics of backyard squirrels. That's why we think you'll have fun with this "squirrel under glass" feeder.

THIS FEEDER provides an unusually clear view of the squirrels that frequent it, because the bold critters actually climb *inside* the feed jar to eat!

James Motsinger of Manor, Texas shares the fun design. His "squirrel under glass" feeder provides a whole lot of entertainment in his backyard. As a side benefit, it helps keep the squirrels from raiding the bird feeders in his yard. Just mount it on the opposite end of your yard away from bird feeders and keep it filled.

James designed the squirrel feeder with holes in the sides large enough for the furry critters to crawl through, but snug enough to make the structure feel like a nesting box.

While squirrels were his target audience, the feeder has attracted a few other interesting visitors, too.

"I've found birds feeding in it, particularly during bad weather," James says. "They seem to like being able to feed where it's dry."

Another plus is that this feeder requires only a minimum of materials. All that's needed is a 6-foot fence board, a handful of screws and a 1-gallon glass jar. If you don't have the glass jar, or don't want to eat a year's supply of pickles to build this feeder, ask local restaurants, schools or other establishments that buy food in bulk if they have a jar to spare.

"Offer to trade a finished feeder for a supply of jars," James suggests. "If you can't find a free jar, a sun tea jar bought at the store will work, too." Just be sure it has an inside diameter of at least 6 inches, so squirrels can dine in comfort.

Here's What You'll Need...

❏ One 6-foot 1-inch x 6-inch "dog-eared" cedar fence board

❏ 2-1/2-inch and 1-5/8-inch galvanized deck screws

❏ One 1-gallon glass jar

Recommended Tools...

❏ Saber saw   ❏ Compass

❏ Rasp or rough sandpaper

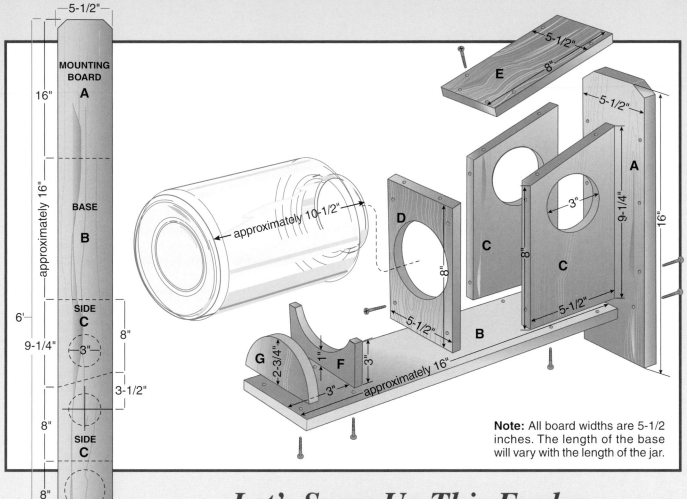

Note: All board widths are 5-1/2 inches. The length of the base will vary with the length of the jar.

Let's Serve Up This Feeder

1. Cut the pieces from a 6-foot 1-inch x 6-inch fence board according to the board layout at left.

2. Make the jar support by tracing the curve of the jar onto the wood. The lowest point of the curve should be 1 inch from the bottom of the board.

Cut along the line with a saber saw. Place the jar on the support to check that it fits well. Trim the sharp corners off the support (about 1/4 to 1/2 inch) and smooth rough edges with sandpaper.

The curved piece remaining from this will become the end piece.

3. Cut entrance holes in both side pieces. Mark a spot about 3-1/2 inches from the highest corner of each board and center the hole from side to side. Draw a 3-inch-diameter circle with a compass, then cut out the holes with a saber saw. Smooth rough edges with sandpaper.

4. Make a hole in the front of the feeder to hold the neck of the jar. This is a tricky step because jars vary in size. Start by determining the *radius* of the jar's mouth. Then lay the jar on its side and measure from the tabletop to the bottom of the mouth. Add these two measurements plus 1 inch. Mark this distance from the bottom of the front board and center.

From this point, draw a circle 1/2 inch larger than the diameter of the mouth. Cut the hole with a saber saw.

5. Assemble the front and sides of the squirrel feeder, then attach the assembled pieces to the base. These joints, and all others, will be fastened with 1-5/8-inch galvanized deck screws. Cedar splits easily, so *be sure to drill pilot holes in each piece before driving in the screws.*

6. Attach the jar support about 3 inches from the far end of the base. Then position the rounded end piece—which keeps the jar from sliding out of the feeder—at the edge of the base. However, make sure there is enough clearance for you to tip the jar out for filling. If it's too tight, use a rasp to round the inside curved edge of this end piece until the jar can easily be removed. If the jar is too loose, move the rounded end farther up the base before attaching it.

7. Predrill holes in the mounting board, then attach it to the feeder with 1-5/8-inch deck screws.

8. If you'd like to make a beveled edge on the roof piece so it tightly meets the mounting board, cut a 15° angle on the back edge with a table saw. Then attach the roof to the sides of the feeder, again using 1-5/8-inch deck screws.

9. Mount the feeder on a tree with 2-1/2-inch deck screws (this is a heavy feeder—you'll need large screws to mount it securely) and fill it with peanuts in the shell, cracked corn or birdseed. Then check your watch. It won't be long before you'll be inviting the neighbors over to admire your "squirrel under glass"!

Invite 'Woody' To a Picnic

Fix an "acorn sandwich" for woodpeckers. It's a novel way to serve suet exclusively to these entertaining backyard birds.

HERE'S SOMETHING that will keep woodpeckers in your neighborhood happy. It's called an "acorn sandwich", and it's designed to give them sole rights to a high-protein suet treat.

Woodpeckers can easily feed from this sandwich by using their long tongues to reach the food deep between the boards. They'll have no problem hanging on to this feeder, either. It's made from rough cedar, giving them sure footing as they eat.

The best part is that other birds, such as pesky European starlings and grackles, can't devour the suet before woodpeckers get their share. That's because as the suet begins to disappear from around the edges of the feeder, it becomes too deep for these other birds to reach. Even squirrels will have a hard time with it.

We recommend buying suet from the butcher at your local grocery during the winter months when it's cooler. It's a treat woodpeckers can hardly resist. In warmer months, fill it with premade suet cakes available at most garden centers, grocery or hardware stores.

You may want to make your own "Acorn Sandwich Treat" (far right, inside the acorn pattern). The recipe was sent to us by Nancy Stone of Friendship, Wisconsin.

"We have many visitors of the woodpecker family come to our backyard thanks to this peanut butter suet,"

she writes. "During the winter when the snow is deep, we sit by a fire and watch downy, hairy, red-headed and even pileated woodpeckers eat their fill. It's a woodpecker winner!"

Make a Woodpecker Smile

1. Make a photocopy of the full-size acorn pattern at right, or simply trace it onto a sheet of paper. The acorn halves can be cut at the same time, but if you prefer cutting each board separately, make two patterns. With a scissors, cut out the paper patterns 1/2 inch beyond the guideline.

2. Cut two 9-inch-long boards from the cedar fence board. If you're cutting both acorn halves at once, place one board on top of the other (rough sides out) and nail them together at the corners with 1-1/4-inch finishing nails.

3. Trace the pattern onto the boards, or use a glue stick to temporarily attach it.

4. Cut out the acorn shape with a band, saber or scroll saw. If the paper pattern is attached to the boards, cut through it along the guideline. Remove the pattern and any excess glue when finished.

5. Cut a 3-inch 3/4-inch x 3/4-inch spacer to place between the two acorn-shaped boards near the top.

6. Drill three 5/16-inch holes through the acorn—two near the top and one at the bottom—for the bolts. The two top holes will be drilled through the acorn and the spacer as pictured in the plan at top right. When drilling the bottom hole, insert a 3/4-inch temporary spacer between the boards to keep them parallel when drilling.

7. Center a screw eye in the top of the spacer. This will be used to hang the feeder.

8. Insert the bolts through one acorn-shaped board and the spacer. Place fresh suet on top of the board and slide the second acorn onto the bolts and squeeze them together. Add a washer and wing nut to the end of each bolt, tighten and hang the feeder from the screw eye. Bon appetit, Woody!

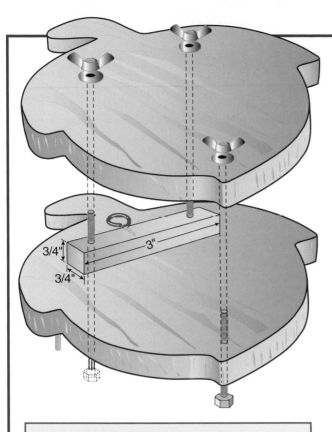

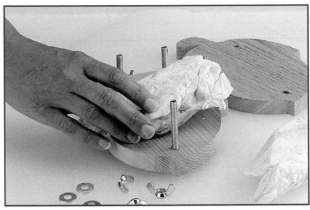

EASY as PB and J. The acorn sandwich is simple to fill. Just remove the wing nuts, take off one side and center the suet between the bolts. Place the side back onto the bolts, squeeze, tighten the nuts and serve a woodpecker lunch.

Here's What You'll Need...

- ❏ 18 inches of 6-inch-wide rough cedar fence board
- ❏ Three 1/4-inch x 3-inch bolts with washers and wing nuts
- ❏ One screw eye

Recommended Tools...

- ❏ Band, saber or scroll saw
- ❏ Power drill
- ❏ Glue stick (optional)

Full-size pattern.
Photocopy at 100%.

Acorn Sandwich Treat

Here's a quick-and-easy recipe that makes a real peanutty treat for your backyard woodpeckers.

1 cup peanut butter
1 cup shortening
1 cup all-purpose flour
4 cups cornmeal

In a mixing bowl, cream peanut butter and shortening. Slowly mix in flour and cornmeal. Store in the refrigerator.

Birds and Their Favorite Foods

Here's a suggested menu to help you attract more birds to your backyard feeders.

Species	Niger (thistle) seed	Cracked corn	White proso millet	Black oil sunflower seed	Hulled sunflower seed	Beef suet	Fruit	Sugar water/ nectar	Meal-worms
Rose-breasted grosbeak				✦	✦				
Black-headed grosbeak				✦	✦				
Evening grosbeak		✦	✦	✦	✦				
Northern cardinal		✦	✦	✦	✦		✦		
Indigo bunting	✦				✦				
Eastern towhee	✦	✦	✦	✦	✦				
Dark-eyed junco	✦	✦	✦	✦	✦				
White-crowned sparrow	✦	✦	✦	✦	✦				
White-throated sparrow	✦	✦	✦	✦	✦				
American tree sparrow	✦	✦	✦		✦				
Chipping sparrow	✦	✦	✦		✦				
Song sparrow	✦	✦	✦		✦				
House sparrow	✦	✦	✦	✦	✦				
House finch	✦	✦	✦	✦	✦				
Purple finch	✦	✦	✦	✦	✦				
American goldfinch	✦	✦	✦	✦	✦				
Pine siskin	✦	✦	✦	✦	✦				
Scarlet tanager							✦	✦	✦
Western tanager							✦	✦	✦
Baltimore oriole							✦	✦	
Red-winged blackbird		✦		✦	✦				✦
Bluebirds							✦		✦
Wood thrush							✦		
American robin							✦		✦
Gray catbird							✦		
Northern mockingbird							✦		✦
Brown thrasher							✦		✦
Ruby-throated hummingbird								✦	
Anna's hummingbird								✦	
Broad-tailed hummingbird								✦	
Tufted titmouse	✦			✦	✦	✦			
Black-capped chickadee	✦			✦	✦	✦			
White-breasted nuthatch				✦	✦	✦			
Carolina wren						✦			✦
Cedar waxwing							✦		
Woodpeckers				✦	✦	✦	✦		
Scrub jay		✦		✦	✦	✦	✦		
Blue jay		✦		✦	✦	✦	✦		
Mourning dove	✦	✦	✦	✦	✦				
Northern bobwhite		✦	✦		✦				
Ring-necked pheasant		✦	✦		✦				
Canada goose		✦							
Mallard		✦							

Source: *Garden Birds of America* by George H. Harrison. Willow Creek Press, 1996.

Chapter 3
Garden Helpers

*W*e can't promise a groundskeeper, but we certainly can make your backyard chores easier with the clever projects on the following pages.

Readers have shared their practical plans for work surfaces that make sense, gadgets to keep your shed or garage tidy and fantastic solutions for saving your back from unnecessary strain. There are even a few plans that will give your plants a hand, too.

So, if you've hoped for some help in the garden, your wish has come true!

Get Carried Away!

This convenient carrier has a split personality. It keeps garden tools within arm's reach or potted plants looking pretty.

TIRED of lugging an unwieldy armload of tools around your garden? Take heart—this helpful carrier is big enough to hold all of your gardening gear and is light enough to carry, too.

It can also be turned into a handsome toolbox-style planter. Just add a few drainage holes, give it a protective coat of exterior paint or stain and fill it with vibrant annuals.

You can move it wherever your yard needs a splash of color. And its portability makes the box perfect for easily moving houseplants outside for the summer and back indoors before the first frost.

Can't decide which option you'd prefer? No problem—it's so simple to make that you won't mind building two!

Let's Start Building

1. From an 8-foot 1-inch x 8-inch pine board, cut the pieces following the board layout at far right. Pine is ideal for this project because it's light, which means even when the carrier is loaded with garden tools, it won't be uncomfortable to move around.

If you're cutting the ends on a table saw, set your miter gauge to 75°, or 15° on a miter box. Both the sides and ends use the full width of the board, which keeps your cuts to a minimum.

2. Predrill pilot holes (see "Workshop Wisdom" above right for a handy tip) before nailing the sides and bottom to the ends. (Pilot holes are necessary whenever you're nailing close to the end of a board because they keep it

from splitting.) Assemble the sides and bottom to the ends with 2-inch finishing nails.

3. The handle brackets measure 2-1/8 inches x 11-1/4 inches. Trim about 1/2 inch off the top corners at a 45° angle.

4. Measure 1-1/8 inches from the top and sides of the handle brackets. This will be the center point for a dowel hole. Drill a hole in each bracket using a 1-1/8-inch spade bit. Drill until the point comes through the other side. Then flip the board and finish drilling.

5. Center, square and fasten the handle brackets to the outside ends of the box with 1-1/4-inch deck screws

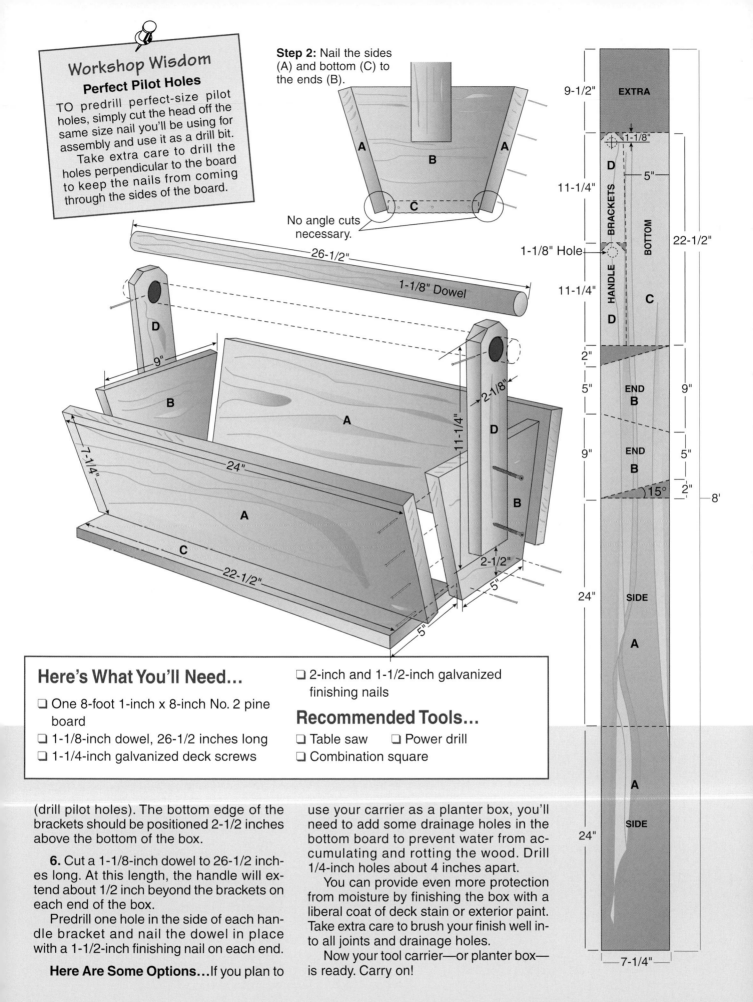

Workshop Wisdom

Perfect Pilot Holes

TO predrill perfect-size pilot holes, simply cut the head off the same size nail you'll be using for assembly and use it as a drill bit.

Take extra care to drill the holes perpendicular to the board to keep the nails from coming through the sides of the board.

Step 2: Nail the sides (A) and bottom (C) to the ends (B).

No angle cuts necessary.

26-1/2"

1-1/8" Dowel

9-1/2" EXTRA

1-1/8"

D

5"

11-1/4" BRACKETS BOTTOM

1-1/8" Hole

HANDLE

11-1/4" D C

22-1/2"

2"

5" END B 9"

9" END B 5"

15° 2"

8'

24" SIDE A

7-1/4"

D

9"

B

A

7-1/4"

24"

A

C

22-1/2"

2-1/8"

11-1/4"

D

B

2-1/2"

5"

5"

24" SIDE A

Here's What You'll Need...

- ❏ One 8-foot 1-inch x 8-inch No. 2 pine board
- ❏ 1-1/8-inch dowel, 26-1/2 inches long
- ❏ 1-1/4-inch galvanized deck screws
- ❏ 2-inch and 1-1/2-inch galvanized finishing nails

Recommended Tools...

- ❏ Table saw   ❏ Power drill
- ❏ Combination square

(drill pilot holes). The bottom edge of the brackets should be positioned 2-1/2 inches above the bottom of the box.

6. Cut a 1-1/8-inch dowel to 26-1/2 inches long. At this length, the handle will extend about 1/2 inch beyond the brackets on each end of the box.

Predrill one hole in the side of each handle bracket and nail the dowel in place with a 1-1/2-inch finishing nail on each end.

Here Are Some Options... If you plan to

use your carrier as a planter box, you'll need to add some drainage holes in the bottom board to prevent water from accumulating and rotting the wood. Drill 1/4-inch holes about 4 inches apart.

You can provide even more protection from moisture by finishing the box with a liberal coat of deck stain or exterior paint. Take extra care to brush your finish well into all joints and drainage holes.

Now your tool carrier—or planter box—is ready. Carry on!

You'll Find Lots of Uses For a Practical Utility Bench

Whether it's used for grilling, potting or storage, this bench will come in handy all year long.

MULTIPURPOSE is the best way to describe this utility table made by Steve Lukach of Pewaukee, Wisconsin.

THIS BENCH is small, lightweight and portable—but don't let its size fool you. It's a real workhorse!

Steve Lukach of Pewaukee, Wisconsin designed the bench for his mother-in-law, Maggie Schimmel, of nearby Wauwatosa.

"Mom wanted a small table that could be used for potting, or as a grill accessory table for our family cookouts, so I made one from some scrap lumber," Steve explains. "She uses it all the time and is always moving it around. The size makes it manageable to use wherever you need it."

But the bench isn't just a fair-weather friend. Apply a coat of deck stain, or make it from pressure-treated lumber, and it is virtually weatherproof. In winter, Maggie uses it to store her extra pots. Come spring planting, they're right where she needs them.

This project is good for beginning woodworkers, since it requires minimal materials and tools. For added strength, you can fasten all the joints with waterproof glue, but the utility bench will be sturdy even without it.

Here's What You'll Need...

- ❑ Four 8-foot 2 x 4's
- ❑ Six 8-foot 2 x 2's
- ❑ One 6-foot 1-inch x 4-inch board
- ❑ 2-1/2-inch galvanized deck screws
- ❑ 2-1/2-inch and 2-inch galvanized finishing nails
- ❑ Deck stain
- ❑ Waterproof glue (optional)

Recommended Tools...

- ❑ Power miter box or table saw
- ❑ Power drill

Let's Start Building

1. Cut out pieces as described in the cutting list at lower right.

2. Assemble the top and bottom frames. Use 32-1/2-inch pieces for the sides and 19-1/2-inch pieces for the ends. The end pieces fit inside the front and back pieces. When the corners are square, drill pilot holes and fasten each corner with one 2-1/2-inch deck screw. These frames will become the upper-level work space and lower-level shelf.

3. Install legs in the inner corners of the frames. The top of each leg should be flush with the top of the upper frame. Attach with 2-1/2-inch deck screws.

Position the lower frame 14-1/2 inches from the bottom of the legs and attach with 2-1/2-inch deck screws.

4. Install 12-1/2-inch spacers between legs. Make them flush with top of the frames. Attach the spacers from the inside with 2-inch finishing nails.

5. Install the 19-1/2-inch 2 x 2's that create the lower shelf. Position outermost pieces against the legs and flush with the top of the frame. Attach them from the

outside of the frame with 2-1/2-inch finishing nails. Space the pieces 3/4 inch apart. (Hint: measure this spacing with a 3/4-inch-thick scrap board.) Attach each piece with a single 2-1/2 finishing nail in each end. The pieces may have moved a bit as you nailed, so reposition them so they're flush and square with the top of the frame and secure with a second nail at the front and back. Attach the 19-1/2-inch 2 x 2's for the top work space the same way.

6. If not using pressure-treated lumber, apply a quality deck stain to protect the bench, brushing well into end grain and joints. Your work is done—now let this bench go to work for you!

Here's a Cutting List to Help...

Note: *The letter after each piece corresponds with labeled parts below.*

From four 8-foot x 2 x 4's, cut:
- Four sides, 32-1/2 inches long (A)
- Four ends, 19-1/2 inches long (B)
- Four legs, 36 inches long (C)

Note: *Cut two sides and one end from each of the first two 2 x 4's. Cut two legs and one end from each of the remaining 2 x 4's.*

From six 8-foot 2 x 2's, cut:
- 24 pieces, 19-1/2 inches long (D)

From one 6-foot 1-inch x 4-inch board, cut:
- Four spacers, 12-1/2 inches long (E)

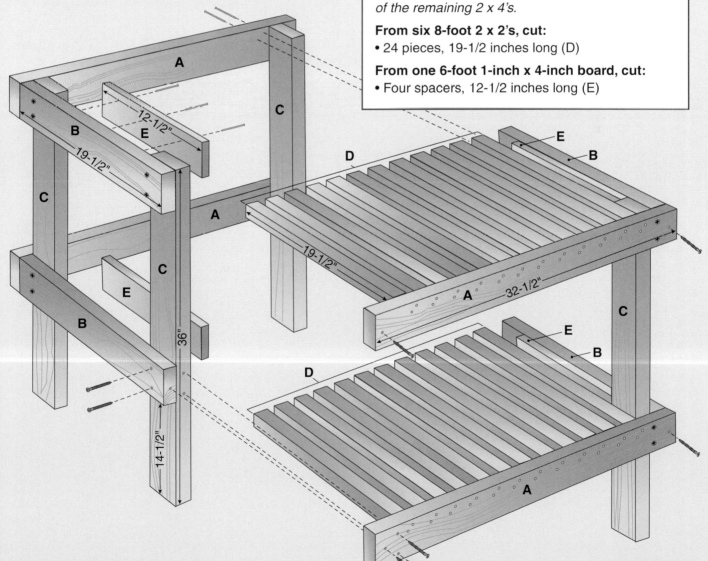

'Picket' Then Plant It In This Unusual Window Box

Your favorite flowers will look great behind this charming picket fence planter.

"DON'T FENCE ME IN" was a sentiment sung by Bing Crosby and the Andrews Sisters. But *you* won't be singing that tune when you add this attractive picket fence planter to your home.

This nifty fenced planter is sure to spruce up any plain old windowsill. Better yet, its simple plans are easily expanded to fit any length of window, and you can choose the style picket that best suits your place!

Your favorite flowers will look lovely from either side of the window when you "fence them in" with your new planter.

Build This Planter...You'll Be Glad You Picked It

1. Measure your windowsill to determine the appropriate length for your window box. Once you decide on the length, cut the back piece of the box from a 1-inch x 8-inch board. Then rip the piece to a width of 6-3/4 inches.

2. Cut the floor of the box from 1-inch x 8-inch board, making it the same length as the back piece. Rip this piece to a width of 6 inches.

3. Cut the front of the box from 1-inch x 8-inch board to a length 3 inches longer than the back and bottom. Rip it to a width of 6-3/4 inches.

4. Cut the ends of the box. Rip a 2-inch x 8-inch board that is 13 inches long to 6 inches wide. Then cut two pieces 6 inches long, using the table saw's miter gauge.

5. Assemble the box. Start by attaching the back to the end pieces, using 2-inch deck screws (make sure the grain runs horizontally on the end pieces and that the tops are flush). It's important to predrill and countersink the holes.

Next, fasten the floor to the end pieces with 2-inch deck screws. Then screw the back piece to the floor with the deck screws. Again, predrill and countersink the holes.

6. Center and fasten the front of the window box to the floor and ends the same way as in the previous step. The piece will extend 1-1/2 inches beyond both ends.

7. Determine the number of pickets needed based on the length of your box. (Select a style that works well with your house. We've provided a few examples at right, or you can design your own.)

The pickets measure 3-1/2 inches wide x 11-3/4 inches tall. They'll be spaced evenly along the face of the box and overhang the bottom by 1-1/4 inches.

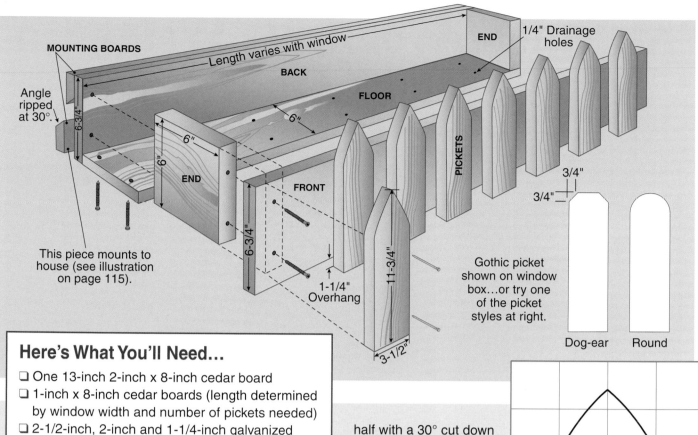

MOUNTING BOARDS

Length varies with window

END

BACK

1/4" Drainage holes

Angle ripped at 30°.

FLOOR

6-3/4"

6"

6"

END

6"

FRONT

PICKETS

3/4"

3/4"

This piece mounts to house (see illustration on page 115).

6-3/4"

1-1/4" Overhang

11-3/4"

3-1/2"

Gothic picket shown on window box...or try one of the picket styles at right.

Dog-ear   Round

Here's What You'll Need...

❑ One 13-inch 2-inch x 8-inch cedar board
❑ 1-inch x 8-inch cedar boards (length determined by window width and number of pickets needed)
❑ 2-1/2-inch, 2-inch and 1-1/4-inch galvanized deck screws
❑ 1-1/4-inch galvanized finishing nails
❑ Waterproof construction adhesive

Recommended Tools...

❑ Table saw
❑ Saber saw
❑ Power drill
❑ Combination square
❑ Countersink
❑ Level

8. Cut the pickets from a 1-inch x 8-inch board. Use a saber saw to cut the tops (or a table saw for the dog-ear style).

If you want to paint the pickets a different color from the box (like in the photo at left), now is the best time to do it.

9. With the window box resting on its back, lay out the pickets across the front. Space them evenly and square to the box. (The end pickets on the box pictured above align with the end pieces of the box.) When set, mark their positions with a pencil line on the same side of each picket.

10. Set a combination square for 1-1/4 inch and position the pickets so they hang below the bottom of the box. Attach the pickets with construction adhesive and 1-1/4-inch finishing nails.

11. Flip the box over and drill 1/4-inch drainage holes in the floor.

12. Rip the window box mounting board 4-1/2 inches wide from a 1-inch x 8-inch board. It should be the same length as the back of the box. Rip the board in

half with a 30° cut down the middle making two pieces.

Fasten one piece with the angle pointing down, flush with the top of the back piece. Use construction adhesive and 1-1/4-inch deck screws. Don't forget to predrill holes in the mounting board so it doesn't split.

13. The other half of the mounting board will be attached to the house or window frame with the appropriate-size screws. Predrill the holes and hang the board using a level to make sure the box sits straight.

Now all you have to do is fill your window box with potting soil that drains well and plant some attractive flowers. (If your spouse has been "impatiently" waiting, you might want to plant some impatiens!)

Before long, your windowsill will be blooming behind the nice, cozy "picket fence" that you put up yourself.

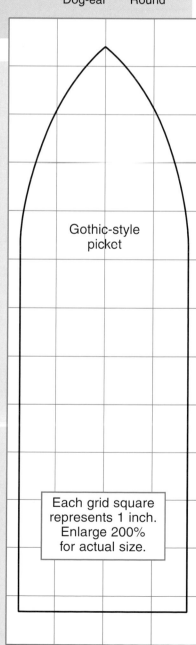

Gothic-style picket

Each grid square represents 1 inch. Enlarge 200% for actual size.

A Project Worth Its Weight in 'Black Gold'

Here's an easy-to-make compost bin that allows you to jump in with both feet!

WHILE many folks simply dump their backyard waste in a heap, this handy bin keeps the goods neatly stacked. It also provides excellent air circulation to efficiently turn clippings, leaves and vegetable waste into rich compost.

As a bonus, the entire bin opens up on any side, making the periodic turnings of the pile an easy and hassle-free task.

This plan is simple enough to get you started, but we've included a few more tips on the next page to help you produce your own gardener's gold.

Start Turning Out This Bin!

1. Cut each 2 x 4 in half to make 16 3-foot pieces.

2. Cut a 3-1/2-inch x 3/4-inch deep notch (known as a rabbet) in both ends of each piece. You can do this on a table saw or with a circular saw.

Make several close cuts (about 1/8 inch apart) across the grain in the notched section. Then, use a hammer and chisel to break out the wood between these cuts. Smooth with a rasp.

3. Fit the notched ends together to make four 3-foot-square frames. Drill holes for two carriage bolts in opposite corners of each notch (see illustrations at top right). Use construction adhesive in each joint before assembling. The nuts should face the outside so that

the bolts won't catch on your clothes when you're turning the pile.

4. Use tin snips to cut the hardware cloth into four 3-foot-square sections.

5. Tack each corner of the hardware cloth to the frame with poultry wire staples. Then staple around the frame every 2 inches.

6. Connect two frames with two door hinges, then put two hook-and-eye gate latches on the other ends. Repeat this step for the remaining two frames.

7. Stand the frames to form a square and latch the sections together. Then fill 'er up!

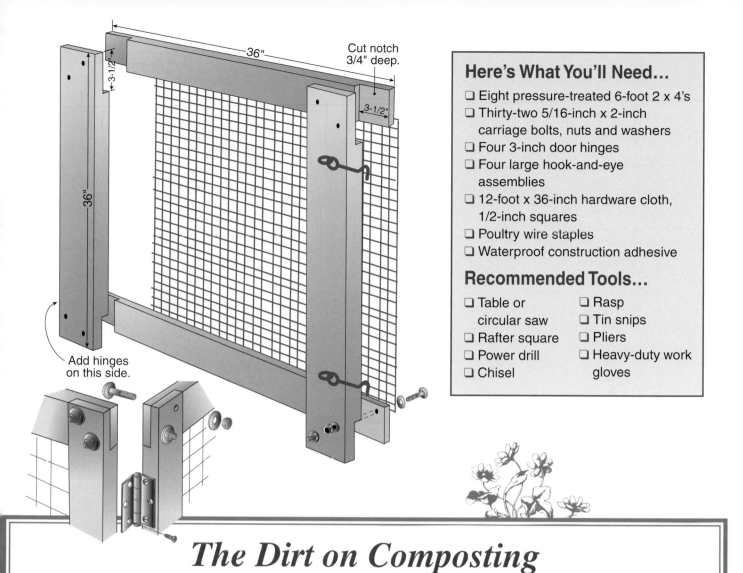

36"

Cut notch
3/4" deep.

3-1/2"

36"

3-1/2"

Add hinges
on this side.

Here's What You'll Need...

❑ Eight pressure-treated 6-foot 2 x 4's
❑ Thirty-two 5/16-inch x 2-inch carriage bolts, nuts and washers
❑ Four 3-inch door hinges
❑ Four large hook-and-eye assemblies
❑ 12-foot x 36-inch hardware cloth, 1/2-inch squares
❑ Poultry wire staples
❑ Waterproof construction adhesive

Recommended Tools...

❑ Table or circular saw
❑ Rafter square
❑ Power drill
❑ Chisel
❑ Rasp
❑ Tin snips
❑ Pliers
❑ Heavy-duty work gloves

The Dirt on Composting

WHAT'S THE BEST and cheapest way to improve your flower gardens? Start by making compost. It's the perfect amendment to garden soil and, best of all, it's free!

Like magic, this "black gold" can be made right at home from yard and kitchen waste. Once these materials break down, they'll serve as a rich additive or mulch that will help your gardens thrive. Here are a few basics to get you started.

The Perfect Ingredients

Equal amounts in weight of green waste (nitrogen sources) with brown waste (carbon sources) will create excellent compost. This balance will provide a perfect mix for rapid decomposition.

What are green and brown wastes? Here are some found at your house:

- Grass clippings (green waste)
- Fallen leaves (brown waste)
- Kitchen scraps, such as eggshells, coffee grounds and fresh fruit and vegetable peelings (green and brown waste)
- Newspaper (brown waste)

There are a few items that you should avoid tossing into a compost bin. These include:

- Dairy products
- Pet waste
- Diseased and insect-infested plants

- Animal products, such as meat, chicken or fish; egg whites or yolks; and bones or skins
- Weeds with seed heads

Finding the proper location for your compost bin is as important as the proper ingredients. Locate it in a level, well-drained area in full sun. Be sure it receives good air circulation and is kept moist enough to help break down the materials. The pile should be moist like a sponge, but not soaking wet.

When's It Ready?

It can take 3 months to 2 years to make finished compost. The more attention you give the pile (frequent turnings, proper ingredients, maintaining proper moisture, etc.), the faster it breaks down.

To turn the pile, simply mix or toss it with a garden fork (see photo at far left), or poke air holes into it with a broom handle.

The process is finished when the bottom of the pile has dark, rich soil that crumbles in your hand.

Compost can be tilled into your garden, used as a mulch, serve as a starter mix for seedlings or for repotting houseplants. You may even try soaking it for a few days in water to make compost tea, which will give your plants an extra fertilizer boost.

There's no time to waste…before you know it, you'll have a bin full of black gold.

Get Organized With This Space-Saving Tool Holder

If you're tired of tripping over long-handled tools, this holder will help you make a clean sweep.

FOR THOSE OF US who are constantly contending with backyard-tool clutter, this handy holder is just the ticket.

It's a great way to organize your rakes, shovels and other long-handled tools—you know, the ones that fall like dominoes every time you trip over them.

The versatile design fits a variety of long-handled garden and yard tools, including those with "D-shaped" handles.

Before getting started, we recommend measuring your tool handles—especially the ones with D-shaped handles—to make sure they'll fit the dimensions shown in the plan at far right. If not, you can easily adjust the grid measurements to fit your own tools.

This project is a perfect one to share with budding woodworkers. It'll give them excellent practice in measuring and assembling.

So go ahead—start building a little organization into your garage...garden shed...carport...basement...

Here's What You'll Need...

- ❏ Two, 6 foot 1-inch x 8-inch No. 2 pine boards
- ❏ Two 8-foot 2 x 2's
- ❏ 2-inch, 1-1/2-inch and 1-1/4 inch finishing nails
- ❏ 1-5/8-inch deck screws

Recommended Tools...

- ❏ Table saw
- ❏ Combination square

Time to Let 'er Rip

1. Rip the sides and ends for the top and bottom frames from the 1-inch x 8-inch pine board according to the board layout at bottom right.

2. Assemble the top and bottom sections by fastening the sides to the ends with 2-inch finishing nails. Be sure to square the corners as you nail. (When nailing close to the end of a board as you are here, it's best to predrill the nail holes using the same size finishing nail as a drill bit. See "Workshop Wisdom" on page 63 for a helpful hint.)

3. Cut four 26-inch lengths from the 2 x 2's. Set these pieces (labeled G in plan at top right) aside.

4. Rip a second 1-inch x 8-inch board into 1-inch strips following the board layout below. These pieces will form the grid that holds your long-handled tools.

The larger openings will provide a 4-1/2-inch space for holding D-handled tools (see photo at left). Measure your tool handles to be sure this space will accommodate them. Adjust the size of the grid as needed.

5. It's time to sharpen your measuring skills. Starting from either end of the 22-1/2-inch side of one of the frames, measure 2-1/4 inches from the *inside edge* of the frame (mark this measurement on the top edge of the frame on both sides).

6. Place one of the 13-inch strips inside the frame so it's centered on the two marks you made and flush with the top of the frame with the 1-inch side facing up. Using the first marks as a starting point, position the remaining six strips 2-3/4 inches apart on center (see plan above right).

7. Nail the strips in place with 1-1/2-inch finishing nails. Before you do, make sure your measurements are accurate. There should be 1-3/4 inches between each strip. Repeat this process for the other frame, which will be identical in spacing.

8. Nail the 1-inch x 22-1/2-inch strips perpendicular and on top of the 13-inch strips you just attached.

To position them, start from either end of the 14-1/2 inch side of one of the frames and measure 2-1/4, 5 and 10-1/2 inches from the *inside edge* (again, mark these measurements on the opposite end of the frame, too). Center three of the 22-1/2-inch-long strips on those marks and check your measurements (all the spaces will be 1-3/4-inches square, except for the D-handled ones, which will measure 4-1/2 inches x 1-3/4 inches) and nail them into place with 1-1/2-inch finishing nails.

9. Every intersection of the grid should be secured with 1-1/4-inch finishing nails. To provide support as you nail, simply cut the end of a scrap piece of 2 x 4 so it fits

snugly under the strips. Repeat this process for the other frame.

10. Use the four 26-inch 2 x 2's cut in step 3 to attach the top and bottom frames. Fasten these pieces with 1-5/8-inch deck screws to the corners of the bottom frame (drive screws through both the sides *and* the ends for added strength). Attach the top in the same manner, but first double check that the spaces in the top grid align with the spaces in the bottom grid.

Your project's complete! Now the only thing left to do is pick up those tools off the garage or shed floor and fill your handy new organizer.

D-handle openings measure 4-1/2" x 1-3/4".

All straight handle openings measure 1-3/4" square.

Each strip 1" wide.

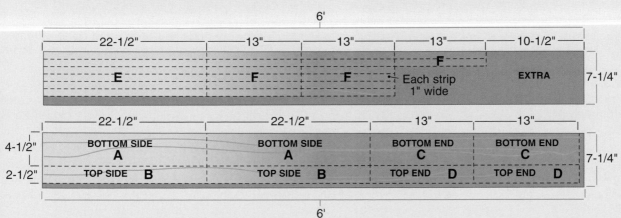

Versatile Clay-Pot Stand Is a Back Saver...and More!

Here's a neat way to add plants along any wall or in a corner. The possibilities for this stand are endless.

THIS HANDY little clay-pot stand is a painless way to brighten your yard—especially if you have a bad back.

The knee-high stand will save you from the deep bending associated with a ground-level garden. You can even tend your plants from the comfort of a lawn chair or a small stool.

Here are many more great features worth pointing out:

• The stand fits neatly against a straight wall (above), or can be turned around and tucked snugly into a corner (at top right).

• There's little to no weeding necessary.

• When the pots are removed, the stand becomes portable. It's light enough to easily move from one place to another.

• The sturdy stand holds its ground on windy days. You won't have to pick up tipped flowerpots.

• It's also ideal when placed near the back door closest to the kitchen—just grow a different herb in each pot for an instant herb garden.

• If you have a taste for fresh vegetables but don't have space for a garden, don't worry. Just find a sunny spot large enough to accommodate this clay-pot stand and fill it with some of the new container vegetables specifically bred for flowerpot gardening.

If that's not enough from one project, here's one more thing to add to the list. When someone asks, "How's your garden growing?" you can actually say, "It's gone to pot"...and smile about it!

Here's What You'll Need...

- ❏ One 8-foot 2 x 4
- ❏ One 8-foot 1-inch x 8-inch No. 2 pine board
- ❏ One 16-inch x 48-inch piece of 3/8-inch or 1/2-inch plywood
- ❏ 2-inch galvanized deck screws
- ❏ 2-inch, 1-1/2-inch and 1-1/4-inch finishing nails
- ❏ Five 6-inch clay pots
- ❏ Waterproof construction adhesive

Recommended Tools...

- ❏ Table saw   ❏ Clamps
- ❏ Saber saw
- ❏ Power drill
- ❏ Compass
- ❏ Combination square

Build Your Pots a Home

1. Find five 6-inch clay pots. You may want to buy new ones from a single source to ensure the pots have the same diameter.

2. Cut the piece of 16-inch x 48-inch plywood to a width of 14-1/2 inches. Then cut the plywood with 45° angles on each end (see illustration below).

Be careful with this board so the pointed corners do not chip when moving it in your work area.

3. With a compass, draw a circle 5-7/8 inches in diameter (2-15/16-inch radius) onto a piece of heavy cardboard or scrap wood. Cut out the circle and check your clay pots for fit. Adjust the diameter if necessary until the lip of the pots sit on the surface of the test piece. Then set your compass for the radius of that hole.

Use the compass to lay out the remaining holes on the plywood as shown in the illustration below, then cut out

each one with a saber saw (see "Workshop Wisdom" on page 55 for a helpful hint).

4. Rip two lengths of 3-inch-wide board from the 8-foot 1-inch x 8-inch board. (Be sure to use a push stick when ripping boards. This will keep your hands a safe distance from the blade.) These become the trim boards around the plywood top.

5. Cut the trim boards to size. You will need to make 45° bevel cuts on each board. See diagram below for the approximate length of each trim board and to determine the direction the angles should be cut. Notice the side trim boards have parallel angles and the front and back boards have opposing angles. (See step-by-step method on following page.)

6. On a flat surface, lay the trim pieces around the *(Continued on next page)*

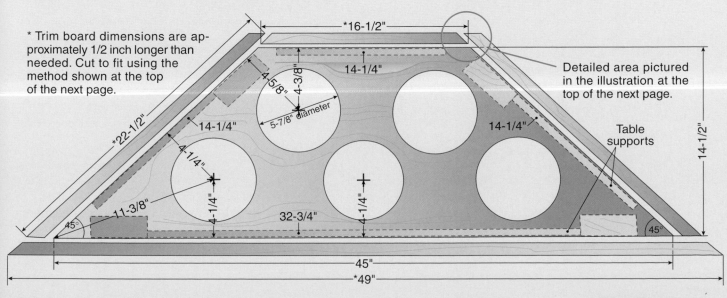

* Trim board dimensions are approximately 1/2 inch longer than needed. Cut to fit using the method shown at the top of the next page.

Detailed area pictured in the illustration at the top of the next page.

Table supports

*16-1/2"
14-1/4"
4-5/8"
4-3/8"
5-7/8" diameter
14-1/4"
14-1/4"
14-1/4"
*22-1/2"
4-1/4"
4-1/4"
4-1/4"
4-1/4"
11-3/8"
32-3/4"
45°
45°
45"
*49"
14-1/2"

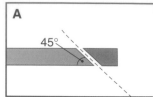

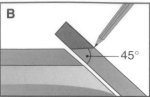

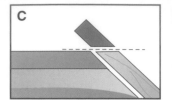

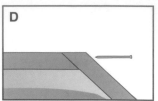

Step 5: To help determine where to cut 45° angles on the trim boards (shown above): **A.** Start by cutting a 45° angle on one piece. **B.** Place it in position, lay the next piece in place and mark where to cut it. **C.** Trim the board. Repeat these steps for the rest of the trim pieces. **D.** To attach the trim, clamp (as shown below), drill pilot holes (make sure they go partially into the next piece) and nail at the corners and into the plywood top with 2-inch finishing nails.

plywood top to make sure they fit together snugly, but don't attach them to the top just yet. Simply mark the depth of the plywood onto each trim board with a pencil. (Do this rather than measure since not all 1/2-inch plywood is exactly 1/2 inch thick.) Later, you will mount support boards along these lines to hold the plywood top flush with the trim boards (see step 8).

7. From the remaining 1-inch x 8-inch board, rip a strip 3/4-inch square (use a push stick) and cut the following table supports:
- One piece 32-3/4 inches long
- Three pieces 14-1/4 inches long (for the other sides)

8. Center the longest and shortest supports on the front and back trim boards and attach them below the pencil line (the line you made in step 6) with 1-1/4-inch finishing nails.

Mount the side supports as indicated in the illustration on page 73 so they do not interfere with the legs.

9. Attach the side trim boards to the plywood top with 2-inch finishing nails. Predrill the holes almost the full length of the nail into the plywood. (See "Workshop Wisdom" on page 63 for a helpful tip.)

Fastening angled pieces can be tricky, but clamping them to your workbench or table will make it much easier (see illustration at right).

10. To make the legs, cut four 17-1/2-inch pieces (they can be longer if desired) from a 8-foot 2 x 4. Add an optional 45° bevel cut to face inward at the bottom of each leg to give them a more finished look.

11. Attach the legs to trim boards (from the inside as shown in the plan at right) with construction adhesive and three 2-inch deck screws.

For each leg, drive in one screw, then square the leg before driving in the others. The screws holding the legs to the longest side will need to be driven in on a slight upward angle because of the tight corners, or you can secure them through the front trim board.

12. To prevent water damage, finish the stand with a coat of deck stain or exterior paint.

Now all you need is potting soil that drains well and a few of your favorite plants to fill those empty pots. Dig in!

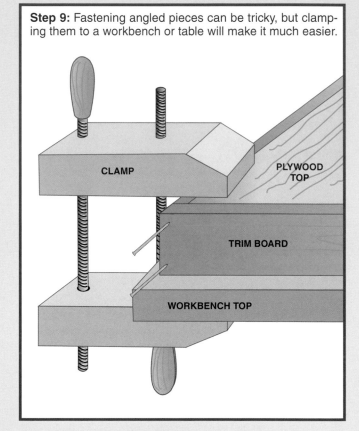

Step 9: Fastening angled pieces can be tricky, but clamping them to a workbench or table will make it much easier.

CLAMP

PLYWOOD TOP

TRIM BOARD

WORKBENCH TOP

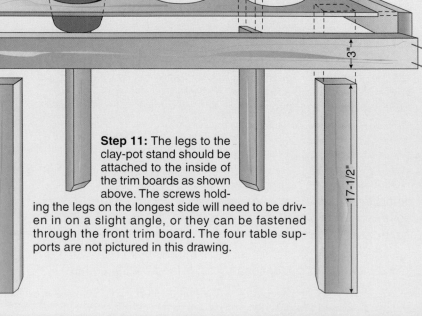

Step 11: The legs to the clay-pot stand should be attached to the inside of the trim boards as shown above. The screws holding the legs on the longest side will need to be driven in on a slight angle, or they can be fastened through the front trim board. The four table supports are not pictured in this drawing.

3"

17-1/2"

A Mighty Vine Helping Hand

Either mounted or standing alone, this easy-to-make trellis lets climbing flowers show their stuff!

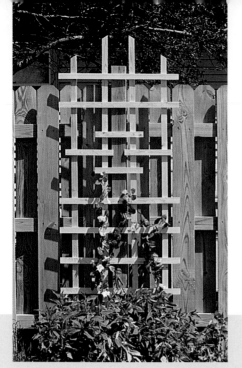

HOW CAN something so simple be so useful? Just ask Pamela Hill of Gilbertsville, Kentucky.

"My trellis was just the thing needed to hide an old tree stump," Pam explains. "I anchored it in front of the stump, then planted clematis and daylilies around its base.

"The clematis climbed the trellis. It's truly a beautiful sight when the flowers are in bloom. The rest of the season, greenery hides the stump."

We thought you'd have use for this project as well. After all, when it comes to growing upwards, nothing could be "viner" than a well-built trellis.

Wrap Your Tendrils Around This Project

1. Rip just enough material off of the 2 x 4's to eliminate the rounded edges. For your safety, use push sticks when cutting the materials needed for this project.

2. From a 2 x 4, rip two outside vertical pieces 3/4 inch x 79 inches. Cut a 30° angle on one end of each piece as shown in plan at right. These pieces are a bit thicker than the rest because they're the main supports. Make sure these supports do not have any large knots or they will be weak.

3. Rip the rest of the 2 x 4's into strips 3/8 inch thick.

4. Cut two of these strips 74-1/4 inches long (pick the ones with the fewest knots). These will be the trellis' center vertical slats. Cut a 30° angle at the top of each piece as shown.

5. From the rest of the material, cut seven 30-inch pieces and four 12-inch pieces for the horizontal slats, eliminating knots whenever possible.

6. Lay out the slats according to the plan at right. Assemble using waterproof construction adhesive and two 3/4-inch brads at each joint. (The joint's strength comes from the adhesive—the brads only hold them in position while the glue dries.) We suggest using a piece of 3/8-inch scrap board for support when nailing.

Be sure to square each piece and double check the measurements before gluing and nailing. And here's a helpful hint…mark the position of each horizontal strip with a pencil line below it so you know where to put the construction adhesive.

Allow the adhesive to dry for 24 hours. When completely dry, flip the trellis over and blunt the points of the brads that protrude.

7. To protect your trellis from weather, give it a coat of deck stain.

8. If free standing, drive the metal pipes 18 to 24 inches into the ground, spacing them 24 inches apart at the outside edge. Place a scrap block on top of the pipe when you hammer. Attach the outer legs of the trellis to the pipes with several 7-inch plastic cable ties, plant a vine and let it climb!

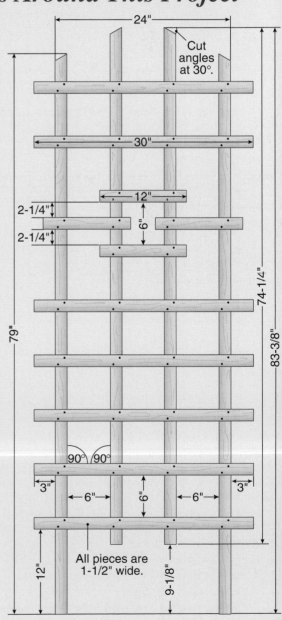

Cut angles at 30°.
24"
30"
12"
2-1/4"
6"
2-1/4"
74-1/4"
83-3/8"
79"
90° 90°
3"
6"
6"
6"
3"
12"
All pieces are 1-1/2" wide.
9-1/8"

Here's What You'll Need…

- ❏ Two 7-foot 2 x 4's (with as few knots as possible)
- ❏ 3/4-inch wire brads
- ❏ Waterproof construction adhesive
- ❏ Six 7-inch cable ties (optional)
- ❏ Two 3-foot pieces of 1-inch pipe (optional)
- ❏ Wood preservative or deck stain (optional)

Recommended Tools…

- ❏ Table saw   ❏ Clamps
- ❏ Combination square

You'll Be Sitting Pretty with These Two-Board Benches

Need a garden seat or a place to display flowers?
These easy-to-make benches fit the bill.

THE USEFUL two-person bench shown above is so versatile that Nellie Anderson of Ocala, Florida predicts most people will not be satisfied making just one.

That's what happened after her husband came up with the simple design. "He's built several of these benches for our garden," she relates. "They're easy to make, and we've found many uses for them."

The Andersons keep one bench outside their kitchen door, where it serves as a potting bench in spring, a display area for annuals in summer and a place to stack empty pots in fall. Another bench in a shady corner provides a welcome spot for the Andersons to relax and admire their garden.

In addition to plans for the long bench, we've included a few modifications so you can build a useful one-person bench like the one pictured above. It has a convenient slot that makes a perfect carrying handle when you have only one free hand.

Whichever project you choose, it's best to use pressure-treated lumber so that the bench won't need a finishing coat to protect it from the weather. If you want to stain or paint it, wait at least a year so the treated wood can thoroughly dry. (See "Workshop Wisdom" at far right for a helpful tip.)

Here's What You'll Need...

Note: *Use pressure-treated lumber.*

❑ One 8-foot 2-inch x 12-inch board
❑ One 8-foot 2 x 4
❑ 3-1/2-inch galvanized deck screws

Recommended Tools...

❑ Hand saw or saber saw   ❑ Rafter square
❑ Table saw   ❑ Power drill

Let's Start Building

1. Check the ends of the 8-foot 2-inch x 12-inch board to make sure they're square.

If they're not, you'll have to square them with a clean straight cut. Just use a rafter square to mark a line about an inch from the board's end and cut.

Then measure two 18-inch pieces for the legs and carefully cut them squarely.

2. Notch each leg by cutting a "V" with a hand saw or saber saw. This will make the bench more stable. Create the V-notch by measuring 4 inches in from each side. Then locate the board's center point and measure 4 inches deep. Connect these points and cut.

3. The rest of the board will be used for the seat. Determine which side should be the top by checking the growth rings on the edge of the board. When assembled, the rings should curve downward like a rainbow (see illustration below). That's important because if the board warps, rain will run off instead of collecting on the seat.

On the bottom of the seat, center the legs 41 inches apart. Position them perpendicular to the seat and fasten with 3-1/2-inch deck screws.

4. Measure the distance between the legs from *where they attach to the seat* and cut a 2 x 4 to that length. Place it 6 inches from the bottom of the legs and fasten it with 3-1/2-inch deck screws.

Want to Make a Single-Seat Version?

To make the smaller single-seat bench, follow the same instructions above, with these modifications:

• Make the seat 16 inches long. Place the legs 1 inch in from the ends of the seat.

• To make the carrying slot, cut holes 3-1/2 inches apart in the center of the seat with a 1-1/4-inch spade bit. Then cut between the holes with a saber saw (see illustration below). Round the edges of the slot on *both sides* of the board with sandpaper, a rasp or a router with a roundover bit.

Whichever project you choose to make, give it a professional look by rounding the edges of the seat. Inspect for splinters, then sit down on your new bench and take a break—you deserve it!

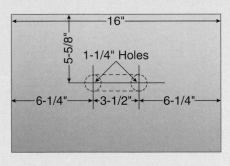

16"

5-5/8"

1-1/4" Holes

6-1/4"   3-1/2"   6-1/4"

Workshop Wisdom
Drying Pressure-Treated Lumber

PRESSURE-TREATED boards (known as "green" or "brown" treated lumber) will often feel very heavy when you purchase them. That's because they're still "wet" with wood preservative.

The extra moisture in the boards will make them difficult to cut, so dry them out for about a week before starting a project.

To dry the treated boards, lay them across scrap strips of wood all the same height so the wet boards rest evenly. This will allow air to circulate on all sides of the boards, drying them quickly. (Wood that dries only on one side at a time is more likely to warp.)

Step 3: The seat board's growth rings should curve downward like a rainbow. This will keep water from puddling on the seat.

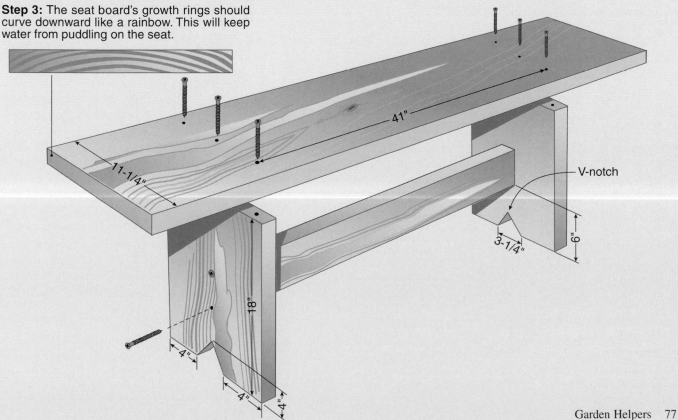

41"

11-1/4"

V-notch

3-1/4"

6"

18"

4"

4"

4"

Mini Shed Keeps Hand Tools Handy

Keep all your garden tools where you need them most —in your garden.

IF YOU find yourself making trip after trip to the garage or shed to gather your garden tools, only to find out you forgot one, you're probably not alone.

One of our staffers, Cliff Muehlenberg of Pewaukee, Wisconsin, solved this problem by designing this miniature toolshed.

"I was working in the yard one day and needed a ball of twine," Cliff remembers. "I had to go to the garage for it. Then I needed my hand pruners, so back to the garage I went.

"That's when I decided to build this mini toolshed. It houses all our small garden tools where we need them most— right in the garden."

The project can be completed in a few hours and takes only minutes to mount. It sits nicely atop a fence post, or can be attached to a post through the back of the shed.

Cliff recommends building the mini shed from rough cedar. It may cost a little more, but it's worth it—cedar resists decay and doesn't need painting.

This design will accommodate most standard garden tools, but before you start building, check the lengths of your hand tools. If yours are too long to fit inside the shed (inside it's 22-5/8 inches from floor to peak), you can easily modify the design.

For your own safety, be sure to hang your tools or secure them to the inside walls so they don't accidentally fall out when the door is opened.

With the time saved not making those extra trips, you'll have more time to spend in the places you enjoy the most—like the garden!

Here's What You'll Need...

- ❑ 9 feet of 1-inch x 10-inch rough cedar
- ❑ 2 feet of 1-inch x 12-inch cedar
- ❑ 1-5/8-inch galvanized deck screws
- ❑ 2-inch and 1-1/2-inch galvanized finishing nails
- ❑ 7/8-inch wire brads
- ❑ Waterproof glue
- ❑ Four brass cup hooks
- ❑ Two small brass-plated hinges
- ❑ One decorative cabinet knob
- ❑ One clothespin
- ❑ One small wood screw
- ❑ One hook-and-eye assembly

Recommended Tools...

- ❑ Table saw
- ❑ Power drill
- ❑ Combination square

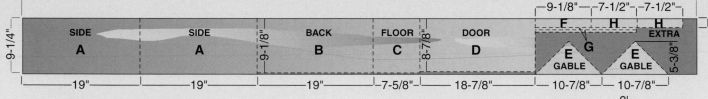

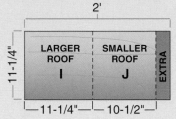

Time for Your Tools...

1. Cut the mini shed pieces by following the board layouts above and at right. To make the gables, cut two 45° angles on each piece to form a peak.

2. Center the gable support (piece F) on the smooth side of one gable. (This piece will be the front gable.) Then attach it with waterproof glue and 1-1/2-inch finishing nails so it extends 3/4 inch below the bottom of the gable.

3. Assemble the back, sides and floor with glue and 2-inch finishing nails. Recess the floor 7/8 inch. Drill pilot holes first (see "Workshop Wisdom" on page 63 for a helpful hint).

4. Attach the back gable to the back wall using glue and 1-1/2-inch finishing nails. Drill pilot holes near the ends of the piece before nailing to keep it from splitting.

5. Fasten the front gable with glue and 1-1/2-inch finishing nails. Attach it from the top of the gable to the sides of the shed. Then nail the sides to the gable support as shown in the plan.

6. Mount and glue the weather strips to the sides of the shed with 7/8-inch wire brads. Set them back 7/8 inch from the front edge of each side piece so they line up with the front edge of the floor. The door closes against the strips, which will keep rain from blowing in.

7. Screw four brass cup hooks into the inside walls to hold your tools.

8. Line up the roof pieces so that the larger piece overlaps the smaller. Predrill holes and attach them to the gables with glue and 1-1/2-inch finishing nails. (You may find it helpful to allow the glue to dry before nailing.)

9. Attach two braces to the inside of the door (positioning them as shown in the plan) with waterproof glue and 1-5/8-inch deck screws. Stagger the screws as shown. The braces will keep the door from warping.

10. Fasten a clothespin with a small wood screw to the inside of the door (drill a pilot hole first) to hold a pair of garden gloves. Attach a decorative cabinet knob to the outside of the door. Then mount the door to the shed with two small brass-plated hinges.

11. Attach a hook-and-eye latch to the door to hold it closed.

12. Mount the shed on a post or a pole used for mounting a bird feeder. You also can hang it on a fence or on the outside wall of a garden shed or garage. Just add a 2 x 4 spacer to the back of the mini shed.

Now gather up those tools and hang 'em up. Next time you're in the garden and need a trowel or hand pruner, it'll be a couple of steps away.

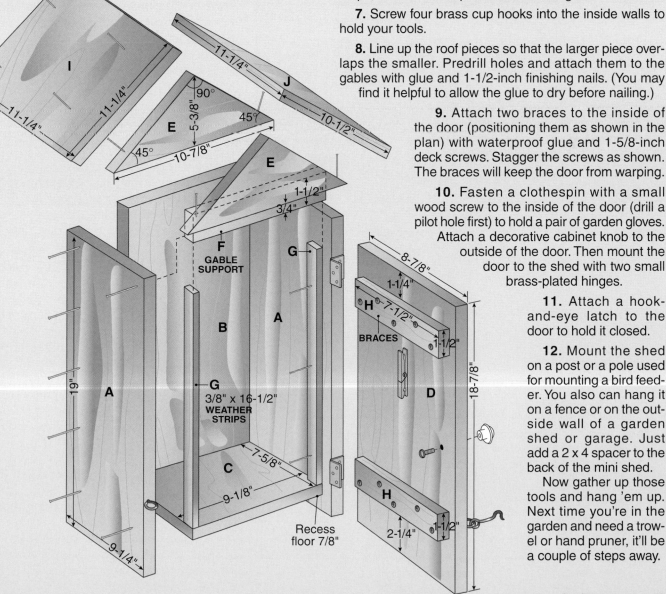

A Potting Bench That Even Organizes Gardening Gear

Hold everything! This clever and practical bench does just that—and may save you a backache, too.

WHEN you're potting plants, getting organized may be the hardest part of the job.

First you have to round up all the materials, then find a convenient place to spread them out. Without a nearby work surface, you may end up doing the job on the ground—and find yourself nursing a sore back the next day.

Sound familiar? Then this attractive and useful potting bench may be just what you need.

The convenient work surface is at a comfortable height, so you won't have to kneel or stoop as you work. A lower shelf provides ample room for storing bags of potting soil and extra pots. And the slats keep dirt from piling up.

The top shelf keeps smaller items close at hand without cluttering your work space. A handy drawer provides extra storage, and it's tucked neatly under the tabletop to protect the contents from rain. Hooks on both sides of the bench keep garden tools within reach.

The bench is made from pressure-treated lumber, which has a high moisture content when first purchased. So give the wood about a week to dry out (see "Workshop Wisdom" on page 77 for a helpful hint). This will make your job a whole lot easier.

Here's one more tip: Don't forget to predrill holes for screws placed near the edges of the wood. You'll spend quite a bit of time drilling pilot holes for this project, but it's worth the extra effort to keep pieces from splitting.

Here's What You'll Need...

Note: *Use pressure-treated lumber unless you are planning to stain the bench when finished.*

- ❏ One 4-foot x 2-foot sheet of 3/4-inch plywood
- ❏ Five 8-foot 2 x 4's
- ❏ One 8-foot 1-inch x 8-inch board
- ❏ Two 8-foot 1 x 2's
- ❏ One 10-inch x 14-inch plastic storage bin
- ❏ 2-1/2-inch, 2-inch, 1-5/8-inch and 1-1/4-inch galvanized deck screws
- ❏ Four hooks
- ❏ Waterproof construction adhesive

Recommended Tools...

- ❏ Table saw
- ❏ Power drill
- ❏ Rafter square
- ❏ Combination square

Here's a Cutting List to Help...

Note: *The letter after each piece corresponds with labeled parts on next page.*

From 4-foot x 2-foot plywood
- Cut the top to 24 inches x 30 inches (A)

From five 8-foot 2 x 4's, cut:
- Four legs, 35-1/4 inches long (B)
- Two inner table supports, 21 inches long (C)

Note: *Cut two legs and one 21-inch support from each 8-foot length.*
- Two lower shelf supports, 30 inches long (D)
- Two lower side spacers, 24 inches long (E)
- One front and one back table support, 27 inches long (F)
- Two outer table supports, 17 inches long (G)
- One drawer support, 21 inches long (H)

From one 8-foot 1-inch x 8-inch board, cut:
- Two side boards, 12 inches long (I)
- One backboard and one top shelf, both 31-1/2 inches long (J and K)

From four 8-foot 1 x 2's, cut:
- 12 shelf strips, 21 inches long (L)
- Four drawer slides, 24 inches long (M)

Let's Start Pottin' It Together!

1. Cut lumber to the lengths indicated in the cutting list above.

2. Bevel, or chamfer, the bottom edges of the four legs at 45°. Take off about 1/4 inch on each edge. This will keep the legs from chipping when the bench is moved.

3. Lay two legs (on the floor) on the 1-1/2-inch sides 30 inches apart. Draw a line 13-3/4 inches from the bottom of the legs. This is where the top of the lower shelf supports should be positioned.

Square and fasten the lower shelf supports to the legs with 2-1/2-inch deck screws. Assemble a second set the same way.

4. Square and fasten the 27-inch front table support

between both front legs and attach with 2-1/2-inch deck screws. Repeat this step with the back table support on the back legs. These pieces are positioned inside the front and back legs (see photo at right).

Step 4

5. Join the front and back legs at the top with the 21-inch inner table supports. These should be mounted between the front and back table supports attached in step 4 (see photo below).

6. Join the lower portion of the front and back legs with the 24-inch lower side spacers. Place these pieces on top of the lower shelf supports attached in step 3 and attach with 2-1/2-inch deck screws (see photo below).

7. Fasten the 17-inch outer table supports at the top between the front and back legs. These should be attached to the inner table supports attached in step 5 with 2-1/2-inch deck screws. (See photo on page 83.)

8. Attach the 12 shelf strips to the lower shelf supports with 2-inch deck screws. Space the strips evenly, with *(Continued on page 83)*

Step 5

Step 3

Step 6

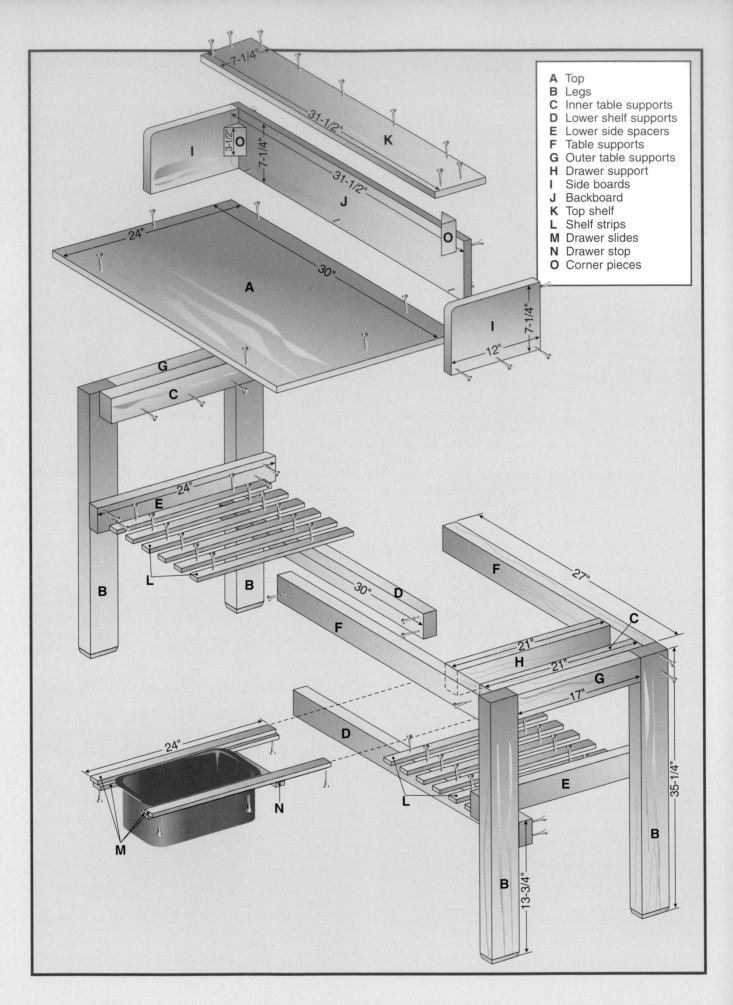

A Top
B Legs
C Inner table supports
D Lower shelf supports
E Lower side spacers
F Table supports
G Outer table supports
H Drawer support
I Side boards
J Backboard
K Top shelf
L Shelf strips
M Drawer slides
N Drawer stop
O Corner pieces

7-1/4"

31-1/2" K

3-1/2" O

7-1/4"

31-1/2"

J

O

24"

30"

A

7-1/4"

12"

I

I

G

C

E

24"

L

B

B

F

30" D

F

F

27"

C

21"

H

21"

G

17"

D

E

B

35-1/4"

24"

N

L

M

B

13-3/4"

B

Step 7

Step 8

about 1/2 inch between each strip. We recommend using a 1/2-inch scrap piece of plywood to help space each strip evenly (see photo above).

9. Assemble two drawer slides. Lay one 24-inch drawer slide board on top of another, but offset them by 1/2 inch to create a "shelf" or step. This will support the lip of the storage bin used for the drawer.

Drill holes for 1-1/4-inch deck screws and fasten the pieces together. (Place screws no closer than 3 inches from the ends to allow room for attaching them to the bench.) Repeat this step for the second slide.

10. Turn the bench upside down.

11. Decide which side of the potting bench you'd like to mount the drawer (we used a Rubbermaid brand tub). Then attach the drawer slides on that side, with one slide butted up against the front and back legs. Drill pilot holes and attach the slide with 2-inch deck screws. Be careful not to over tighten.

Put the drawer into place to determine the position of the second slide assembly. Allow about 1/4 inch extra "play" so the drawer slides easily. Attach the second slide.

12. Center the 21-inch drawer support on its edge *between* the drawer slides. The piece is positioned so that it's flush with the bottom of the front and back table supports. Attach with 2-1/2-inch deck screws through the front and back table supports. This will keep the drawer from dropping down when opened.

13. Insert the drawer into the slides and push it back to about 1 inch behind the front of the bench. Measure the distance from one drawer slide to the other and cut a scrap of 1 x 2 to that length to make a drawer stop. Predrill and attach the stop to the drawer slides with 1-1/4-inch deck screws.

14. Fasten the plywood top to the framework with 2-inch deck screws.

15. Cut round corners on the two 12-inch side boards. Use a quart paint can or a coffee can as a template. Cut with a saber saw and sand smooth.

Attach the sides to the outer table supports (not the plywood top) with 1-5/8-inch deck screws, positioning it so that the top of the sides are 5 inches above the work surface and flush with the rear edge.

16. Attach the backboard. Fasten it to the back table support with 1-5/8-inch deck screws. Attach it to the side boards.

17. To keep soil from building up in the back corners, cut optional corner pieces. Glue them to the backboard and side boards with waterproof construction adhesive.

To do this (see illustration below), set your table saw blade at 45°, lay a 2 x 4 flat on the saw's table and trim off the end. Measure 2-3/4 inches from the pointed end of the 2 x 4 and draw an opposing 45° angle with a combination square along the edge on the opposite side of the board. Line up the mark with the saw's blade and cut another 45° angle. Repeat to make the second corner piece and glue them in the corners.

18. Attach the top shelf to the side boards and backboard. Predrill holes and fasten with 1-5/8-inch deck screws.

19. Install hooks on the sides of the bench to hold garden tools. Then round up the potting gear that's cluttering your garage or shed. You now have a practical place to put all of it!

Step 17: Cutting corner pieces…it's easy as A, B, C!

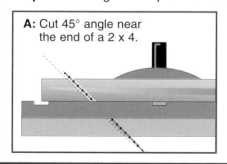

A: Cut 45° angle near the end of a 2 x 4.

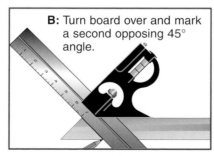

B: Turn board over and mark a second opposing 45° angle.

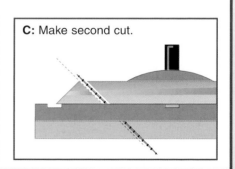

C: Make second cut.

Give Your Plants a Head Start

*Why wait for the weather to warm up when you can jump-start
your garden with this cold frame?*

TO GET A JUMP on the gardening season, there's nothing more practical than a simple cold frame.

Just a few winter hours spent in the workshop will produce this easy-to-make windowed frame that lets the warm sunshine in and helps keep the frigid air out—especially on chilly evenings.

We've seen several cold frames, and this one is inspired by many of the best ideas our readers sent in.

The frame is built on an angle to capture the most light, especially when it's placed facing South. And the metal straps are a sturdy and secure way to make sure the open lids will stay that way. That's a comforting thought when you're working below the open panels.

On warm sunny days, the straps allow you to open the lids to several positions, letting hot air escape so your plants won't wilt from excess heat.

We used pressure-treated wood for this project, which will keep the frame in business for many gardening seasons to come. Just give the wood a week or so to dry out before actually building with it.

One word of warning—we were tempted to build our cold frame with old storm windows stored away in an editor's garage. For safety reasons, we opted to use Plexiglas instead. It may cost a bit more, but when it comes to safety, particularly when young ones are around, it's money well spent.

Here's What You'll Need...

Note: *Use pressure-treated lumber.*

- ❏ One 4-foot x 8-foot sheet of 3/4-inch plywood
- ❏ Two 6-foot 5/4-inch x 6-inch treated deck boards (That's a true 1-inch-thick board, but lumber yards call it 5/4 inch.)
- ❏ Two 8-foot 2 x 4's
- ❏ Two 30-inch x 36-inch x 1/8-inch sheets of clear Plexiglas

- ❏ Two 36-inch perforated rigid metal straps
- ❏ One 48-inch x 1-1/16-inch brass piano hinge
- ❏ Two 3/8-inch x 1-1/2-inch bolts, four washers and two nuts
- ❏ Four 1/4-inch x 2-1/2-inch bolts, eight washers and four nuts
- ❏ Two 3/8-inch x 4-inch bolts
- ❏ Two 2-inch round plastic knobs
- ❏ Waterproof construction adhesive

- ❏ 1/2-inch No. 8 sheet-metal screws (to attach Plexiglas)
- ❏ 2-inch, 1-5/8-inch and 1-inch galvanized deck screws

Recommended Tools...

- ❏ Table saw
- ❏ Circular saw
- ❏ Hacksaw
- ❏ Power drill
- ❏ Countersink
- ❏ Rafter square
- ❏ Grinder or file

Heat Up the Workshop With This Cold Frame!

1. Rip just enough stock off two 5/4-inch x 6-inch deck boards to eliminate the rounded edge from both sides. Then rip both boards to widths of 2-1/2 inches. You'll end up with four pieces measuring 2-1/2 inches x 72 inches.

2. From each of these four pieces, cut a section 30-1/4 inches long and another section 36-1/4 inches long. These will be used to make the window frames.

3. Cut 2-1/2-inch half-lap joints (see plans on next page) on both ends of the frame boards. These joints, which are half the stock's thickness deep (approximately 1/2 inch), can be made on the table saw quicker with a dado blade, but you can also use a regular saw blade by making more passes.

4. Assemble the window frame on a flat surface using a rafter square to make sure each corner is 90°. Apply adhesive to each corner and interlock the half-lap joints. Fasten with two 1-inch deck screws on each corner. Predrill the holes first so you don't split the frame.

Here's a tip: Start by squaring and putting one screw in each corner. Check the frame with the rafter square. Then add a second screw to each corner. Make a second frame the same way.

5. Drilling holes in the Plexiglas must be done very carefully so it does not crack. Drill larger holes than the 1/2-inch sheet-metal screws so they easily fit through the holes. A sharp twist drill will work fine but *do not apply pressure* as you drill. If you have a variable speed drill, use a medium speed. Drill holes about 5 to 6 inches apart, starting about 1-1/2 inch from the corners of the Plexiglas.

6. Cut the plywood and 2 x 4's as shown in the plywood board layout at right and in the plan on page 86. From the 2 x 4's, cut two pieces 23 inches long for the back of the box, two more pieces 11-3/4 inches long for the front of the box and one piece 50-3/8 inches for across the back of the box.

7. Attach the 23-inch-long 2 x 4's to the back plywood piece, indenting 3/4 inch from the edges. Position the 2 x 4's so the wider (3-1/2-inch) side is against the plywood and fasten them with 2-inch deck screws. Here's another

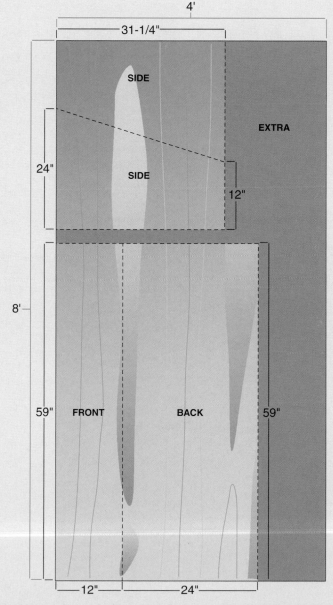

tip: Use a piece of 3/4-inch-thick scrap plywood to help set the indent needed to properly position the 2 x 4's.

Attach the 11-3/4-inch 2 x 4's to the front plywood piece, again indenting 3/4 inch from the edges.

8. Attach the plywood sides to the back and front 2 x 4's with 2-inch deck screws. Be sure to square all the cor-

(Continued on next page)

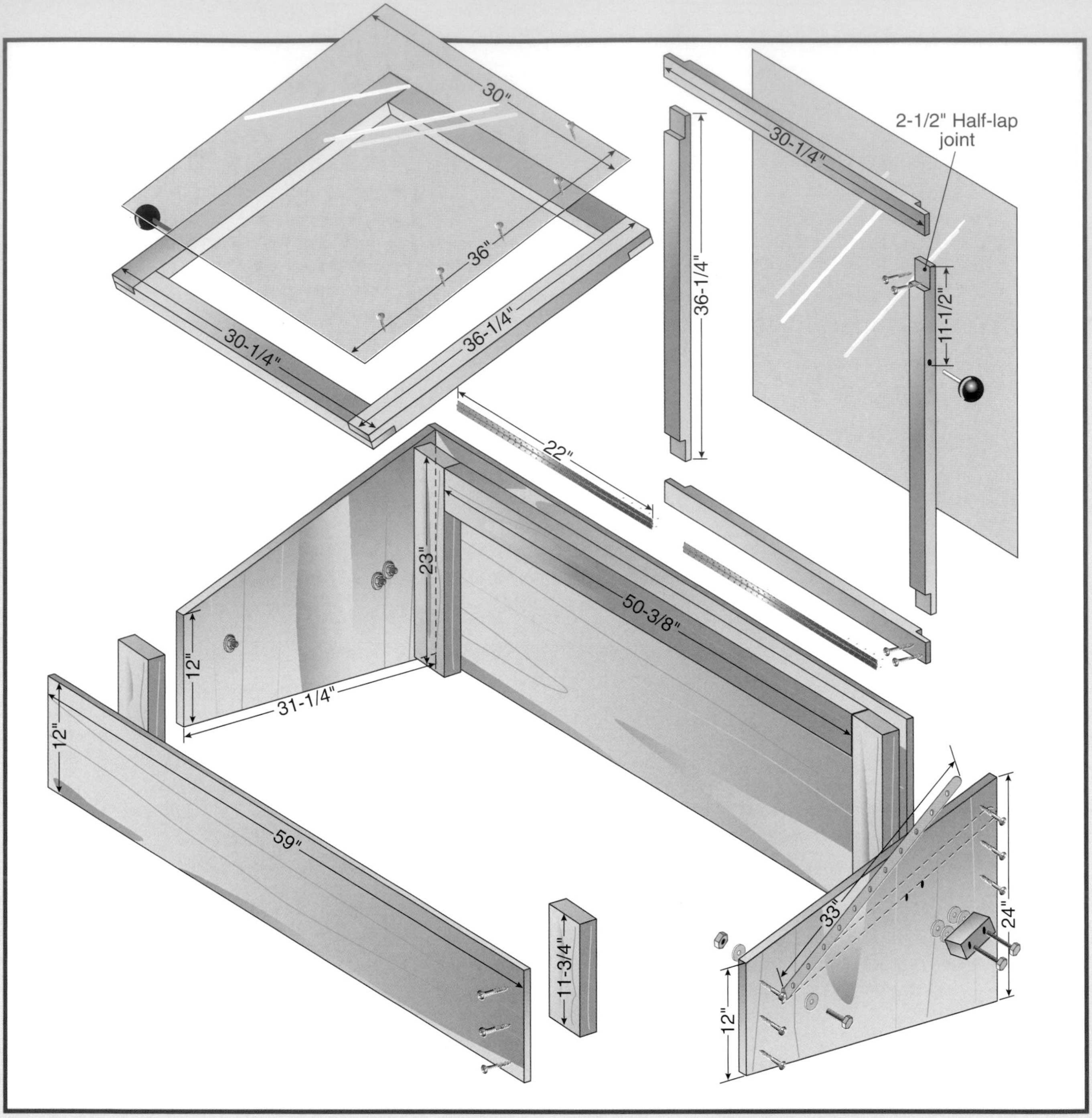
30"
36"
30-1/4"
36-1/4"
30-1/4"
2-1/2" Half-lap joint
36-1/4"
11-1/2"
22"
23"
50-3/8"
12"
31-1/4"
12"
59"
11-3/4"
33"
24"
12"

ners as you assemble. This will avoid problems later.

9. Attach the 50-3/8-inch 2 x 4 across the back wall. Position it flush with the tops and between the back vertical 2 x 4's. Attach through the back wall with 1-5/8-inch deck screws. This piece keeps the frame square.

10. Cut the piano hinge into two pieces 22 inches long with a hacksaw. Attach one hinge to the back of each window frame (one of the 30-1/4-inch sides) along the edge.

Lay windows in position on top of the cold frame—you may need an extra set of hands here. Allow about 1/2 inch between the two windows in the center.

11. Cut the metal straps 33 inches long and round the ends with a file or grinder. Attach each strap to a side with 3/8-inch x 1-1/2-inch bolts, washers and nuts as shown.

12. On the outside edge of each window frame, drill a 3/8-inch hole 1-1/2 inches deep and 11-1/2 inches from the front corner for locking pins. The pins will hold the metal straps in place when the windows are propped open.

To make the pins, cut the heads off each 3/8-inch x 4-inch bolt with a hacksaw and file the ends smooth. Then screw a plastic knob onto the threads of each bolt.

13. To make a rest for the metal straps, which are used when the windows are closed, cut two 3-inch-long pieces from a 2 x 2. Predrill two holes through each and attach to the sides of the box with 1/4-inch x 2-1/2-inch bolts. Place two washers stacked between the 2 x 2 and the side boards on each bolt.

Go ahead—it's time to start planting, even if there is a threat of frost!

Chapter 4
Backyard Accents

*L*ooking for ideas to make your place truly stand out? Well, look no further. This chapter is packed with the types of projects that will have your friends and neighbors asking, "Where did you get that? I want one, too!"

If you're not already convinced, this chapter proves our readers certainly aren't short of creativity. They've provided everything you'll need to brighten up your windows…gardens…patios and decks…mailbox…doorstep… the list goes on and on.

The Neatest Seat
In the House

*This birdhouse bench is a perfect porch decoration that's
sure to quickly become a family favorite.*

YOU'D HAVE a hard time finding a decorative bench that packs more old-time country charm than this one does.

The birdhouse bench pictured above was inspired by a well-weathered bench spotted at a bed-and-breakfast in the heart of Amish country—Holmes County, Ohio. The beautiful bench had so much home-spun appeal we decided to make our version out of un-treated lumber.

You can give it even more of a nostalgic feel by mak-ing it with hand tools and using galvanized nails (where appropriate) instead of the more modern deck screws.

This is a fun project to build, and a particularly good choice for working alongside young woodworkers as they hone their skills. Any hammer marks made during the learning process will just add more character to the bench—and you'll appreciate the memory of how they got there.

When you're finished, stain or paint the wood for a more formal look, or leave it as is and let nature and time "finish" it for you.

Before starting this project, make sure your lumber is dry. If it feels heavy, wet and cold, give it time to dry out before building this family treasure.

Here's What You'll Need...

- ❑ Two 8-foot 4 x 4's
- ❑ Three 8-foot 2 x 4's
- ❑ Five 8-foot 1-inch x 8-inch boards
- ❑ 3-1/2-inch and 2-1/2-inch galvanized nails or 3-1/2-inch, 2-1/2-inch and 1-1/4-inch galvanized deck screws
- ❑ 1-1/2-inch galvanized finishing nails
- ❑ 1-1/4-inch wire brads

Recommended Tools...

- ❑ Table saw
- ❑ Saber or coping saw
- ❑ Rafter square
- ❑ Combination square

Let's Start Building

1. Cut a 4 x 4 in half, giving you two 48-inch-long pieces for the back posts.

2. Use a combination square to mark two 45° angles on one end of each post to form the peaks of each decorative "birdhouse". Make the angle cuts with a miter saw or a hand saw.

If you're using a hand saw, draw the 45° lines, then use the combination square to extend the lines straight along the adjacent sides of the post. This will provide a guideline to help you cut straight.

3. For the front posts, cut a 4 x 4 into two lengths of 27-3/4 inches and set them aside.

BENCH WITH CHARACTER. You can add your own one-of-a-kind touches to this birdhouse bench by painting it (as shown below) or staining it, so its clever design speaks for itself (as pictured at top left).

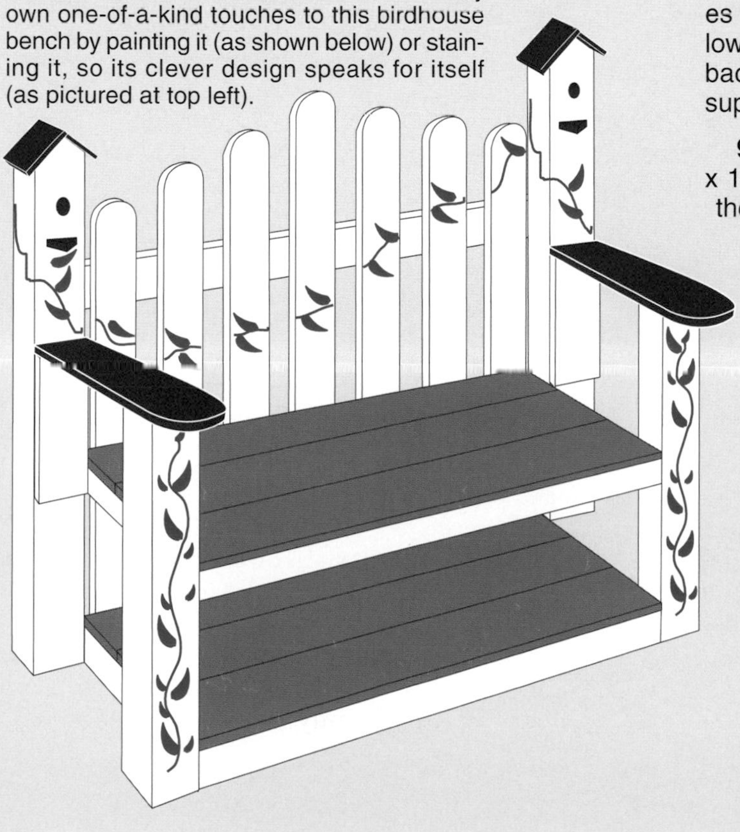

4. Build the seat and bottom frames from 2 x 4's. These frames will be the same size, so from three 8-foot 2 x 4's, cut four pieces 17 inches long and four pieces 38-1/2 inches long.

On a flat surface, assemble the rectangular frames (as pictured in the plan on the next page) with 3-1/2 inch nails or 3-1/2-inch deck screws. Make sure to square each frame as you assemble it.

If using nails, blunt them first by turning them upside down and hitting the tip lightly with a hammer. This will help keep the 2 x 4's from splitting. If the wood still splits, drill pilot holes.

5. Attach the bottom and seat frames to the 4 x 4 posts. Start with the bottom first, squaring the frame to each post (clamp to hold in place). Predrill holes in the frame, then attach to the posts with two 3-1/2-inch deck screws.

To help as you attach the seat frame, temporarily tack a small block of wood to the inside of each 4 x 4 post 14-1/4 inches from the bottom. Then set your seat frame on the blocks, square the posts and clamp in position. Drill pilot holes and fasten. Remove the blocks from the post when finished.

6. From 8-foot 1-inch x 8-inch boards, cut six bottom shelf and seat boards measuring 38-1/2 inches long.

7. Before nailing the boards in place, orient the growth rings so the curves resemble a rainbow (see the next page for an illustration of this). If the boards begin to cup, the water will run off.

Fasten the boards to the bottom frame with 2-1/2-inch nails or 1-1/4-inch deck screws. Begin with the front board, positioning it flush with the front of the frame. Fasten the back board (flush with the back of the frame) next, then center the third board between the two.

Nail the seat boards in place using the same method.

8. Make a seat support measuring 3 inches x 14 inches from a 1-inch x 8-inch board. Center the support below the seat boards and between the frame's front and back boards. Use 1-1/4-inch deck screws to fasten the support to all three seat boards.

9. Cut two rear arm supports measuring 3-1/2 inches x 13-1/2 inches from a 1-inch x 8-inch board. Fasten them to the faces of the back posts with 1-1/4-inch deck screws or 2-1/2-inch nails so the bottom of the supports are 14-1/4 inches from the bottom of the posts.

10. Make the pickets by ripping two 1-inch x 8-inch boards into 3-1/2-inch-wide boards. Cut the center picket 49 inches long. Then cut two measuring 46 inches long, two 43 inches long and two 40 inches long.

11. Create the rounded picket tops by tracing a pint paint can on one end of a single picket. Carefully cut along the curved line with a saber or coping saw and sand smooth. Then use that picket as a pattern for the others.

12. Before attaching the pickets, locate and mark the center of the bottom frame on its back

(Continued on next page)

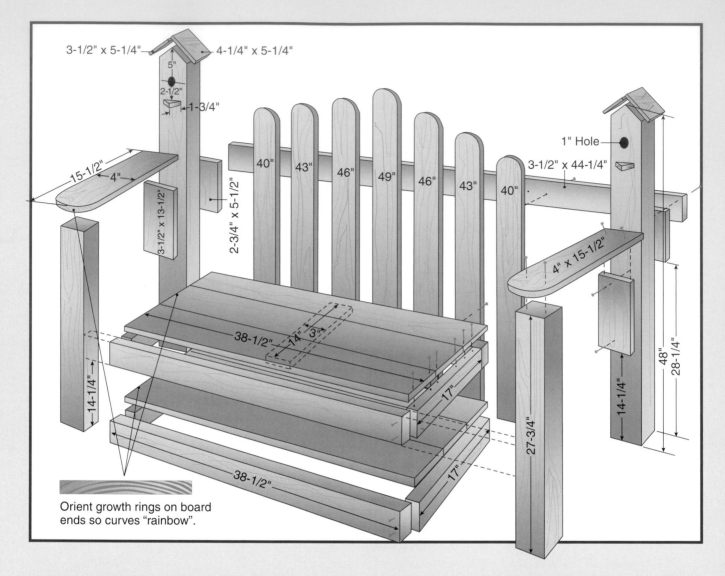

3-1/2" x 5-1/4" 4-1/4" x 5-1/4"

5"

2-1/2"

1-3/4"

1" Hole

3-1/2" x 44-1/4"

15-1/2"   4"

3-1/2" x 13-1/2"

2-3/4" x 5-1/2"

40" 43" 46" 49" 46" 43" 40"

4" x 15-1/2"

48"

28-1/4"

14-1/4"

14-1/4"

38-1/2"   14" 3"

17"

27-3/4"

38-1/2"   17"

Orient growth rings on board
ends so curves "rainbow".

board. Then center the longest picket on this mark 1 inch from the bottom and square it to the seat with a rafter square. Screw or nail the picket to the seat and bottom frames just enough to hold it in place. Then lightly tack the two shortest pickets close to the back posts. Evenly space, square and tack the four remaining pickets, placing each one 1 inch from the bottom.

Step back to make sure they all look straight and are properly spaced. If everything looks good, drive the fasteners home.

13. From a 1-inch x 8-inch board, cut two spacers measuring 2-3/4 inches x 5-1/2 inches. Attach them to the back side of the rear posts so the bottom of the spacers sit 28-1/4 inches from the bottom of the posts. Drill pilot holes and attach them to the rear posts with 1-1/4-inch deck screws or 2-1/2-inch nails.

14. From a 1-inch x 8-inch board, make a horizontal picket support measuring 3-1/2 inches x 44-1/4 inches.

15. Center and attach the picket support to the spacers with 2-1/2-inch deck screws or nails. Screw the pickets to the horizontal support from the back with 1-1/4-inch deck screws or nails. If you use nails, fasten from the seat side.

16. Cut two armrests measuring 4 inches x 15-1/2

inches from a 1-inch x 8-inch board. You can either round the ends (we used a quart paint can as a template), leave them square or dog-ear the corners.

With 2-1/2-inch finishing nails, fasten the armrests to the front post and back arm support. Drill pilot holes first and let the outermost edge of the armrest overhang the post by about 3/8 inch.

17. Make a decorative birdhouse entrance hole in the face of each back post. Measure 5 inches down from each peak and bore a 1-inch hole centered about 1 inch deep with a spade bit.

18. Cut triangular "perches" from the corner of a scrap board. Measure 1-3/4 inches in each direction from a corner of the board, then cut between the top points to make a triangle. Cut the pieces and attach the perches 2-1/2 inches below the center of the holes. Predrill holes through the perches to keep them from splitting. Nail them into place with 1-1/4-inch wire brads.

19. Cut the roof pieces from a 1-inch x 8-inch board. The two wide roof sections measure 4-1/4 inches x 5-1/4 inches, and the two narrow pieces measure 3-1/2 inches x 5-1/4 inches. The wide roof will overlap the narrow roof at the peak. Fasten with 1-1/2-inch finishing nails.

Now have a seat and admire your handiwork!

On-the-Go Chair

Once you try this sturdy one-board chair, you might give up on rickety lawn chairs for good.

THIS NIFTY little deck or patio chair is so easy to make—and use—you'll probably want to build several.

Despite its rigid look, this chair is surprisingly comfortable. It can also be toted and stored with ease, making it ideal for outdoor events like parades, tailgate parties and picnics.

The design comes from Sharon Smith of Blue Springs, Missouri. "We met a young woman whose husband had brought her a similar chair from Africa," Sharon explains. "I immediately fell in love with the chair because it was so unique…and comfortable!"

So Sharon and her husband, G.B., designed their own one-board chair. "We've made many chairs and painted everything imaginable on the backs and seats," Sharon relates. "They're as fun to decorate as they are to make."

Here's What You'll Need…

❏ One 6-foot 5/4-inch x 12-inch No. 2 pine board

Recommended Tools…

❏ Saber saw
❏ Power drill
❏ Rafter square
❏ 1-1/4-inch spade bit
❏ Router with a 3/8-inch roundover bit

Let's Start Building

1. Check both ends of the board to make sure they're square. If not, use a rafter or combination square to draw a straight cutting line. Then saw the ends of the board square, removing as little as possible.

2. To make the chair back, cut a piece from the board 39 inches long.

3. Round the corners on one end of the board. To do this, set a pint paint can on the corners of the board and trace a pencil line around the bottom of the can. Cut on the line with a saber saw. This end will become the top of the chair back.

4. Use the remaining 33-inch board for the seat. Round the corners on one end as in the previous step.

5. On the opposite end from the rounded corners, notch the seat board to create a "tongue" measuring 20 inches x 6-1/8 inches.

6. Cut a rectangular slot in the chair back for the tongue portion of the seat board to fit through. The slot starts 9 inches from the bottom of the chair back and is centered from side to side. With a saber saw, cut the slot 6-1/4 inches wide and 1-1/8 inches deep.

7. To make the handle, use a 1-1/4-inch spade bit to drill 1-1/4-inch holes 3-1/2 inches apart.

8. Cut between the two holes with a saber saw, then soften the edges of the handle on both sides of the board with sandpaper or a router with a 3/8-inch roundover bit.

9. Round the edges of the seat board and seat back. Only round the seating portion of the chair. The leg area below the seat should have straight edges for stability.

10. Protect the chair with a coat of deck stain or add the special design of your choice.

After it dries, take your new chair to the nearest shady tree…and relax!

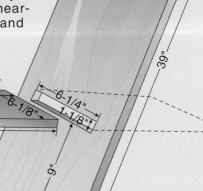

Growing Up, Up, Up!

If you want to show off your prized potted plants, this three-tiered stand is a step in the right direction.

DISPLAYING plants has never been easier than with this space-saving stand inspired by a suggestion from one of our staffers, Mary Isaacson of West Allis, Wisconsin. (That's her pictured at right.)

"I thought a stepladder-type stand would look nice and allow several plants to be displayed in a small space," Mary says. "It would be especially pretty with plants like ivy that would cascade over the sides."

So we took her to task and made this three-tiered plant stand that's an attractive showcase not only for trailing plants, but also for small annuals, herbs, seedlings…the list is endless.

Its wide shelves provide a stable platform for potted plants, and it also folds up so it can easily be stored without taking up a lot of room.

Since its small size makes it portable, the stand is also perfect for displaying tender tropical plants that need to be moved inside over winter.

A word of caution…This plant stand is designed for display use only and should not to be used as a stepladder.

Here's What You'll Need…

- ❑ 12 feet of 1-inch x 8-inch No. 2 pine board
- ❑ 1-5/8-inch, 1-1/2-inch and 1-1/4-inch galvanized deck screws
- ❑ 1-1/4-inch finishing nails
- ❑ 7/8-inch wire brads
- ❑ Waterproof construction adhesive

Recommended Tools…

- ❑ 20-inch x 25-inch brown kraft paper or a sliding bevel
- ❑ Power drill
- ❑ Countersink bit (optional, see "Workshop Wisdom" at far right)

Here's the Step by Step

1. Cut out the plant stand pieces as shown in the board layout at bottom right.

2. Carefully align both sets of legs to ensure they open at the same angle before joining them to the leg supports. You can do this using the kraft paper method below, or with a sliding bevel—a tool made specifically for copying angles. (A sliding bevel is available for about $6 at any hardware store.)

Kraft paper method: Tape the kraft paper onto your work table so it's flush with the table edge closest to you.

Draw a line (at least 24 inches long) perpendicular to the table edge in the center of the paper. Lay one pair of legs on the paper as pictured at right, with the inside corners meeting at the drawn line and the outer corners flush with the edge of your work surface. The distance between the drawn line to the innermost point at the *bottom* of each

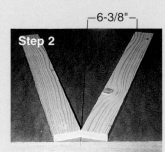

Step 2

6-3/8"

leg (the ends farthest from you) should be 6-3/8 inches.

3. Tack a scrap board (at least 16 inches long) across the bottom of the legs to hold them in place. Leave this temporary board attached until the project is built.

4. Place one leg support at the top end of the legs (the end closest to you). Attach the support with 1-1/4-inch deck screws as shown in the diagram at right, making sure the pivot screw is in the proper position. The position of the two screws on the other leg does not matter. *The leg with one screw pivots so the stand can be folded.* Predrill and countersink these holes.

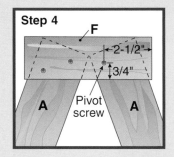

Step 4

5. Use the same method in steps 2, 3 and 4 to assemble the second set of legs. Again, attach the leg support using two screws in one leg and one in the other. *However, the pivot screw must be in the opposite leg.* This will ensure the pivot screws are on the *same side* of the ladder when it's assembled.

6. The shelf supports are located 8 and 16 inches from the bottom of each leg. Mark these locations on the inside of each leg at the outermost edge.

Place a long straight edge between these marks and on the front and back legs, then draw a line. (You can also use a sliding bevel. Just copy the angle from the bottom of the leg support.)

Glue *the top* of the shelf supports along the drawn lines and secure with 1-1/4-inch finishing nails. The back of the supports should be flush with the inside edge of each leg.

7. Nail the shelf stops to the back edge of each shelf with 7/8-inch wire brads and construction adhesive. The stops should be above the top surface of the shelf by about 1/8 to 1/4 inch. This will keep potted plants from sliding off the back of the shelves.

8. Stand both sets of legs about 15 inches apart (recruit a helper for this step). *Make sure the legs with the pivot screw are on the same side.* Center and attach the top shelf to the leg supports with four 1-5/8-

inch deck screws. Predrill and countersink pilot holes.

9. Glue the middle and bottom shelves to the shelf supports and clamp until the glue dries. The back edge of the shelves should be flush with the back ends of the shelf supports.

10. Predrill and countersink a 1-5/8-inch deck screw into the ends of each shelf, fastening from the outside of the legs. Be careful you don't miss the end of the shelves with your screws.

11. Remove the scrap board attached in step 3. Then paint or stain the stand as desired.

When dry, you're ready to step up and arrange an eye-pleasing display of your favorite potted plants.

> ## Workshop Wisdom
> ### For a Professional Look...
>
> DECK SCREWS are self-countersinking. However, when a finished look is desired (such as in the case of this plant stand), we recommend you countersink the screw heads.
>
> To do this, drill pilot holes first. After you drill the holes, drill them again with a countersink bit. You'll be very pleased with the professional look.

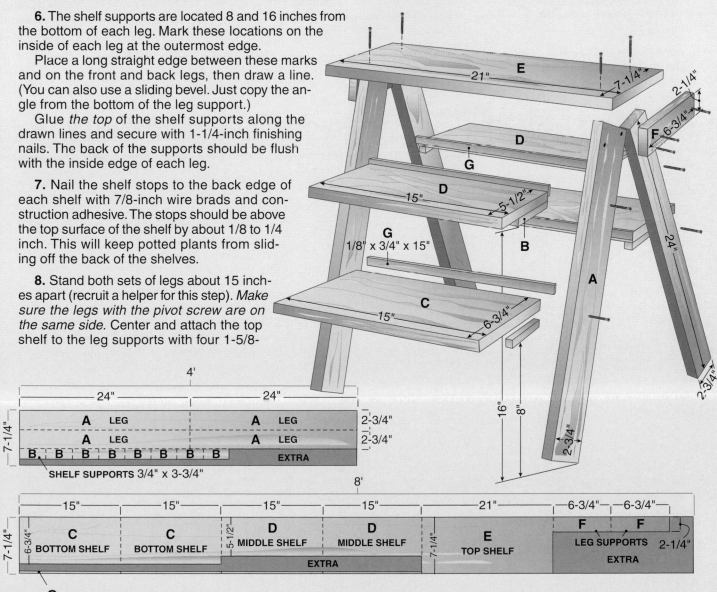

Pyramid Trellis Takes Gardening to New Heights

With this 7-foot trellis, your vining plants will have nowhere to go but up.

MARY LEE and Allen Millikin have built several trellises since their retirement, but this design was their first, and it's still the one they prize most.

"We admired a trellis like this at my cousin's house, then saw one just like it in a magazine," recalls Mary Lee of Ruther Glen, Virginia. "It was selling for $79 in the magazine, but our cost was around $20—quite a difference—and much more rewarding since we built it ourselves!

"One year we planted several mandevillas at its base. Since the trellis is 7 feet tall, we were able to see the top of it, with those beautiful blooms, while sitting in our easy chairs inside the house."

We recommend building this trellis with pressure-treated wood for two reasons: It's long-lasting for outdoor projects, and it won't need a coat of stain. Pressure-treated lumber does have high moisture content, though, so it's important to let it dry thoroughly before you begin building.

Ready to improve the view from *your* easy chair? Then read on! ⚒

Onward and Upward!

1. From four 2 x 2's, cut four 84-inch-long legs. Cut at 90°.

2. Cut horizontal spacers from the remaining 2 x 2's. All these pieces should be cut at 6°, with the angles opposing. Cut four pieces each to these lengths (length given is for the widest side of the piece): 18-1/2 inches; 13-1/8 inches; 8-3/8 inches; and 4-1/8 inches.

3. Rip just enough wood from the two 6-foot 5/4-inch x 6-inch deck boards to eliminate both rounded edges. Then rip the boards 1-1/8 inch wide—you'll get four pieces

from each board. From these, cut four pieces 60 inches long and eight pieces 36 inches long. Cut two 45° angles on one end of each to make a decorative peak.

4. Measure and mark positions of the four spacers on the legs. To do this, lay all four legs together, with sides touching and tops and bottoms aligned. Measure and mark as shown in the illustration below right. Work from the bottom up. Set aside two of the legs.

5. Lay the other two legs on your workbench, with their sides touching. Keep the legs together at the tops (a heavy-duty rubber band around the tops will help) while spreading them apart at the bottom. Center the longest spacer at the lowest mark on the legs, the second-longest spacer at the second mark, and so on. Fasten the spacers using 2-1/2-inch screws (drill pilot holes first). Start at the bottom and work your way up. As you screw the spacer to one leg, clamp the other down or nail a board behind it on your bench so you have something to push against. When positioning these screws, leave room for the screws you'll use to attach adjacent spacers (see illustration above right). Assemble the other set of legs the same way.

6. Stand the two sets of legs upright on a level floor, with the tops touching. Spread the bottom legs to make room for the spacers that hold the two sets together. Hold the tops together temporarily by wrapping with duct tape. Drill a pilot hole and fasten the longest spacer between

Here's What You'll Need...

Note: *Use pressure-treated lumber.*
- ❏ Six 8-foot 2 x 2's
- ❏ Two 6-foot 5/4-inch x 6-inch deck boards
- ❏ One 2-inch x 6-inch x 6-inch board (finial platform)
- ❏ One decorative finial
- ❏ One 3/16-inch x 2-1/2-inch dowel screw
- ❏ 3-1/2-inch, 2-1/2-inch, 2-inch and 1-5/8-inch galvanized deck screws

Recommended Tools...

- ❏ Table saw   ❏ Power drill
- ❏ Duct tape

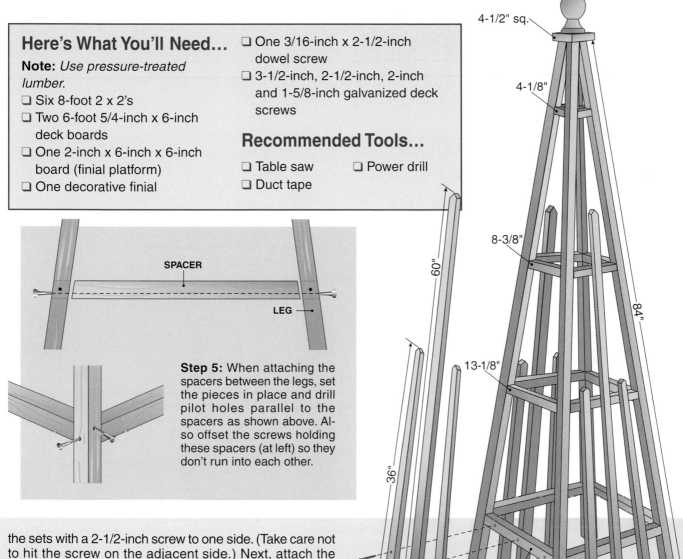

SPACER

LEG

4-1/2" sq.

4-1/8"

8-3/8"

60"

84"

36"

13-1/8"

18-1/2"

1-1/8"

Step 5: When attaching the spacers between the legs, set the pieces in place and drill pilot holes parallel to the spacers as shown above. Also offset the screws holding these spacers (at left) so they don't run into each other.

the sets with a 2-1/2-inch screw to one side. (Take care not to hit the screw on the adjacent side.) Next, attach the *shortest* spacer on the same side. Fasten the second and third spacers last. Attach spacers on the opposite side in the same order.

7. Make a 4-1/2-inch-square finial platform from a 2-inch x 6-inch scrap of pressure-treated lumber. (You can find these pieces in the scrap bin at most building centers for a small fee.) Rip the piece to 4-1/2 inches first, then cut a piece 4-1/2 inches long from the board.

8. Find the center point of the platform by drawing lines that connect the opposite corners with a straight edge. Mark the center where the lines intersect with an awl. Predrill a hole for the 3/16-inch dowel screw (also called a double-ended wood screw) in the spot you've marked. Sand the platform for a rounded appearance.

9. Attach the platform to the legs. Predrill holes on the platform for 3-1/2-inch screws. Angle the holes so they run parallel to the legs. Screw the platform into the top ends of the legs.

Attach a dowel screw for the finial in the center of the platform, then thread a decorative finial onto the screw.

10. Center the longest vertical "spear" on each side and attach to the spacers with 1-5/8-inch deck screws. Center short spears between the legs and the long spears, then fasten to the spacers with deck screws. The bottom of each spear should be about 1 inch off the ground. This will ensure that the trellis rests on the legs instead of the spears.

If you plan to use the trellis in a windy spot, you may want to anchor it. Drive two pipes into the ground, then attach the trellis to them with cable ties or hose clamps.

Remove the duct tape and get something growing!

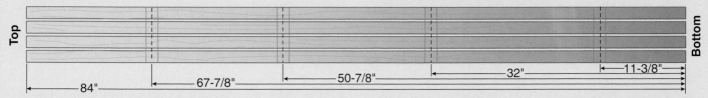

Top   Bottom

84"   67-7/8"   50-7/8"   32"   11-3/8"

Step 4: Lay legs together and mark. These are the centers where the spacers will attach.

A New Spin on Backyard Decorations

The slightest breeze will set this handsome "wind screw" in motion.

Let's Start Cutting And Cutting...

1. Cut scrap boards into four 8-inch lengths. From these boards, you will be ripping the narrow strips for the project.

2. A table saw is about the quickest way to cut the narrow strips. If you have a "thin kerf" blade, you won't waste as much material.

For safety reasons, you will need to custom make a "zero-clearance" throat plate for your table saw before ripping these strips. This will keep the thin pieces of wood from falling into the saw as you're cutting. To make a zero-clearance throat plate:

2a. Unplug your saw and remove the existing throat plate.

2b. Trace the shape of this existing plate onto a piece of plywood, hardboard or Plexiglas. The thickness of this material should come as close as possible to the distance from the throat-plate supports to the surface of your saw's table.

2c. Cut out the new throat plate as carefully as possible with a saber saw or band saw. Install the new throat plate so it's flush with the table surface (make sure the blade is all the way down before installing). You may need to sand or file the underside of the new throat plate where it sits on the supports until it is level with the surface.

2d. With the blade all the way down, plug in your saw. Use a push stick to hold the new throat plate in

INSPIRED by letters and photos from several readers, we've duplicated this hanging ornament that makes a handsome addition to your deck, patio, porch or any other area with a breeze.

When the wind blows, the "wind screw" rotates gracefully—a soothing sight you'll be able to appreciate year-round.

We used redwood for ours, but you can use just about any type of scrap wood.

This project will result in a substantial pile of sawdust, so we recommend wearing a dust mask as you rip the narrow strips. But all the cutting is worth it once you see the completed decoration set in motion.

place. Then turn on the saw and slowly raise the blade. It will cut through the throat plate as you raise it. Stop raising the blade when its height exceeds the thickness of the material you're cutting by 1/4 inch.

3. Set your table saw fence slightly more than 1/8 inch from the blade. We recommend attaching a board to the table saw fence first. This is known as an auxiliary fence and will protect the metal fence.

Using push sticks, guide the wood through and past the blade to avoid "kickback". You will actually cut through the push stick with the first cut.

You'll need a stack of about 10-1/2 to 11 inches of these cut strips for the project.

4. Drill a 5/32-inch hole in the center of each strip. We recommend setting up a "jig" to ensure all the holes are drilled in the same location. This will save time and increase accuracy.

Make the jig from a 5-inch x 9-inch scrap board. Nail two 3/4-inch-thick trim pieces in the shape of an "L" onto the board. This "L" will hold each piece in the same position as you drill.

On a test strip of wood, find the center point for the hole. If using a drill press, place the test strip into the jig and line up the center point with the 5/32-inch drill bit. Then clamp the jig to the table of the drill press.

Drill a hole in the test strip and measure to make sure it's centered (adjust if necessary). When the hole is properly located, clamp the jig in place and drill the remaining strips two at a time.

If using a hand-held drill, mark the center point where each piece should be drilled on the jig.

5. Place a fender washer and nut at one end of the threaded rod. Then fill 10-1/2 to 11 inches of the rod with wood strips.

6. Add the other fender washer and the 1-inch rod-coupling nut to the other end of the threaded rod, turning the coupling in about 1/2 inch. Then tighten the other nut at the bottom.

7. Turn a 1/8-inch nut onto the screw eye and add a lock washer. Turn the screw eye into the rod coupling until it meets the threaded rod. Tighten the small nut against the rod-coupling nut—the lock washer and nut keeps the screw eye from coming loose as the wind screw turns.

8. Attach a large heavy-duty ball-bearing-type fishing swivel to the screw eye. (We found the ball bearing swivels turned with the slightest breeze.)

9. Connect a wire, cable or a fishing leader to the swivel and hang the ornament so nothing interferes with its motion. Use material that's strong—the constant twirling will really put it to the test.

10. Fan out the wooden pieces into a spiral and tighten the bottom nut a bit more. (Don't make it too tight or the wood pieces may crack.) Your new wind screw ornament is ready to take a spin.

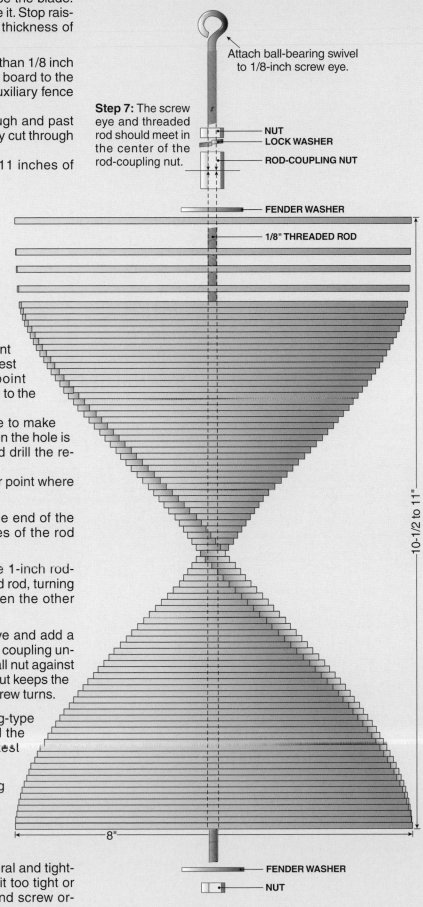

Attach ball-bearing swivel to 1/8-inch screw eye.

Step 7: The screw eye and threaded rod should meet in the center of the rod-coupling nut.

NUT
LOCK WASHER
ROD-COUPLING NUT

FENDER WASHER

1/8" THREADED ROD

10-1/2 to 11"

8"

FENDER WASHER

NUT

A Butterfly High-Rise for Your Backyard

Here's a real conversation piece for your garden. In fact, your friends will be full of questions about this whimsical butterfly house.

OVER THE YEARS, our magazines have received a lot of mail about butterfly houses. Do they really work? How do you attract butterflies to them? What should be placed inside?

So we set out to do our own research on these "flying flower" abodes to find some answers. As of yet, we have not been able to confirm that garden-variety butterflies will actually take up residence in these popular butterfly houses.

But don't let that discourage you from making this project. We're fairly certain placing a butterfly house in your garden will attract quite a few comments and generate lots of interest, even if it doesn't really attract butterflies.

Spread Your Wings With This Project!

1. From the 8-foot 1-inch x 8-inch board, cut the pieces as shown in the board layout at far right. If you do not plan on painting your butterfly house, we recommend using cedar, which will weather well.

2. Cut 60° angles on a table saw to form a peak on the front and back pieces.

3. Locate and cut 5-inch slits as shown in diagram at far right. Use a 3/8-inch bit to drill holes 5 inches apart at the top and bottom of each slit. Then cut between the holes with your saber saw. The slits can also be made with a router mounted to a router table, using a 3/8-inch straight bit.

4. Since wasps like to use these butterfly houses, we recommend stapling a piece of roofing paper or other dark material on the inside over the entrance slits. This will keep unwelcome insects out.

5. Attach sides to back with 1-1/2-inch finishing nails, setting the heads just below the surface.

6. Glue a 3-inch-long 2 x 2 to the inside of the back piece, making sure the bottom of it is recessed 1 inch. Clamp and allow to dry.

7. Nail the floor in place through the sides. The floor should sit up against the block attached in the previous step. (The floor will be recessed 1/4 inch.)

8. Drill a 7/8-inch hole in the rear corner of the floor and into the block approximately 2-1/2 inches deep.

9. Nail the front to the sides with 1-1/2-inch finishing nails, setting the heads just below the surface.

10. Make a 30° bevel cut on the top edge of each roof piece to form the peak. To make this cut on a table saw, tilt the blade 30°. Hold the board upright on end against the fence and push the piece through the saw blade. To do this safely and accurately, make an auxiliary fence like the one pictured at right.

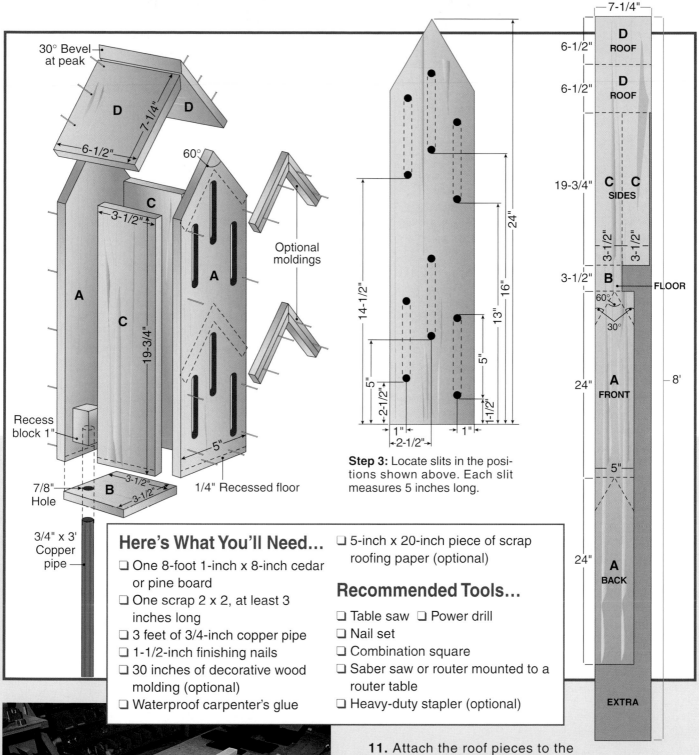

30° Bevel at peak

D

D

7-1/4"

6-1/2"

60°

Optional moldings

C

3-1/2"

A

A

19-3/4"

C

Recess block 1"

7/8" Hole

B

3-1/2"

3-1/2"

5"

1/4" Recessed floor

3/4" x 3' Copper pipe

7-1/4"

6-1/2"

D ROOF

6-1/2"

D ROOF

19-3/4"

C C SIDES

3-1/2"

3-1/2"

3-1/2"

B

FLOOR

60°

30°

24"

A FRONT

8'

5"

24"

A BACK

EXTRA

24"

14-1/2"

16"

13"

24"

5"

5"

2-1/2"

1-1/2"

1"

1"

2-1/2"

Step 3: Locate slits in the positions shown above. Each slit measures 5 inches long.

Here's What You'll Need...

- ❏ One 8-foot 1-inch x 8-inch cedar or pine board
- ❏ One scrap 2 x 2, at least 3 inches long
- ❏ 3 feet of 3/4-inch copper pipe
- ❏ 1-1/2-inch finishing nails
- ❏ 30 inches of decorative wood molding (optional)
- ❏ Waterproof carpenter's glue
- ❏ 5-inch x 20-inch piece of scrap roofing paper (optional)

Recommended Tools...

- ❏ Table saw ❏ Power drill
- ❏ Nail set
- ❏ Combination square
- ❏ Saber saw or router mounted to a router table
- ❏ Heavy-duty stapler (optional)

Step 10: Use a 2 x 4 as a movable auxiliary fence to help cut the beveled peak. Fasten a push piece to the 2 x 4 and perpendicular to the table saw. Then clamp the roof to the movable fence. Push the fence, roof and push piece through the blade. (Note: Make sure your clamp is tight and positioned as shown.)

MOVABLE AUXILIARY FENCE

PUSH PIECE

ROOF

11. Attach the roof pieces to the top of the butterfly house with 1-1/2-inch finishing nails, setting the heads just below the surface.

12. If adding optional moldings as pictured above, cut 30° angles at the peaks and attach with 1-1/2-inch finishing nails.

13. Hammer the 3/4-inch copper pipe about 12 to 18 inches into the ground. Use a scrap block of wood on top of the pipe while hammering to prevent damaging the top of the pipe.

Make sure the pipe is straight and slide the house onto it. Then show your friends and family you've put out the welcome mat for butterflies!

Soothe Your Soul with a Pint-Sized Pond

No room for an elaborate backyard water garden? Think small—turn a barrel into a tiny pool of serenity.

MOST OF US would love having a soothing pond right outside the back door. Unfortunately, ponds can be expensive as well as a lot of work to install. And many yards simply don't have the space for them.

"Don't let that stop you though," says Christine Davis of Platte City, Missouri. "Do what I did—make a small garden pond from an old wooden barrel.

"It doesn't cost much and fits just about anywhere. Mine's even small enough for our deck," she informs. "Plus, the experience may give you the confidence to eventually try your hand at building a larger pond." (When you're ready to advance, turn to page 141.)

Christine's design is remarkably simple, requiring only a half wooden barrel and a sheet of heavy-duty plastic. If you don't mind spending a little more money, you can simplify the project even further by substituting a rigid preformed plastic insert in place of the plastic liner.

Submerged and floating leaved plants are the best choices for a pond this size. The leaves of submerged plants sit at least partially below the water level. These plants act as filters, keeping the water clear and oxygenated. Floating leaved plants, like water lilies, do their part by shading the water, which discourages algae growth.

So go find an old barrel. They're available at most garden centers, nurseries and hardware stores. In just a few hours, you could be enjoying a refreshing tropical paradise in your own backyard.

Here's What You'll Need...

❑ Half wooden barrel ❑ 1/2-inch staples
❑ One 10-foot x 25-foot roll of heavy-duty plastic
❑ Cinder blocks, bricks or plastic pots

Recommended Tools...

❑ Scissors ❑ Staple gun

Let's Make a Splash

1. Cut a 10-foot length from the roll of heavy-duty plastic. Thoroughly check the inside of the barrel for anything sharp that may puncture the plastic.

Fold the plastic in half to create a double thickness and center it inside the half wooden barrel. Have someone help smooth and press the liner along the bottom and sides of the barrel. Cut off the excess liner at the top of the barrel, leaving about 12 inches overlapping the rim.

2. Select a location for the barrel. Once it's filled with water, it'll weigh over 200 pounds, making it too heavy to move, so it's best to spend a few extra minutes finding a suitable location.

Most pond plants prefer full sun, so choose a spot that receives at least 5 to 6 hours of sunlight a day. Try to keep the pond away from trees that will drop a lot of debris.

3. Begin filling the barrel with water, smoothing the plastic as the water rises. The pressure will force the liner against the inside of the barrel. When it's about half full, turn off the water and trim the plastic around the rim again, leaving only 1 or 2 inches overlapping the top.

4. Fold the excess plastic toward the inside wall and

Step 1: Smooth liner into barrel and cut off excess plastic.

Step 3: Fill barrel half full, smoothing the plastic as you go.

attach it to the inside of the rim with a staple gun and 1/2-inch staples. Place the staples about 4 inches apart. Make sure they go through all the layers of plastic.

5. Finish filling the barrel until the water is just below the staples.

6. Let the water warm up before adding your plants. If you have treated water, add a water conditioner to remove the chlorine, or just wait a few days for it to evaporate.

7. Begin placing the plants in the pond. To position plants at the proper levels, you may need a few cinder blocks, bricks or plastic pots (black ones blend in well) for them to rest on. Add these items carefully so you don't damage the liner.

A couple of goldfish will also create additional interest, or you may want to try installing a small fountain. But keep in mind that water lilies and many other floating plants do best in calm water.

All that's left is finding a comfortable chair nearby to enjoy your tiny tropical paradise.

Step 4: Fold excess plastic toward inside wall and attach it to the inside rim with a staple gun.

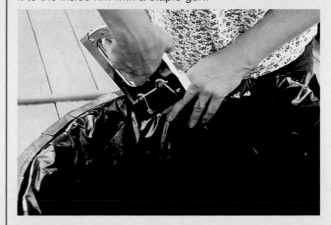

Step 7: Use cinder blocks, bricks or plastic pots to give your plants a boost. Be careful not to damage the plastic liner.

Let Your Imagination Take Wing

Easy to make and easy on the eyes, these fanciful feathered friends will bring cheerful notes to your garden.

WANT TO ADD a little wooden wildlife to your gardens? Give this plan a try. These charming bird ornaments are a snap to create and add a welcome touch of whimsy to any garden or yard.

R.L. Porter of Des Plaines, Illinois came up with the design while recuperating from an accident. "I'd seen some decorative birds similar to these 3 or 4 years ago and thought making some might be good therapy," he recalls. Since then, he's made several of these garden companions for neighbors and relatives.

For the most striking effect, R.L. suggests placing them among flowers, along borders or at the edge of a low bush. "They also look good indoors, stuck in among large potted plants," he adds.

Once you make one, you won't be satisfied until you've made a whole flock of these birdie companions.

WINGED WONDERS. R.L. Porter of Des Plaines, Illinois designed these easy-to-make garden decorations. Because they move with the breeze, they bring both color and action to your garden.

Project Takes Wing

1. Photocopy the pattern, or carefully trace it onto a sheet of paper (make two copies of the wings). Trim each paper pattern with scissors, leaving 1/2-inch white space outside the cutting lines.

2. Position the patterns on a 13-inch 1-inch x 6-inch board (see board layout above right). If you plan on painting them, we recommend using pine. The wood grain should run parallel with the longest dimension of each pattern. Glue each pattern in place with rubber cement or glue stick.

Here's What You'll Need...

- ❏ One 13-inch 1-inch x 6-inch rough-cut cedar or No. 2 pine board
- ❏ One 3/16-inch steel rod, about 3 feet long
- ❏ Rubber cement or glue stick
- ❏ Waterproof construction adhesive
- ❏ 1-1/4-inch finishing nails or brads
- ❏ Paint or outdoor stain (optional)

Recommended Tools...

- ❏ Saber, band saw or scroll saw
- ❏ Power drill

Step 2: The wood grain runs parallel with the longest dimension of each piece.

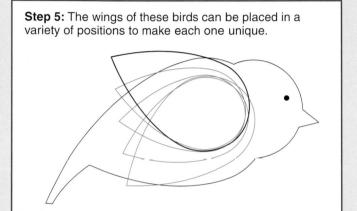

5-1/2"

13"

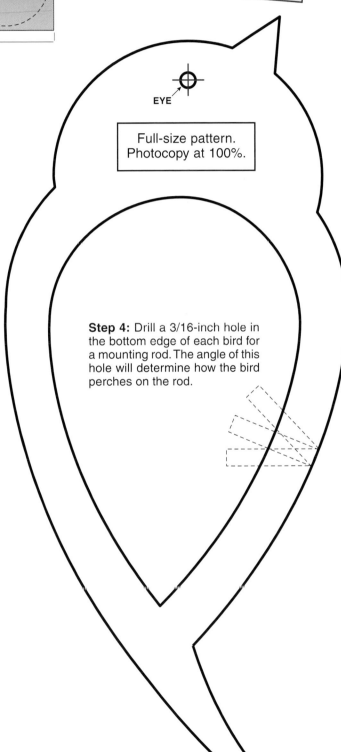

EYE

Full-size pattern.
Photocopy at 100%.

Step 4: Drill a 3/16-inch hole in the bottom edge of each bird for a mounting rod. The angle of this hole will determine how the bird perches on the rod.

Step 5: The wings of these birds can be placed in a variety of positions to make each one unique.

3. Mark the eye of the bird with an awl, then drill a straight hole through the wood at this point with a 3/16-inch bit.

4. Cut out all the pieces with a saber or band saw, cutting through the paper pattern along the cutting lines. Drill a 3/16-inch hole in the bottom edge of the bird for the steel rod.

5. Peel away the paper patterns and rub off any rubber cement remaining on the wood. Attach the wings in the position you like best with waterproof construction adhesive. Tack each wing in place with 1-1/4-inch finishing nails or brads.

6. If using pine wood, paint the bird whatever color you desire. Bright colors will make it stand out in the garden.

R.L. likes to use rough-cut cedar for his wooden birds. To give them an instant weathered look, he adds a little black acrylic paint to a bucket of water and dips the completed birds into the mixture. This darkens the wood slightly to give the just-cut edges an aged appearance.

7. Mount the bird on a 3/16-inch steel rod about 3 feet long. The rod will have an oily coating (it's there to inhibit rust). R.L. wipes this coating off with a cloth so the rods rust, giving them a more weathered look.

8. Find a spot in your garden that could use a wooden feathered friend. Push the rod into moist soil and let your new garden companion take flight.

WOODEN WELCOME. Frederick Keifer of Berwick, Pennsylvania designed and built this one-of-a-kind garden gate from pruned and fallen branches.

A 'Tree-mendous' Garden Gate

Give fallen tree branches a new lease on life—build this one-of-a-kind, charming entryway to your backyard.

THE GENTLE flow of spreading branches gives this garden gate a rustic charm all its own. The best part is, no matter how many readers build one like it, there will never be two exactly alike.

Frederick Keifer of Berwick, Pennsylvania designed the lovely gate pictured above. He liked it so much, he decided to add more fallen branches to the fence it's attached to.

"I've never seen another gate like it," Frederick says. "But I'm sure there are other readers who'd like to make an original one for their yard, too."

Frederick recommends searching for branches about 1 to 1-1/2 inches in diameter. Branches this size are fairly easy to nail to the gate's frame and look very proportional.

To help keep those carefully chosen branches from splitting, be sure to predrill holes first before nailing them in place.

Also keep in mind…it's best to always use dry branches for this project. If you'd like to use branches from a recent pruning, we recommend giving them a few weeks to dry out. Otherwise, they may split after they're attached to the frame and begin to dry.

We've added larger corner supports and a third hinge to our plan at right. This way your gate will be as sturdy as a mighty oak no matter how many times it's slammed. 🔨

Here's What You'll Need...

- ❑ Two 8-foot 2 x 2's
- ❑ 1/2-inch or 3/8-inch plywood (7-1/2 inches x 16 inches minimum)
- ❑ One 4-foot 1-inch x 2-inch furring strip
- ❑ 1- to 1-1/2-inch-diameter branches
- ❑ Three 3-1/2-inch flat hinges
- ❑ 3-1/2-inch, 2-inch and 1-5/8-inch galvanized deck screws
- ❑ One hook-and-eye latch
- ❑ Waterproof construction adhesive

Recommended Tools...

- ❑ Power drill
- ❑ Rafter square

Ready to Branch Out?

1. Measure both the top and bottom of your gate opening. Use the narrower dimension as the width of the gate.

2. Cut two 8-foot 2 x 2's (be sure they're straight) into four equal lengths 3/4 inch less than the gate opening.

3. Lay the pieces in place on a flat surface, with the top and bottom boards *running the width needed.*

4. Screw the top and bottom pieces into the sides with one 3-1/2-inch deck screw in each corner. Drill pilot holes for a tight hold (see "Workshop Wisdom" on page 155 for a helpful hint).

Before securing each corner, apply waterproof con-

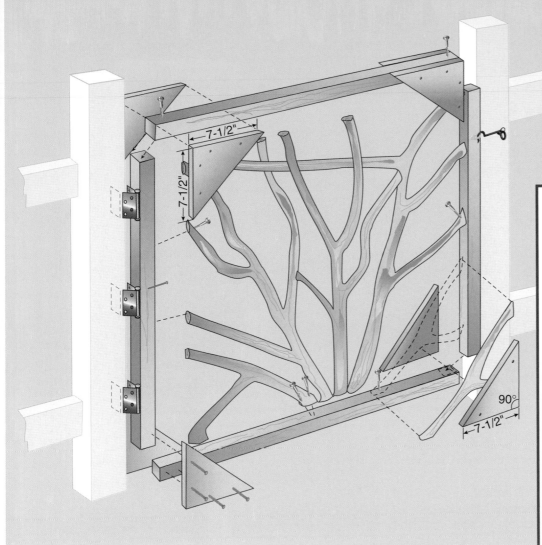

7-1/2"

7-1/2"

90°

7-1/2"

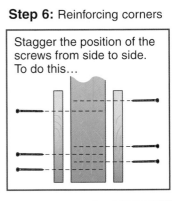

Step 6: Reinforcing corners

Stagger the position of the screws from side to side. To do this…

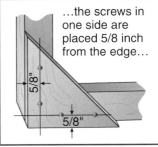

…the screws in one side are placed 5/8 inch from the edge…

5/8"

5/8"

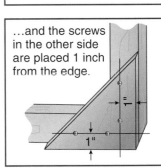

…and the screws in the other side are placed 1 inch from the edge.

1"

1"

struction adhesive between the joints and square them up. Then drive in the deck screw. If the wood splits, scrap it and use a different piece. There's no strength in split lumber.

Follow the same procedure for each of the remaining corners.

5. For strength, all four corners of the gate need to be reinforced on both sides with triangular corner supports. Cut eight right-angle (90°) triangles from 1/2-inch or 3/8-inch plywood. The two sides forming the right angle should measure 7-1/2 inches each.

6. Attach these corner supports with construction adhesive and 1-5/8-inch deck screws. Square and drill pilot holes before securing the screws.

We recommend predrilling holes through both pieces when using 2 x 2's because they're easy to split. Use a 7/16-inch drill bit and drill 1-1/4 inches deep. (See "Workshop Wisdom" on page 25 for a helpful hint.)

After attaching the four corner supports on one side, flip the gate over and repeat on the other side. Be careful to position the screws on the second side in slightly different positions from where they are on the first side (see illustration above right).

Set the gate aside for 24 hours to give the adhesive plenty of time to dry. This is a good time to search your branch pile for interesting pieces you'd like to use in the gate.

7. Attach three 3-1/2-inch flat hinges on the edge of the gate as shown in the plan.

8. Cut the branches to fit the gate frame, lay them in place and determine where you want to attach them (see sketch above). Predrill holes in branches and fasten them to the frame with 2-inch deck screws. The screws should fit loosely into the pilot holes.

Have a helper hold the gate upright while you screw the branches in place. It's best to screw against a firm surface such as a workbench.

9. Attach the hinges to a fence post. A gate stop made from a 4-foot 1-inch x 2-inch furring strip will provide a surface for the gate to close against.

10. Install a hook-and-eye latch to hold the gate closed. The eye should be on the gate with the hook on the post.

Once your neighbors see the newest addition to your yard, don't be surprised if they ask you to build a gate for them. Why, you might even have to open a branch office!

Little Log Snowman Will Brighten the Holiday Season

Here's a project husbands and wives can merrily make together.

FROSTY THE SNOWMAN's got nothing on this festive fellow! The little log snowman at right is the creation of Dick and Ona Marie Amman of Beulah, Colorado.

In sharing their plan, Dick says, "This is an excellent husband-wife craft project. I do the rough cuts and assembling, and Ona Marie does the decorative detail work."

What started out as a simple Christmas gift idea for a few relatives has become quite a seasonal business for Dick and Ona Marie.

Why not try their project? Whether working as a team or solo, you'll find it a good way to use up some scraps from your workshop or craft room...and melt a few hearts as you spread some welcome holiday cheer.

SUN'S SHINING...S'NO PROBLEM. This snowman decoration made from landscape timber will stay around all winter. Ona Marie and Dick Amman of Beulah, Colorado share their plan for this friendly fellow.

Here's What You'll Need...

- ❑ One 18-inch 3-inch x 4-inch piece of landscape timber (or any round log, fence post, etc.)
- ❑ One 2-foot 1-inch x 6-inch pine board
- ❑ 1-5/8-inch galvanized deck screws
- ❑ 1-inch wire brads
- ❑ Waterproof construction adhesive
- ❑ Glue stick
- ❑ Black buttons
- ❑ One 5/16-inch dowel, 2-1/4 inches long (for nose)
- ❑ One 3/16-inch dowel, 2-1/2 inches long (for pipe)
- ❑ One piece of corncob (for pipe, available at craft stores)
- ❑ Black, white and orange or red exterior paint

Recommended Tools...

- ❑ Saber saw or scroll saw
- ❑ Hot-melt glue gun
- ❑ Power drill   ❑ Pocketknife

Let's Build a Snowman!

1. Cut landscape log to proper lengths. The body is 14 inches high and the hat crown is 4 inches high.

2. From the 1-inch x 6-inch board, cut the 7-inch x 5-1/2-inch base.

3. Photocopy or trace the full-size patterns on page 108 for the arms, feet and hat brim. With a scissors, cut out the patterns 1/2 inch beyond the guide-lines (see "Workshop Wisdom" on page 103 for a helpful hint). Paste the patterns onto the 1-inch x 6-inch board with a glue stick.

4. Cut out the pieces with a saber saw or scroll saw and sand any rough edges.

5. Paint the pieces with exterior paint. The body and arms are white, and the hat, feet and base are black. The nose, which is whittled to a "carrot" point, can be painted orange or red.

6. Attach the base to one end of the log body with two 1-5/8-inch deck screws.

7. Fasten the hat brim onto the top end of the log body with 1-5/8-inch deck screws. Glue the hat crown in place on top of the brim with waterproof construction adhesive.

8. Attach each of the arms with a 1-5/8-inch deck screw, locating them about 9-1/2 inches above the base. Drill pilot holes through the arms so the wood doesn't split.

9. Attach the feet to the log with construction adhesive or a 1-5/8-inch deck screw. Center the piece as shown in the plan at right.

10. Tack black buttons into place with wire brads to make the eyes and mouth of the snowman.

11. Drill a 5/16-inch hole for the nose. Put some glue in the hole and insert the 5/16-inch dowel.

12. Drill a 3/16-inch hole for the pipe. Glue the 3/16-inch dowel in place. After it's dry, add a piece of corncob on the end for the pipe bowl.

13. Decorate the rest of the snowman as you desire. A hot-melt glue gun is a handy tool when it comes to dressing it up. Have fun and use your imagination. There's plenty of time because this snowman won't melt!

(Patterns on next page)

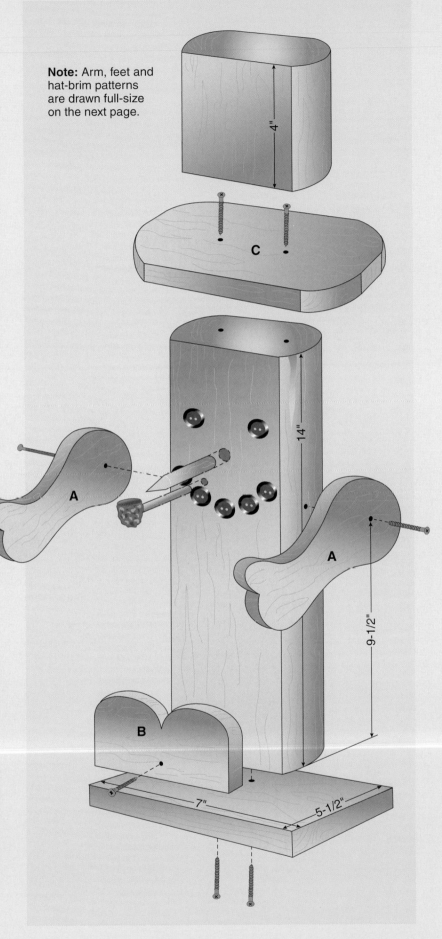

Note: Arm, feet and hat-brim patterns are drawn full-size on the next page.

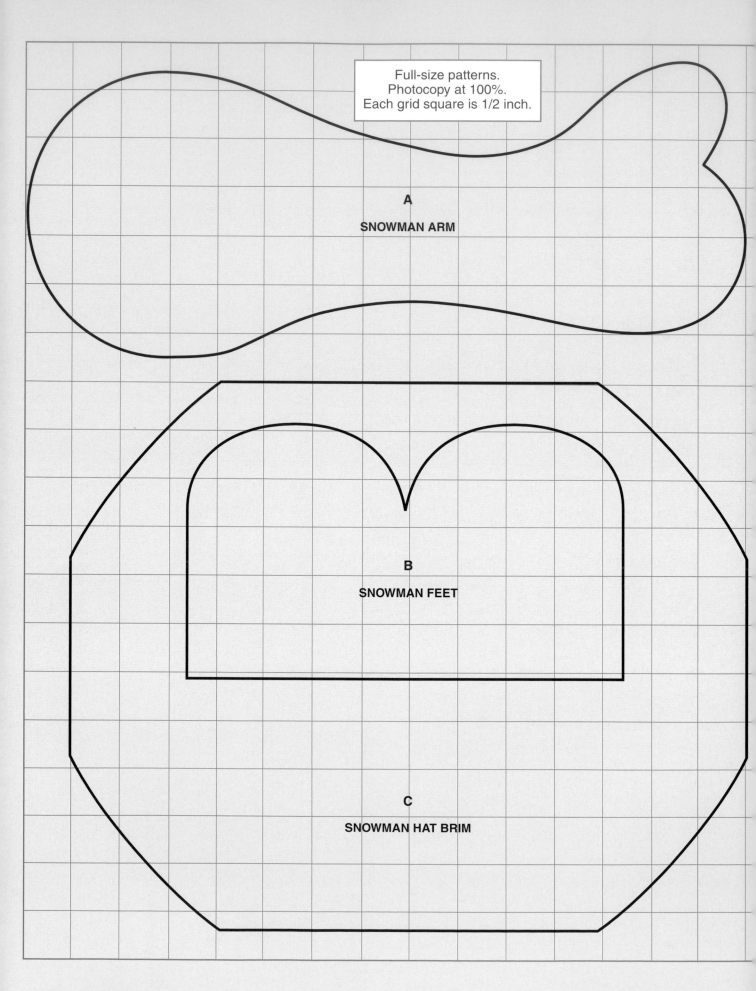

Full-size patterns.
Photocopy at 100%.
Each grid square is 1/2 inch.

A

SNOWMAN ARM

B

SNOWMAN FEET

C

SNOWMAN HAT BRIM

Wooden Luminaries Let Your Light Shine

His wooden version of the traditional Mexican Christmas lantern adds a warm glow to frosty nights.

WARM WELCOME. Don Clarke (that's him above) of Keuka Park, New York came up with this bright idea to add some inviting light to your front porch or back deck.

THIS PROJECT gives an old holiday tradition an interesting new twist.

Luminaria are Mexican Christmas lanterns formed with paper bags. Don Clarke of Keuka Park, New York replaced the customary bag with a sturdy wooden frame, then placed a candle in a canning jar to protect the wood from scorching.

We've included four patterns, representing each season, for delicate cutout designs you can use on the front of your wooden luminary (see page 111 for patterns). If you're handy with a scroll saw, try making a design of your own. But keep it simple and cut out openings just big enough to let light shine through.

(Step-by-step instructions begin on next page)

Let's Start Luminatin'

1. Cut all the pieces from a 3-foot 1-inch x 6-inch pine board.

Don likes to make these luminaries from boards 3/8 inch thick because they look more proportional. (He planes the board down to this thickness before cutting the pieces.)

If making from optional 3/8-inch stock, cut the sides 4-5/8 inches wide. However, if you want to use regular 3/4-inch-thick stock, make the sides 5 inches wide.

In either case, the base of the lantern is 4-1/4 inches square.

2. Select a side free of knotholes for the front of the luminary. Choose one of the patterns provided, or create one of your own. Photocopy the patterns at 200%, or draw them using the grid to help. Then trace or glue (with a glue stick) the design onto the wood. (Position the design about 1/4 inch to the left of center.)

3. Cut out the pattern with a scroll or coping saw.

4. Glue and nail the sides together with 1-1/2-inch finishing nails. Drill pilot holes so you don't split the boards.

5. Sand the sides. Don suggests rounding off all the edges for a softer look. Apply two or three coats of exterior polyurethane gloss inside and out, lightly sanding between each coat.

6. Put a candle inside a large-mouth 1-quart canning jar and set the jar inside the box. Now find a nice spot for your luminary and let it warm up your backyard!

Here's What You'll Need...

Note: *This material list is for one luminary.*

- ❑ One 3-foot 1-inch x 6-inch pine board
- ❑ 1-1/2-inch finishing nails
- ❑ Waterproof carpenter's glue
- ❑ Glue stick (optional)
- ❑ Exterior polyurethane gloss
- ❑ One large-mouth 1-quart canning jar
- ❑ One candle

Recommended Tools...

- ❑ Table saw
- ❑ Power drill
- ❑ Scroll saw or coping saw

Note: Dimensions given are for wood measuring 3/4 inch thick. If planing wood to 3/8 inch thick, as Don does, the width of the side boards should be 4-5/8 inches.

Workshop Wisdom
Cope with a Hand Saw

IF YOU'D LIKE to try this project but don't have a scroll saw, don't worry. A coping saw will do the job very well. It may take a little more time and patience, but the end result will be just as pleasing. If you don't have a coping saw, they're available at hardware stores for less than $10.

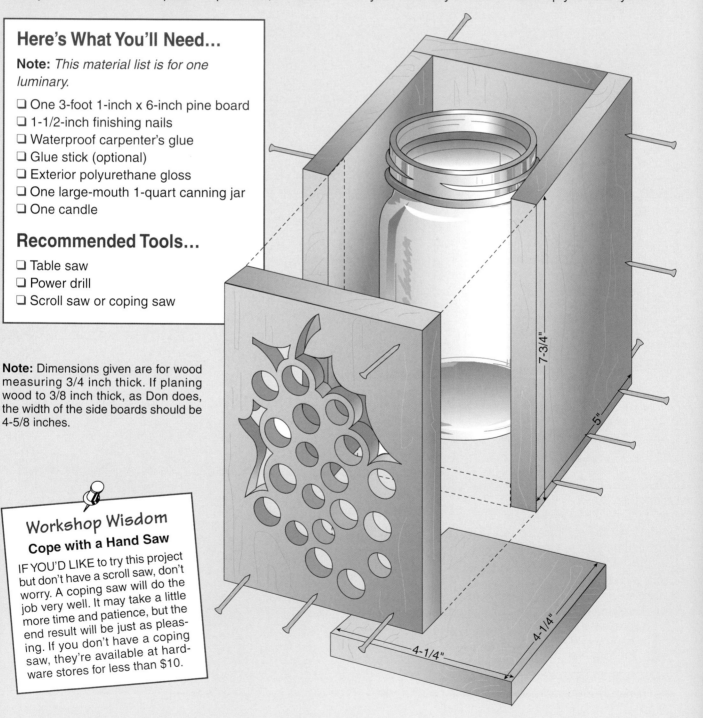

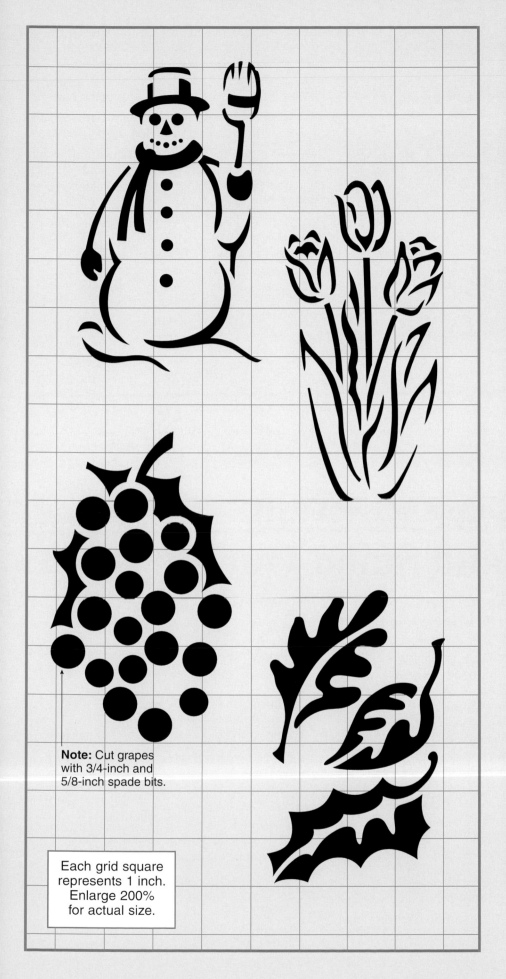

Note: Cut grapes with 3/4-inch and 5/8-inch spade bits.

Each grid square represents 1 inch. Enlarge 200% for actual size.

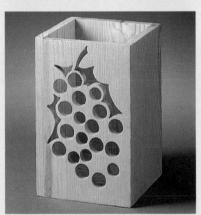

FOUR SEASONS of fun are represented by the patterns used to make the above deck lanterns. Looking for more? Try paging through kids' coloring books for new ideas.

Deck Flower Box Will Stand Up and Stand Out

Not just another pretty planter, this one will last for years—and continue looking great doing it.

ALL DECKED OUT.
Tim Setterington of Kingsville, Ontario came up with a colorful way to deck-orate his deck.

YOU'LL NEVER need to worry about accidentally kicking this deck flower box over. The wind won't tip it, either.

With the bottom and ends built from hefty 2-inch x 10-inch cedar, this solid, durable and (best of all) maintenance-free flower box is guaranteed to last for years.

Tim Setterington of Kingsville, Ontario designed the flower box to add both beauty and safety to his new deck, without interfering with the gorgeous view.

"We're backyard birders," Tim explains. "We didn't want to spoil the view with railings, so I created these flower boxes to line the edges of the deck. They're large enough to keep visitors from accidentally stepping over the edge, and they're fun to fill with color all year long." (Check local deck-building codes to see if railings are required.)

To keep the flower box looking neat through the years, the trim is attached with nails *and* waterproof construction adhesive, so there's no need to tack it back in place every spring.

So if your goal is to deck out your deck, there isn't a better project to start with than this one.

Here's What You'll Need...

- ❑ One 6-foot 2-inch x 10-inch cedar board
- ❑ One 8-foot 1-inch x 10-inch cedar board
- ❑ Two 8-foot 1-inch x 6-inch rough cedar boards
- ❑ 3-inch and 2-inch galvanized deck screws
- ❑ 1-1/2-inch galvanized finishing nails
- ❑ Waterproof construction adhesive

Recommended Tools...

- ❑ Table saw
- ❑ Combination square

Deck Out the Deck

1. Cut the bottom and ends from a 6-foot 2-inch x 10-inch cedar board. The bottom should measure 9-1/4 inches x 38 inches. Each end should be 9-1/4 inches square.

Drill pilot holes through the ends and attach them to the bottom with 3-inch deck screws.

2. Cut the two sides of the box, each measuring 41 inches long, from a 8-foot 1-inch x 10-inch cedar board. (You may have to rip the sides to the same width as the end pieces.)

3. Square and attach the sides to the ends and bottom of the box. To do this, drill pilot holes through the sides for 2-inch deck screws. Locate these screws 3/4 inch from the bottom edge of each board (these screws will be hidden when you attach the decorative moldings later) and, at each end, 1 inch from the top and bottom. Center a third pilot hole from top to bottom.

4. Rip one 8-foot 1-inch x 6-inch cedar board into four molding strips 1-5/8 inches wide (use push sticks for safety when cutting). From these boards, cut:
• Six molding strips, approximately 42-3/4 inches long. (Lengths will vary with thickness of cedar being used.)
• Six molding strips, approximately 11 inches long. (Lengths will vary with thickness of cedar being used.)

5. Attach three of the 11-inch moldings on each end with waterproof construction adhesive and 1-1/2-inch finishing nails, setting the nail heads just below the surface.

The top molding should be flush with the top of the box, the bottom molding flush with the bottom, and the third molding centered between them.

6. Attach three 42-3/4-inch moldings to each side, lining them up and nailing in place using the same method as in the previous step. If necessary, trim side moldings flush with end moldings.

7. Rip 2-3/4-inch-wide top trim boards for each end from a second 8-foot 1-inch x 6-inch cedar board. To determine the length, measure the *inside* dimension of the box from side to side. Center and attach them with construction adhesive and 2-inch deck screws.

8. Use the rest of the 1-inch x 6-inch board to make 2-1/4-inch-wide top trim boards for the sides. Cut the pieces to fit flush with the end trim boards. Attach as in the previous step.

9. Cut feet for the bottom of the box from leftover cedar. You'll need three measuring about 1-5/8 inches x 11 inches. Center, glue and screw one to each end and one in the center.

10. Sand the edges smooth, add a few 1/4-inch drainage holes in the bottom, and your new deck flower box is ready for planting.

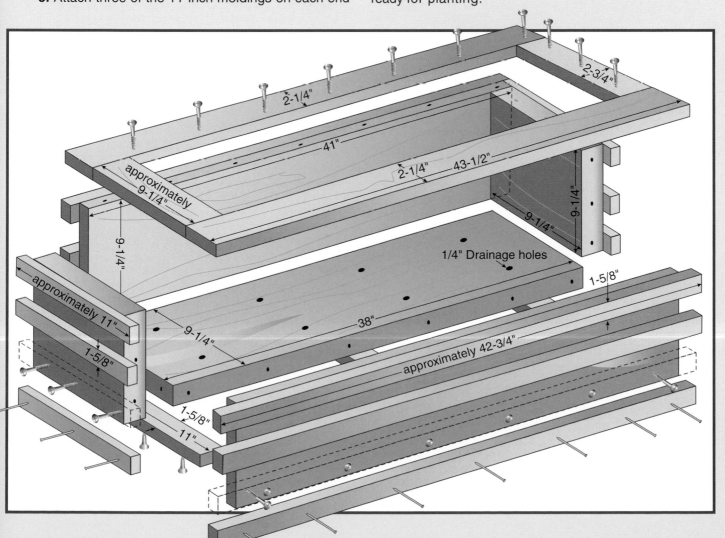

Spice Up Your Windowsill

You can hang this herb garden right outside your kitchen window.

HERE'S A PROJECT that is doubly satisfying. That's because this window-box herb garden will not only perk up your sill, it will also add some zest to your cooking.

It can be sized to fit any window, but it makes the most sense to hang it near the kitchen, where you can snip whatever herb best complements the meal of the day.

Growing herbs in pots is a great way to keep them under control and have a variety right at your fingertips. It also eliminates many chores of large-scale gardening.

If herbs aren't your thing, that doesn't mean you have to write off this project. The clever design is perfect for holding pots of colorful annuals, too.

In fact, you can easily extend the growing season by planting early spring bloomers, such as violas, then as they begin to fade, swap the pots with new ones filled with summer annuals. Late in the season, change the pots again, adding ones filled with chrysanthemums, which will brighten your windowsill until the first frost. ✎

Here's What You'll Need...

- ❑ 1-inch x 8-inch rough cedar board (the length will be determined by the width of your window)
- ❑ One 2-inch x 8-inch rough cedar board, 15 inches long
- ❑ 2-1/2-inch and 2-inch galvanized deck screws
- ❑ 2-inch galvanized finishing nails
- ❑ Waterproof construction adhesive
- ❑ 6-inch clay flowerpots ❑ Glue stick

Recommended Tools...

- ❑ Table saw ❑ Power drill
- ❑ Saber or band saw ❑ Level
- ❑ Combination square

Let's Build a Window Garden

1. Measure your window to determine the overall length of your window box.

2. Make two photocopies of the end-support pattern at right (outlined in red). With a scissors, cut out the paper patterns 1/2 inch beyond the guidelines. Tack each pattern to the 2-inch x 8-inch board with a glue stick. Place the straight sides flush with the corners of the 2-inch x 8-inch board. (Notice that the grain runs horizontally.) If necessary, square the corners of the board first.

Cut out each end support with a saber saw or band saw and sand the edges smooth.

3. Cut the top to length from a 1-inch x 8-inch board.

4. Cut the back to length from a 1-inch x 8-inch board, making it 7 inches shorter than the top. Rip it 5-1/4 inches wide.

5. Locate the center points for the pot holes in the top board. To do this, draw a line the length of the board 1/8 inch off center (*closer* to the front). Then mark the

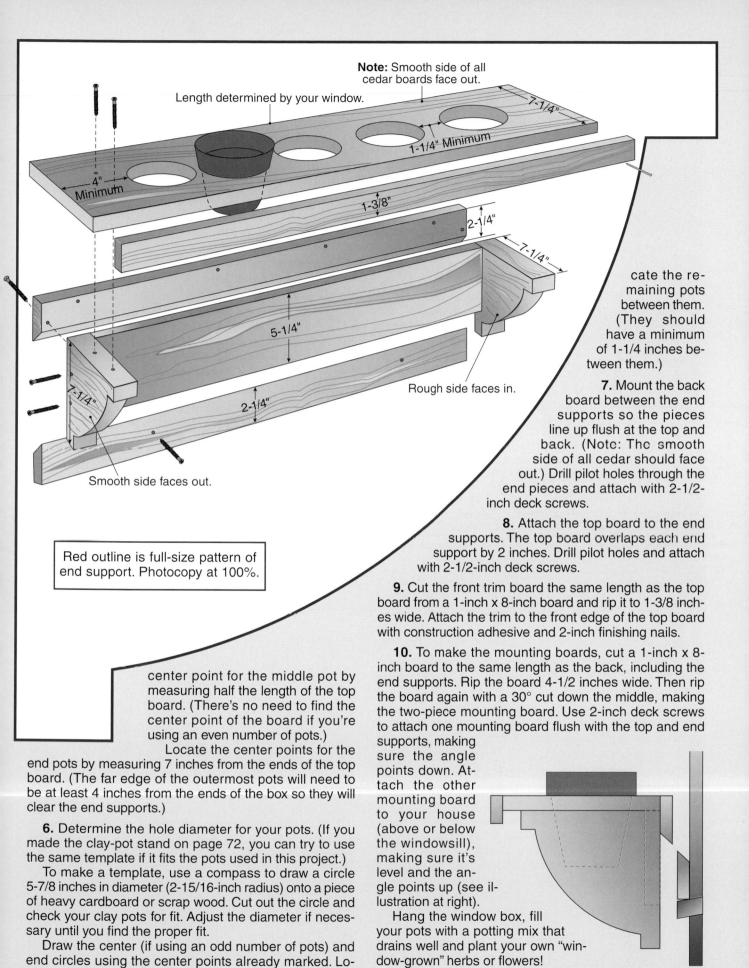

Note: Smooth side of all cedar boards face out.

Length determined by your window.

7-1/4"

1-1/4" Minimum

4" Minimum

1-3/8"

2-1/4"

7-1/4"

5-1/4"

2-1/4"

7-1/4"

Rough side faces in.

Smooth side faces out.

Red outline is full-size pattern of end support. Photocopy at 100%.

cate the remaining pots between them. (They should have a minimum of 1-1/4 inches between them.)

7. Mount the back board between the end supports so the pieces line up flush at the top and back. (Note: The smooth side of all cedar should face out.) Drill pilot holes through the end pieces and attach with 2-1/2-inch deck screws.

8. Attach the top board to the end supports. The top board overlaps each end support by 2 inches. Drill pilot holes and attach with 2-1/2-inch deck screws.

9. Cut the front trim board the same length as the top board from a 1-inch x 8-inch board and rip it to 1-3/8 inches wide. Attach the trim to the front edge of the top board with construction adhesive and 2-inch finishing nails.

10. To make the mounting boards, cut a 1-inch x 8-inch board to the same length as the back, including the end supports. Rip the board 4-1/2 inches wide. Then rip the board again with a 30° cut down the middle, making the two-piece mounting board. Use 2-inch deck screws to attach one mounting board flush with the top and end supports, making sure the angle points down. Attach the other mounting board to your house (above or below the windowsill), making sure it's level and the angle points up (see illustration at right).

Hang the window box, fill your pots with a potting mix that drains well and plant your own "window-grown" herbs or flowers!

center point for the middle pot by measuring half the length of the top board. (There's no need to find the center point of the board if you're using an even number of pots.)

Locate the center points for the end pots by measuring 7 inches from the ends of the top board. (The far edge of the outermost pots will need to be at least 4 inches from the ends of the box so they will clear the end supports.)

6. Determine the hole diameter for your pots. (If you made the clay-pot stand on page 72, you can try to use the same template if it fits the pots used in this project.)

To make a template, use a compass to draw a circle 5-7/8 inches in diameter (2-15/16-inch radius) onto a piece of heavy cardboard or scrap wood. Cut out the circle and check your clay pots for fit. Adjust the diameter if necessary until you find the proper fit.

Draw the center (if using an odd number of pots) and end circles using the center points already marked. Lo-

Let the Birds Handle the Air Mail

Receiving bills will be a little less painful when you pull them from this unique mailbox.

YOU'LL BE checking for the mail several times a day just to admire your handiwork after you build this fun and functional mailbox cover.

It's a decorative project that brings your handyman skills from the backyard right out to the front, where everyone in the neighborhood can appreciate it.

This mailbox cover has a functional flower box on each side, so you can add some brilliant color to your curbside.

We added a decorative, non-functional birdhouse perched on top just for fun. You're sure to get the stamp of approval from your mail carrier, who won't be harassed by feisty nesting birds when delivering *your* bills.

Neither Rain, Sleet, Snow Nor Dark of Night Shall Keep Us from Completing this Project!

1. Cut out the pieces for the mailbox cover according to the board layouts at the bottom of page 118.

2. Cut the arched opening for the mailbox door in the front gable piece. To do this, center the back end of the mailbox on the front gable so the top is 2-7/8 inches below the peak. Trace around the mailbox with a pencil. Hold your pencil perpendicular to the board and against the mailbox as you trace. This will give you 1/4-inch margin around the mailbox door, which is needed for it to open and close properly.

3. Start assembling the flower box by attaching the main sides (A) to the flower box floors (F) with 1-5/8-inch deck screws. (See "Workshop Wisdom" at right for a helpful hint.) Next, attach the flower box sides (E) to the outside of the flower box floors (F). Align the sides flush with the bottoms of the floors.

(Continued on page 118)

Here's What You'll Need...

Note: *All lumber is from No. 2 pine boards.*

- ❏ 14 feet of 1-inch x 4-inch board
- ❏ 7 feet of 1-inch x 8-inch board
- ❏ 4 feet of 1-inch x 10-inch board
- ❏ 2-inch and 1-1/2-inch galvanized finishing nails
- ❏ 3-1/2-inch, 1-5/8-inch and 1-1/4-inch galvanized deck screws
- ❏ Twelve 1/2-inch No. 8 sheet-metal screws
- ❏ Two 3/4-inch No. 8 sheet-metal screws
- ❏ One standard mailbox, 19 inches long, 8-3/4 inches high and 6-1/2 inches wide
- ❏ 2-inch x 2-inch piece of 1/4-inch hardware cloth (optional)
- ❏ Waterproof glue

Recommended Tools...

- ❏ Table saw
- ❏ Nail set
- ❏ Power drill
- ❏ Band or saber saw
- ❏ 1-inch spade bit
- ❏ Level
- ❏ Bar clamps

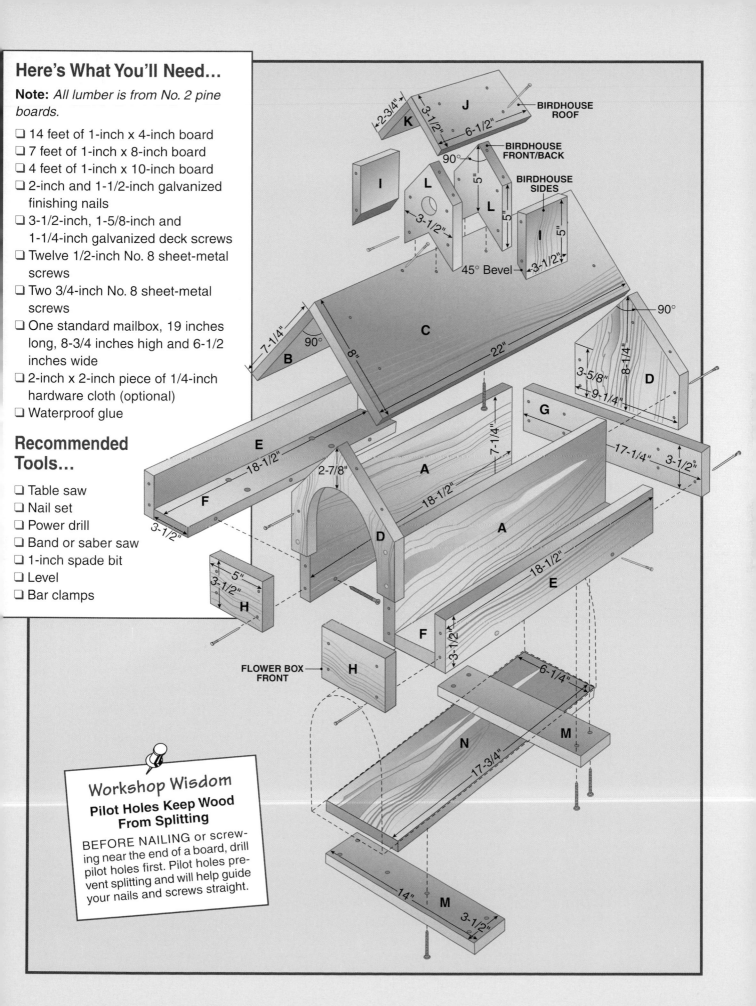

Workshop Wisdom
Pilot Holes Keep Wood From Splitting
BEFORE NAILING or screwing near the end of a board, drill pilot holes first. Pilot holes prevent splitting and will help guide your nails and screws straight.

4. Join the two flower box sides/floors with the back piece (G). Drill pilot holes first.

5. Nail one flower box front piece (H) in place with 1-1/2-inch finishing nails. Do not drive the nails "home" just yet. Before nailing on the second front piece, position the front gable (with the arch) in place to make sure the edge of the doorway lines up with the front pieces of the flower box. Make any necessary adjustments and nail the second front piece in place. Drive all nails home.

6. Predrill and nail the back gable piece to the main sides with 1-1/2-inch finishing nails.

7. Position the roof pieces so the wider one overlaps the narrower. Predrill holes and nail them to the gables using 1-1/2-inch finishing nails. Set the nails.

8. Drill a 1-inch entrance hole on the birdhouse front. Since the birdhouse cupola is decorative, cover the hole from the inside with a piece of hardware cloth, or simply drill only partway through the board (see "Workshop Wisdom" on page 25 for a helpful hint).
Assemble cupola with 1-1/2-inch finishing nails according to plan on page 117.

9. Center the assembled cupola on the main roof and trace its bottom edge onto the roof. Measure 3/8 inch inside these lines, then center a mark with an awl in the positions shown in the plan on page 117. Drill pilot holes *vertical* to the ground at these marks. Place the cupola on the roof and fasten from beneath with 1-5/8-inch deck screws.

10. Prepare the mailbox for installation by removing its flag and flag bracket.

11. Position the mailbox base (N) atop the post to which it will be mounted. Mark the outline of the post on the bottom of the board. Drill four holes inside this marked post outline for the screws that will mount the board to the post. Predrill and fasten it to the post with four 3-1/2-inch deck screws. It must be secure. Now fasten the mailbox to this base, with the board positioned to the rear of the mailbox so it doesn't interfere with the opening of the door. Use 1/2-inch No. 8 sheet-metal screws. Note: If the top of the post is not square, the mailbox will sit crooked. Level the box with wood shims until it sits straight from front to back and side to side.

12. Attach the flower box to the mounted mailbox. First, position one bottom strip 4 inches from the front, centered side to side. Fasten with only *one* 1-5/8-inch screw to the bottom of the flower box floor. Then position and fasten the strip to the other flower box floor. Check position of mailbox before fastening to the mailbox base. Add two more screws to each location. Fasten the back bottom strip the same way.

13. Attach the flag and bracket to the right side of the flower box with 3/4-inch No. 8 sheet-metal screws. Now wait patiently for the mail to come.

HELPING HANDS. Because there are a number of pieces to be assembled in this project, use clamps wherever possible to help hold boards in position. It's often easier to glue the pieces together first, then assemble them with finishing nails after the glue has dried. This will keep the pieces from slipping out of position as you nail.

Workshop Wisdom
More Soap, Less Elbow Grease
KEEP A BAR of soap in your toolbox. Before driving in screws, rub a little soap on the threads. They'll turn easier.

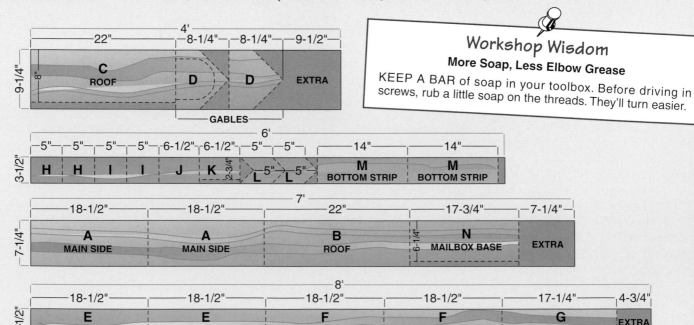

ANDREW SOUCY of Leominster, Massachusetts has a barrel of fun making these wheelbarrows.

A Wheely Neat Idea

This wheelbarrow will surely never see a day of hard work. But as a flower planter, it can handle a load of beautiful blooms.

YOU COULD CALL Andrew Soucy of Leominster, Massachusetts a bit of a tinkerer. That's how this clever woodworker came up with the plan for a classic wooden wheelbarrow that's sure to give your front lawn a nostalgic feel.

"I saw one like it and made some sketches," Andrew says. "Then I threw in some of my own ideas and began making my own."

Andrew has made over 30 small decorative wheelbarrows like the one pictured above. Several of them have old iron wheels, but the favorite of gardeners in his area is the wooden-wheeled version like the one here.

"I've sold a lot of these wheelbarrows, and people always seem to want the ones with wooden wheels," he says. "I guess it just gives them a bit more old-fashioned character."

(Step-by-step instructions begin on next page)

Here's What You'll Need...

- ❑ 12 feet of 1-inch x 12-inch No. 2 pine
- ❑ Two feet of 1-inch x 6-inch No. 2 pine
- ❑ Two 8-foot 2-inch x 3-inch studs (these pieces actually measure 1-1/2 inches x 2-1/2 inches)
- ❑ One scrap piece of 2 x 2
- ❑ 2-1/2-inch and 1-5/8-inch galvanized deck screws
- ❑ One 1/2-inch x 8-inch carriage bolt, one nut and one washer
- ❑ Waterproof glue

Recommended Tools...

- ❑ Table saw
- ❑ Band or saber saw
- ❑ Rasp or coarse sandpaper
- ❑ Compass
- ❑ Combination square

Roll Out the Barrow

1. Cut out pieces according to the board dimensions below. Also, from two 8-foot 2-inch x 3-inch studs, cut:
- One yoke, 4-1/2 inches long (Cut opposing 12° angles. See dimensions below.) (E)
- Two handles, 58 inches long (Cut one end at 12°.) (F)
- Two legs, 12 inches long (Cut one end at 10°.) (G)

2. Cut two floor pieces 18-1/2 inches long from a 1-inch x 12-inch board. Rip the boards to 11 inches wide—one rip cut should be at 15°. This beveled edge will be positioned at the front of the box. Then bevel the ends of the boards 10° (see front view detail at far right for the proper direction of these cuts).

Lay the two floor pieces in position side by side with the ends facing toward you. Butt the boards together and temporarily tack the ends closest to you 1 inch from the front edge of your workbench. This will keep them in position as you assemble the box.

3. Attach one side to the cut edge of the floor boards. To do this, stand the appropriate side piece on the workbench in front of you so it runs along the length of the floor. Fasten it flush to the floor with 1-5/8-inch deck screws. (*When assembling all pieces in this project, drill pilot holes first to keep the wood from splitting.*)

Then stand the front piece in position on top of the floor. (Be sure to place it on the end cut 15° in step 2.) Fasten the side to it with 1-5/8-inch deck screws.

4. Stand the back piece on top of the floor. Attach the side to it using 1-5/8-inch deck screws.

5. Fasten the second side to the floor, front and back. To do this, unfasten the box from your workbench and turn the side to be completed toward you. Fasten the side with 1-5/8-inch deck screws.

6. Turn the box upside down and secure the floor to the front and back boards.

7. Shape handle grips with a saber saw, taking 3/8 inch off the top and bottom of the handles (see plan at right).

Then use a rasp or coarse sandpaper to round the ends of the grips.

8. Lay the two handles side by side on a flat work surface with the handle grips on the same end. Place the yoke against the angled ends of the handles. Space the handle grips 24 inches apart, measuring to the outside edge. The angle on the yoke should match the angle of the handles. Drill pilot holes and attach the yoke to the ends of the handle with 2-1/2-inch deck screws.

9. Lay the box on top of the handles. The front of the box should be set 18-1/2 inches back from the front of the yoke. Center the sides of the box between the handles. Fasten the box (from the inside) to the handles with 1-5/8-inch deck screws.

10. Locate and bore a hole for the wheel's axle through each handle. To do this, measure 9 inches from the front of the yoke along the top of each handle. Lay a straight edge across both handles and draw a line connecting these marks. This will provide a guideline to follow as you drill the axle holes. It is important that these holes line up.

With a combination square, carry the 9-inch lines down the outer sides of the handles. Measure 1-1/4 inches down from the top of the handles to locate each hole's center point. Drill a straight 1/2-inch hole through each handle, following the guideline you drew at the top of each handle. It's easier to drill a smaller pilot hole first before using the 1/2-inch bit.

11. Attach legs to the inside of the handles. The angle cut butts the floor of the box, and each leg should be flush with the back edge of the box. Square the legs perpendicular to the ground. Fasten with 2-1/2-inch deck screws.

12. Cut out an 11-inch round disk (D) from each 11-1/4-inch square piece. Find the center point of each piece by connecting the opposite corners of the square with a line drawn along a straight edge. Set a 5-1/2-inch radius on a compass and draw a circle on each board. Use a saber saw or band saw to cut out each disk.

13. Glue the two disks together and secure with 1-5/8-inch deck screws to make one wheel. Place the screws

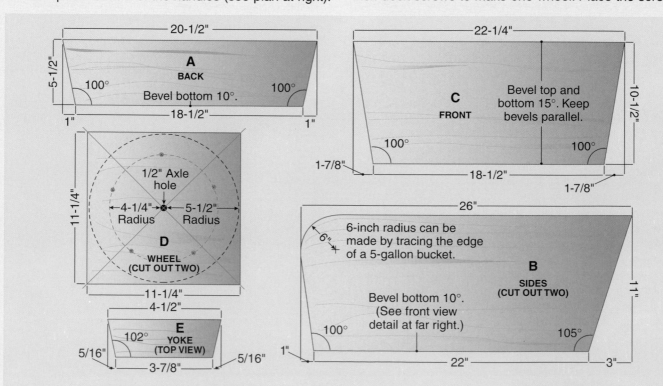

about 1-1/4 inches from the edge of the wheel. You can quickly locate this distance by drawing a 4-1/4-inch radius circle on each side of the wheel. Drive five evenly spaced screws into one side of the wheel (space the screws about 5 inches apart). Then turn it over and drive five more screws into the side of the wheel, spacing the screws *between* the ones on the opposite side.

14. Drill a 1/2-inch axle hole in the center of the wheel.

15. Make axle spacers from a 2 x 2. To do this, mark the center on one end of the 2 x 2. (Remember, you can quickly find the center by connecting the opposite corners with straight lines.) At the center point, drill a 1/4-inch hole as deep as possible. Enlarge the hole to 1/2 inch.

Cut off a 1-1/4-inch piece from the 2 x 2 at 12°, or use the measurements shown in the illustration at top right. The 1/2-inch hole should be bored through the entire piece.

Continue drilling a 1/2-inch hole deeper into the end of the 2 x 2 and cut off another 1-1/4-inch piece at 90°. This piece will already have a 12° angle on one end.

16. Glue the spacers in place between the handles. Line up the 1/2-inch axle holes in the spacers with the 1/2-inch holes drilled in the handles in step 10. The angled ends should be glued to the handles with waterproof glue. Use the carriage

bolt to help line up the holes.

17. When the glue is dry, insert the wheel between the handles and assemble the axle (carriage bolt) and hardware as pictured. Be careful not to overtighten the bolt or the wheel will not turn.

18. Apply a coat of deck stain to the wheelbarrow to protect it from the elements. Apply liberally, especially at the edge of the wheel and the bottom of each leg because these pieces will be in contact with the ground. Make sure to brush the stain well into all joints.

19. Drill several 1/4-inch drainage holes in the bottom of the box and fill with potting soil and colorful plants. Your friends and neighbors are sure to be wheely impressed when the wheelbarrow's filled to the brim with blooms.

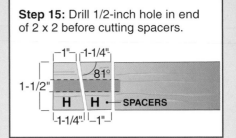

Step 15: Drill 1/2-inch hole in end of 2 x 2 before cutting spacers.

1" 1-1/4" 81° 1-1/2" H H SPACERS 1-1/4" 1"

B

A

1/4" Drainage holes

Bevel both ends of floor boards 10°. (See front view detail below.)

22"

C

15° Bevel

B

18-1/2"

Front view detail of box

B C B

FLOOR

Note direction of 10° bevels.

1-3/4"

2-1/2"

Cut ends at 10°.

24"

F

G

6"

Step 7: Shape the handle grips with a saber saw, removing 3/8 inch from top and bottom of the handles. Round ends with a rasp or coarse sandpaper.

12"

11-1/2"

G

H

H

F

D

H

E

9"

58"

102°

Cut ends at 12°.

Chapter 5
Just for Kids

*H*ere's a chance to not only make some "cool" projects with your children and grandchildren, it's also an opportunity to build some great memories, too.

We've included a handful of projects that are so simple, kids will be able to complete them with just a little adult supervision.

There are also a few that take a bit more skill, but are sure to create lasting impressions in your little ones' minds, such as a sturdy "kid-size" picnic table and the pony they've always longed for.

Kids Will Have a Picnic
With This Table of Their Own

*You'll have no trouble getting children to eat their meal
if you serve it on this sturdy outdoor picnic table—just their size.*

"I BUILT my first kid-size picnic table from scrap lumber sometime in the mid-1960's, and it served my children well," says Stanley Badzinski of New Berlin, Wisconsin. "When they outgrew that table, I hung it in the garage.

"Years later, I gave it to my daughter, whose 3-year-old son enjoyed it for several more years. Since then, I built another for my other daughter's children."

Unlike some picnic tables that have a tendency to tip when two people sit on the same side, this one is plenty sturdy."It can hold more than 200 pounds on one side," Stan explains.

"You should've seen the look on my son-in-law's face when I told him to have the three kids sit on one side as I knelt on the other. He nearly panicked when I got off, but the table didn't budge because I designed it so the legs are spread well under the seats."

Go ahead and build this miniature version for your little tikes. They'll appreciate having a picnic table just their size.

(Step-by-step instructions begin on next page)

Here's What You'll Need...

- ❏ 12 to 14 8-foot 1 inch x 3-inch furring strips (these actually measure 3/4 inch x 2-1/2 inches)
- ❏ 2-inch, 1-5/8-inch and 1-1/4-inch galvanized deck screws
- ❏ Exterior paint or stain

Recommended Tools...

- ❏ Miter box, table saw or hand saw
- ❏ Power drill
- ❏ Rafter square
- ❏ Combination square
- ❏ Clamps

This Will Be a Picnic to Build!

1. Cut the 1-inch x 3-inch furring strips to the sizes indicated in the cutting list below. There should be enough extra material so you can cut around some of the larger knotholes as you size the pieces. Double-check all measurements before cutting multiple pieces.

2. Sand and round all edges before assembling to remove splinters or sharp edges.

3. Place the eight tabletop boards (B) face down on a flat work surface and align the ends with a rafter square.

4. Line up two tabletop cleats (D) flush with the ends of the tabletop boards. Attach the cleats to the outermost boards with 1-1/4-inch deck screws, placing one screw in each of the four corners. Square and insert a second screw in each corner.

5. Evenly space the remaining tabletop boards and fasten them to the cleats with two 1-1/4-inch deck screws on each end. Screw through the cleats and into the top boards.

6. The center tabletop cleat (D) with the 45° angles on each end should be positioned vertically on the underside of the table and held in place from the top with 1-5/8-inch deck screws.

To screw this piece in place from the top without missing the cleat below, find the center of the table end for end. Draw a centered line across the table using a rafter square.

Using the line as a guide, bore a perpendicular pilot hole in each tabletop board, *drilling from the top*. Center the tabletop cleat below the pilot holes and clamp in place. Fasten with 1-5/8-inch deck screws.

7. Make the bench seats by placing three 39-inch seat boards (B) together. Square the ends of the boards. There should be a slight gap between each.

Evenly space three seat cleats (G) on each bench and fasten with 1-1/4-inch deck screws. Again, fasten the seat boards with two screws in each cleat.

8. After the bench seats are assembled, trim about 1 inch off each corner at 45° to protect little knees.

9. Build the leg frames to support the tabletop and benches. To create the proper leg angle, line up the legs (C) with the top edge and ends of the table supports (F). Attach the legs to the table and seat supports (F and A) with 1-1/4-inch deck screws.

10. Turn the table upside down and fasten table supports (F) to tabletop cleats (D) with 1-5/8-inch deck screws. Then install the 18-3/4-inch diagonal braces (E) to the seat supports (A) and center tabletop cleat (D) with 2-inch deck screws. The braces need to be offset by 3/4 inch to give you enough room to screw through the center cleat into each diagonal brace. Drill pilot holes first.

11. Attach the benches to the seat supports (A), drilling pilot holes through the benches and into the top edge of the support. Fasten with 1-5/8-inch deck screws.

12. Protect the table with exterior paint or stain. When it dries, this cute little table, as well as your little ones, will be ready for a lunch!

Here's a Cutting List to Help...

Note: *The letter after each piece corresponds with labeled parts on the next page.*

From the 1-inch x 3-inch furring strips, cut:
- Two seat supports, 40 inches long (A)
- Eight tabletop boards and six seat boards, 39 inches long (B)
- Four legs, 25 inches long (Cut both ends with 22-1/2° parallel angles.) (C)
- Three tabletop cleats, 21 inches long (Make *one* with 45° opposing angles.) (D)
- Two diagonal braces, 18-3/4 inches long (Cut with 33° parallel angles.) (E)
- Two table supports, 19-3/4 inches long (Cut with 22-1/2° opposing angles.) (F)
- Six seat cleats, 7-1/2 inches long (G)

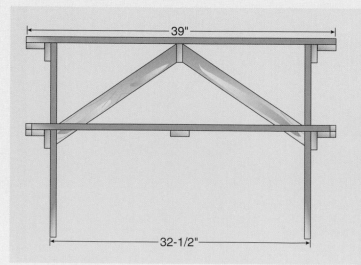

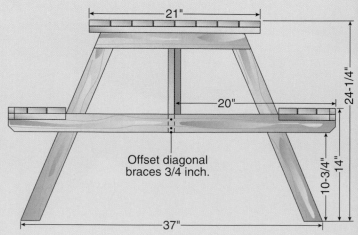

Offset diagonal braces 3/4 inch.

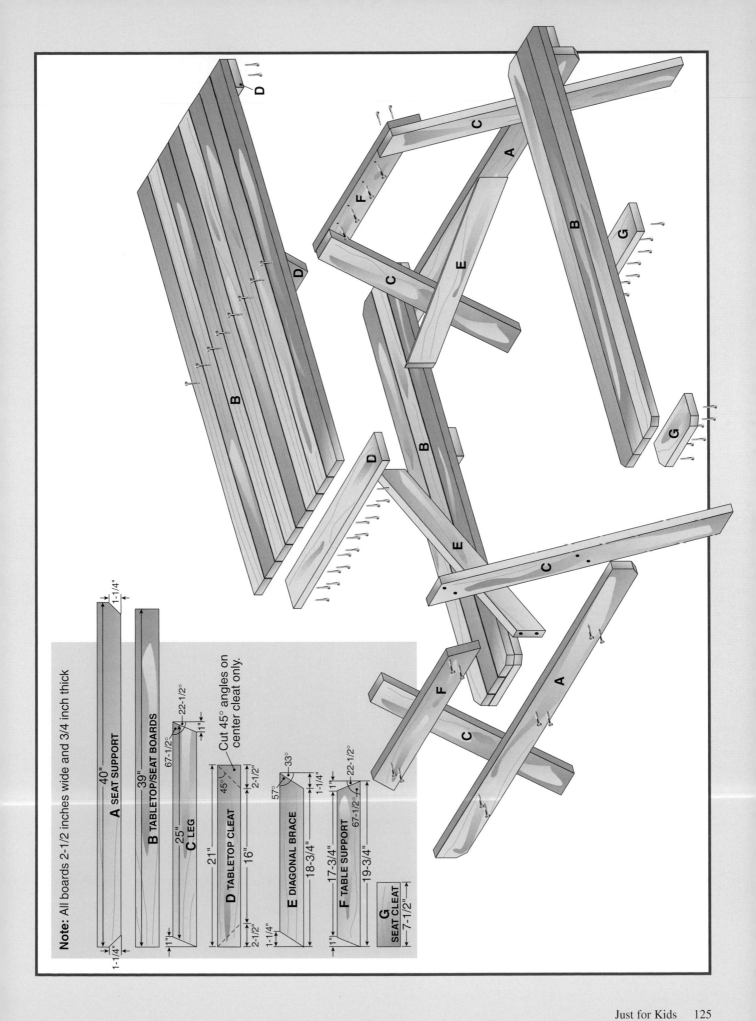

Note: All boards 2-1/2 inches wide and 3/4 inch thick

A SEAT SUPPORT
40"
1-1/4"
1-1/4"

B TABLETOP/SEAT BOARDS
39"

C LEG
67-1/2°
22-1/2°
1"
25"
1"

D TABLETOP CLEAT
45°
2-1/2"
2-1/2"
21"
1-1/4"
Cut 45° angles on center cleat only.

E DIAGONAL BRACE
57°
33°
1-1/4"
16"
1"

F TABLE SUPPORT
22-1/2°
1"
67-1/2°
18-3/4"
17-3/4"

G SEAT CLEAT
7-1/2"
19-3/4"

Log Feeder a Project for Fledgling Woodworkers

Youngsters will find this "peanut butter log" as much fun to fill as it is to make.

EVEN THE YOUNGEST WOODWORKERS can sink their teeth into this quick project—then birds and squirrels can dig in, too.

This "peanut butter log" requires the bare minimum of materials and just a few simple tools. We borrowed the design from Rob Curl of Brookfield, Wisconsin, who built his log feeder in just an hour. Even more impressive is the fact he was only 10 years old at the time!

Peanut butter is a great way to attract a wide variety of birds to your feeders, including chickadees, nuthatches and woodpeckers.

If you've heard that peanut butter poses a choking hazard to birds, don't worry. *Birds & Blooms* Contributing Editor George Harrison, a noted bird expert, says that's a myth. In fact, he feeds peanut butter to birds in his own yard.

This simple project will provide hours of enjoyment for your family. Just wait until you see a squirrel hanging upside down to eat as the feeder swings through the air like a circus trapeze. Enjoy!

Here's What You'll Need...

- ❑ One round log, about 18 inches long and 3 to 4 inches in diameter
- ❑ Rope or chain for hanging
- ❑ One screw eye

Recommended Tools...

- ❑ Hand-turned brace-and-bit set or power drill and spade bit

Easy as 1, 2, 3

1. Place the log in a vise and drill random holes 1 inch or larger along its length. The depth of the holes isn't important.

Younger children can make the holes with a hand-turned brace-and-bit set. Older children and adults can use a power drill with a spade bit, but be careful—a large-diameter bit in a power drill can be hard to control. Whichever method you choose, be sure to wear safety glasses. Attach a screw eye to one end of the log.

2. Fill each hole with peanut butter using your fingers or a butter knife.

Dipping a knife into the peanut butter jar while filling the feeder may leave bits of bark and wood behind, so here's a tip: Buy a *big* jar of an inexpensive brand and label it "for the birds".

3. Attach a rope or chain and hang the feeder from a tree limb. It's ready for visitors—just give them a little time and they'll find it. You'll soon be adding more peanut butter as birds and squirrels empty the holes.

Step 1

Step 2

Step 3

A PROJECT FOR ALL AGES. Rob Curl of Brookfield, Wisconsin demonstrates how easy this project is. Just bore 1-inch or larger holes into a round log (top left), fill them with peanut butter (left) and hang the feeder from a tree limb (above). Watch the birds come and get it!

A Birdhouse For Beginners

With its classic good looks, this one-board birdhouse will fit in anywhere.

WHILE THIS BIRDHOUSE is as simple as it gets, it has a lot going for it. It can be made very quickly…uses minimal materials and tools…and boasts a sleek look that will make any budding woodworker proud to say, "I built it myself!".

"We've had a simple one-board birdhouse like this in our yard for the past 3 years, and have had occupants each spring," says Loron Holden of Lillian, Alabama.

We simplified Loron's design a bit so even kids can take on this project with a little help from an adult. So clear off your workbench, grab your hammer and tape measure and start showing that young woodworker-in-training how it's done. ✎

Let's Saw That Board!

1. Using the full width of the 1-inch x 6-inch board, cut out the pieces as shown in the board layout below.

2. Drill a centered entrance hole about 2-1/2 inches from the top of the front piece. See the "Build a Better Birdhouse" chart on page 39 for recommended hole sizes and placement.

3. Attach the front to the sides with 1-5/8-inch deck screws. Predrill the holes in the front piece to prevent the wood from splitting.

After nesting season when it's time to clean out the birdhouse, remove these screws for easy access.

4. Attach the back to the sides with 2-inch finishing nails. Be sure each nail goes in straight. We recommend predrilling holes using the method described in "Workshop Wisdom" on page 63.

5. Cut about 1/2 inch off each corner of the floor for drainage.

6. Recess the floor 1/4 inch up from the bottom of the house, then attach it with 2-inch finishing nails from the sides and back. *Do not nail the floor from the front or you won't be able to open it for cleaning.*

7. Attach the roof to the sides with 1-5/8-inch deck screws.

You're finished—your board is now a birdhouse. Nice job!

Here's What You'll Need...

- ❏ One 5-foot 1-inch x 6-inch No. 2 pine board
- ❏ 1-5/8-inch galvanized deck screws
- ❏ 2-inch galvanized finishing nails

Recommended Tools...

- ❏ Power drill
- ❏ Appropriate-size spade bit
- ❏ Hand saw

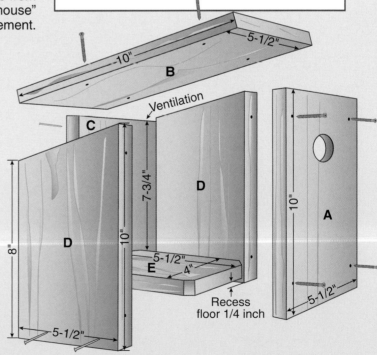

Don't Trash Cans— Build a Bird Feeder

If you're looking for an easy fund-raising project, this feeder is a sure bet for turning trash into cash.

A RECYCLER'S DREAM, this unique bird feeder is created entirely from items that might otherwise end up in the garbage. You can even make several at once with only a little additional effort.

Weston Thorsen of Brookings, Oregon says the design was a natural outgrowth of his upbringing. He was taught that "everything can be used more than once".

"I serve meals at our local Elk's lodge," Weston says. "After each meal, I used to remove the tops and bottoms of large cans and flatten them for the trash. I thought this was a waste, so I came up with another use for the cans."

Before long, he was building feeders by the dozen. "It only takes a few minutes to paint about 50 cans," he says. "It's a great way to use leftover spray paint."

Here's What You'll Need...

- ❑ One large food or coffee can
- ❑ Scrap lumber
- ❑ Spray paint
- ❑ Small nails
- ❑ Wire coat hanger
- ❑ Dowel or tree branch (optional)

Recommended Tools...

- ❑ Can opener
- ❑ Half-round file
- ❑ Saber saw

Because the feeders are easy to make, it's an ideal fund-raising project for Scout troops, 4-H clubs and school projects. It's also perfect for kids to make their own gifts.

If you don't have any large cans on hand, check with local schools, churches and restaurants. You can also use a coffee can to make a smaller version. Either way, it's a fun way to feed your feathered friends cheaply.

This One's in the Can

1. Clean cans, removing the labels and glue. Then use a can opener to remove the bottom lids and file down any sharp edges.

2. To paint several cans at one time, slip them end-to-end along scrap boards (6- to 10-foot boards work well) and rest each end on top of a sawhorse.

3. Paint the cans with spray paint. Walk along them, spraying as you go. When you get to the last can, rotate them a bit and spray again. Do this until the cans are completely painted. Use newspapers or a drop cloth to catch any overspray.

Weston gives his a tie-dyed look by switching between several different colors as he walks along the rows of cans. (This is an especially good way to finish up partially used cans of paint.)

4. Cut partial circles from scrap wood to make ends for the feeders. Measure 2-1/4 inches from the edge of the board and draw a straight line along its length (see the diagram at right). Then place the edge of the can along the line and trace the inside lip. Each feeder will need two of these wooden pieces.

If all your cans are the same size, cut one wooden piece from the board and use it as a template for the rest. Weston also rounds the top of the end boards as pictured above, but this isn't necessary if you want to keep it simple.

5. Add an optional perch to each partial circle if desired. Use dowels or fallen tree branches. Weston made square perches cut from old pallet wood and chiseled out each hole.

6. Sand the edges of the wood pieces and paint or stain if desired. When the finish dries, nail the pieces into the open ends of the cans. The pieces will line up better if you place one end of each piece even with the seam of the can. Be sure to drill or punch pilot holes in the can.

7. Cut a wire coat hanger just below the twisted area and straighten it out. With a drill or large nail, make a hole in the top of the feeder near each end. Insert the ends of the hanger through the holes and bend them back around the rim. Make sure the cut ends of the wire are on top of the feeder as pictured above, pointing toward the center. This will keep birds safe from sharp ends.

Fill the feeder with seed, hang it up and get ready… birds *can* not resist it!

Step 4: Trace the inside of a large can as the bottom edge sits on a line 2-1/4 inches from the edge of a board. Cut with a saber saw and use the cutout as a pattern.

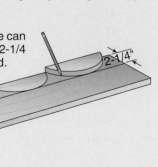

'Old Paint' Will Never Get Tired

Here's a lasting gift sure to please any little girl or boy.

RIDE 'EM COWBOY. Every kid's dream is to have a pony of his or her own. Make a wish come true with this horse swing.

Here's What You'll Need...

- ❑ One 6-foot 1-inch x 12-inch board (preferably clear pine, which is free of knots)
- ❑ One 8-foot 1-inch x 6-inch board (also clear pine)
- ❑ Two 8-inch sections of 1-inch wooden dowel (an old broom handle will work fine)
- ❑ Enough rope to suspend the horse in two places from an overhead support
- ❑ Twine (for the tail)
- ❑ Three 5/16-inch x 3-inch machine bolts, 10 washers and three lock nuts
- ❑ 2-inch galvanized deck screws
- ❑ Glue stick
- ❑ High-gloss exterior paint (you choose the colors)

Recommended Tools...

- ❑ Spade bits (the same size as the dowel or broom handle and rope)
- ❑ Router with 1/4-inch or 3/8-inch roundover bit (optional)
- ❑ Metal file
- ❑ Saber saw
- ❑ Power drill
- ❑ Countersink bit
- ❑ Paint pen

THIS HOBBYHORSE comes from some fine bloodlines going back almost 50 years.

"When I was a child, one of my mother's cousins made a hobbyhorse for my brother and me," recalls staffer Tom Curl of Brookfield, Wisconsin. "Then, about 20 years ago, I made one for my brother's three sons. They loved it as much as I did when I was young!"

Tom has pictures of children in two generations of his family riding the horses, which are sturdy enough to last for many years.

Lucky for us, he found the old, faded pattern he worked from stored away in his workshop and shared it with us.

Besides being a kid's dream, "Old Paint" has many other notable qualities—he's easy to care for, requires no feeding and his stall never needs cleaning!

Saddle Up and Let's Go

1. Photocopy the patterns on pages 130-132 at 200%, or draw off 1-inch squares on the 1-inch x 12-inch board. Glue the pattern onto the board or sketch out Old Paint's outline onto the grid.

Don't worry if you don't get the drawing exactly right, the result will probably still look like a horse. If not, then you can tell your eager youngster you decided to make Louie the Llama or Callie the Cow. (However, if the result looks like Charlie the Chicken, then perhaps you should split the wood to create kindling for next winter's fireplace and start over with a new board.)

2. Mark the round ends on the 1-inch x 6-inch body rails with a
(Continued on next page)

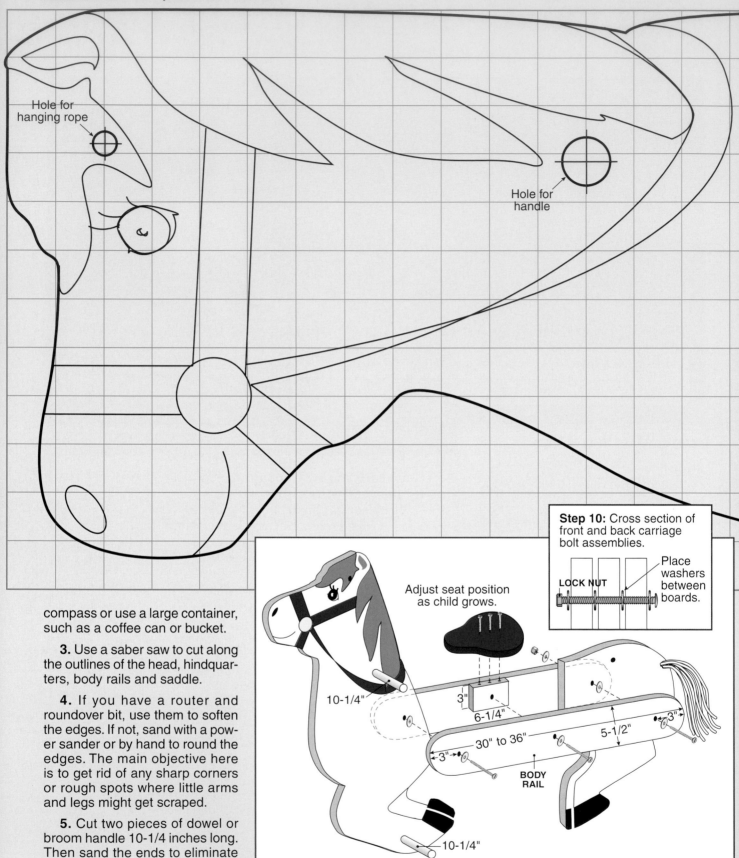

Hole for
hanging rope

Hole for
handle

Step 10: Cross section of
front and back carriage
bolt assemblies.

LOCK NUT

Place
washers
between
boards.

Adjust seat position
as child grows.

10-1/4"

3"

6-1/4"

30" to 36"

5-1/2"

3"

3"

**BODY
RAIL**

10-1/4"

compass or use a large container,
such as a coffee can or bucket.

3. Use a saber saw to cut along
the outlines of the head, hindquarters, body rails and saddle.

4. If you have a router and
roundover bit, use them to soften
the edges. If not, sand with a power sander or by hand to round the
edges. The main objective here
is to get rid of any sharp corners
or rough spots where little arms
and legs might get scraped.

5. Cut two pieces of dowel or
broom handle 10-1/4 inches long.
Then sand the ends to eliminate
sharp edges.

6. Drilling the holes for the handle and footrest is a bit
complicated—this is the one spot where accuracy *is* important. If you make the holes too small, you'll destroy the

round pieces as you pound them in. If the holes are too
large, the handle and footrest will be wobbly.

We recommend drilling a hole with a spade bit in a

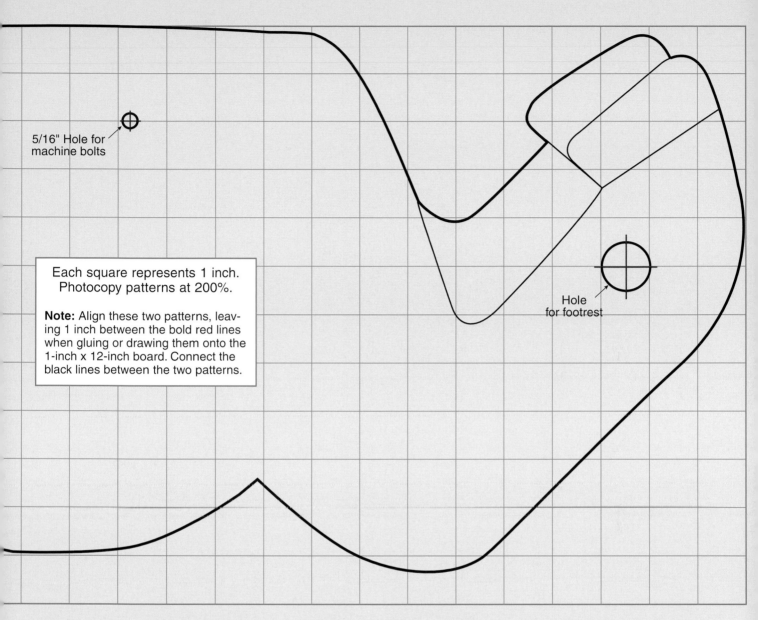

5/16" Hole for
machine bolts

Each square represents 1 inch.
Photocopy patterns at 200%.

Note: Align these two patterns, leaving 1 inch between the bold red lines
when gluing or drawing them onto the
1-inch x 12-inch board. Connect the
black lines between the two patterns.

Hole
for footrest

scrap board first to test the dowel or broom handle for
fit. Make adjustments if necessary. To get a clean hole
with a spade bit, drill from one side until the tip comes
through the other side. Then flip the board and finish
the hole.

7. Paint Old Paint. Unless it's a gift, your youngster
may want to select the color of his or her dream horse.

8. After a couple coats of the body paint are dry,
paint the saddle, mane, bridle and hooves. You can use
a paint pen to add the eyes, nose, mouth and other outlines and accents.

9. Drill a hole in the hindquarters for the twine tail. Pull
strands through the hole and bend in half. Then tie a
piece of twine around the strands to hold them in place.
Trim with a scissors if needed.

10. When it's time to assemble the horse, drill the
5/16-inch holes in the places shown on the patterns.
Again, don't worry if they're a bit out of place. Old Paint
will gallop along just fine.

Assemble the parts as shown in the diagram at left us-

ing lock nuts to ensure that the constant movement doesn't
allow them to loosen and the horse to fall apart.

11. Cut a 6-1/4-inch x 3-inch block from a scrap board
that's the same thickness as Old Paint's head and
hindquarters. Mount this board lengthwise along the bottom of the saddle using three 2-inch deck screws. Drill pilot holes and use a countersink bit to make sure the
screws are below the surface of the seat so youngsters
can't scratch themselves or snag their clothes.

12. Attach the saddle to the body rails. It's best to have
the youngster carefully sit briefly on the seat to see exactly where it should be attached (you can move the seat
back as the child grows).

Drill a 5/16-inch hole through the rails and block attached to the saddle and secure it with a bolt, washers
(on each side) and a lock nut.

13. Use rope to suspend Old Paint from a sturdy
support—then back off as your delighted cowpoke
rides off into the sunset.

(Patterns continued on next page)

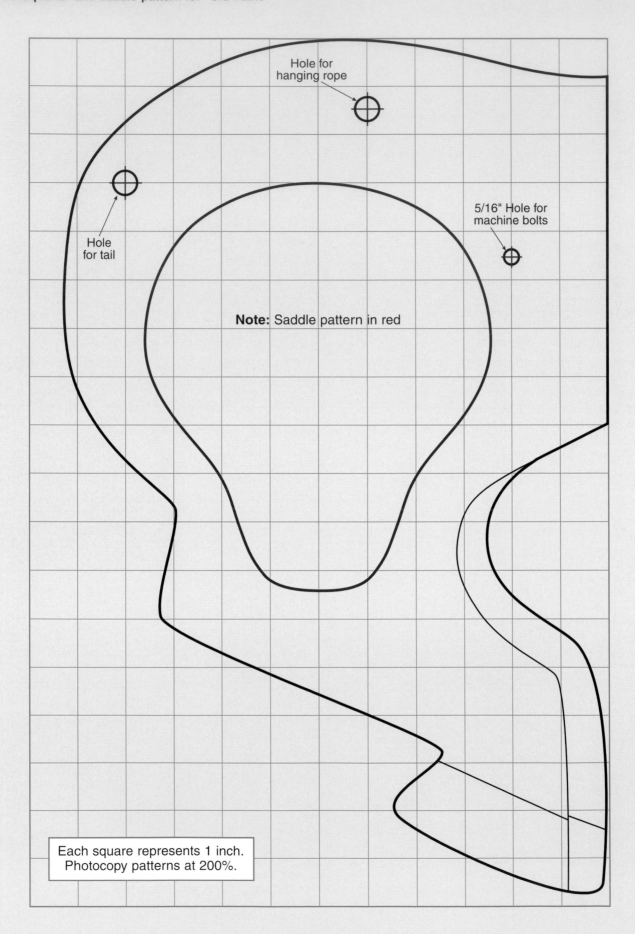

Hole for
hanging rope

Hole
for tail

5/16" Hole for
machine bolts

Note: Saddle pattern in red

Each square represents 1 inch.
Photocopy patterns at 200%.

Make Some Concrete Memories

These quick and easy-to-make stepping-stones will last a lifetime...
and lead you on a trip down memory lane.

HERE'S a great project to personalize your garden as well as give your kids or grandkids something fun to do on a warm summer day.

"A friend suggested putting my children's handprints and footprints in concrete stepping-stones," writes Charlene Schneckenberger of East Aurora, New York. "It was such a great idea, I ended up making a stone for each member of our family, including our dog, 'Molson'.

"We used wood stencils to add our names," she says. "Then we personalized each stone by making an impression with objects—such as a dog biscuit for Molson."

Beads, buttons and other small objects can also add color to your stepping-stones. Just press them into the concrete while it's still wet.

"We placed our garden stones by a swing I love to sit in. They're now the focal point of our backyard—and we'll always treasure this keepsake."

These stepping-stones make perfect gifts for Mother's Day, Father's Day, or just to celebrate those lazy days of summer when there's "nothin' to do".

Here's What You'll Need...

- ❑ One 6-foot 2 x 4
- ❑ 2-1/2-inch galvanized deck screws
- ❑ One 40-pound bag of concrete mix (approximately half a bag for each 13-inch-square stone)

Recommended Tools...

- ❑ Power drill
- ❑ Hand saw
- ❑ Large bucket
- ❑ Garden hose
- ❑ Spatula or wide putty knife (to smooth concrete)

STUNNING STEPPING-STONES can be made in your own backyard. Just pour concrete into a premade form, add handprints or footprints and decorate with buttons, beads or other personalized items.

Create a Great Impression

1. Cut four 14-1/2-inch-long pieces from a 2 x 4 to make a 13-inch-square concrete form. (You can adjust the size of these pieces to make larger or smaller forms.)

2. Lay out the boards on edge to form a square (each board should overlap the end of the next piece). Drill pilot holes and fasten them together with 2-1/2-inch deck screws. Set the form on level ground or place it on a piece of cardboard or scrap plywood.

3. Mix concrete in a large bucket according to the manufacturer's directions. If using quick-drying concrete, work fast—it begins to set in minutes.

4. Pour the concrete into the form so it's at least 2 inches thick. Smooth the surface with a spatula or wide putty knife.

5. Press hands or feet into wet concrete. Rinse hands immediately with a garden hose because materials in concrete mix are dangerous to the eyes. (Read the package label for other warnings.) Decorate as desired.

6. Let the concrete dry completely and remove the stepping-stone from the form. Be careful not to crack the stones...loosen the form screws first and carefully pull the boards apart.

7. Bury the stepping-stone in a visible place so it sits flush with the ground.

Tighten the form screws and you're *set*

to make another priceless stepping-stone, as well as a priceless memory.

Chapter 6
The BIG Stuff

$\mathcal{L}$ooking for a challenge?
If you've mastered some of the projects in the earlier chapters, you may want to tackle one or more of these workshop wonders.

While most will surely take more than a weekend to complete, we're certain your efforts will be worthwhile. The best part is, not all of the projects are just for looks. There are plenty of practical ones as well.

So have a cup of coffee and study the plans first. Then take your time…you'll enjoy every minute spent building one of these backyard treasures.

Gated Arbor Turns Garden Into an Elegant Retreat

Make your yard a serene hideaway with this handsome arbor.

THE MOST INVITING gardens are those that calm the spirit. They allow you to forget your worries for a while, and remind you of the value of spending quiet time in a beautiful place.

This garden gate arbor provides a welcoming entryway for such a special place—or a good way to begin creating one.

Ted Stanfield of Sharon, Connecticut designed the arbor to complement a tall cedar fence in his yard. When his wife, Dorothy, first saw it, her reaction was a single word—"Wow!"

"That's been the reaction of many others who've seen the arbor, too," Dorothy adds proudly.

Ready to wow your neighborhood? Then get busy…but allow yourself plenty of time, as this project may take a couple of weekends to complete.

(Step-by-step instructions begin on page 138)

YOU'LL WOW 'EM. Ted Stanfield of Sharon, Connecticut shares the plans for the arbor he built in his backyard. It's guaranteed to impress your friends and neighbors.

ARCHED ARBOR ASSEMBLY
(Step-by-step instructions begin on page 138)

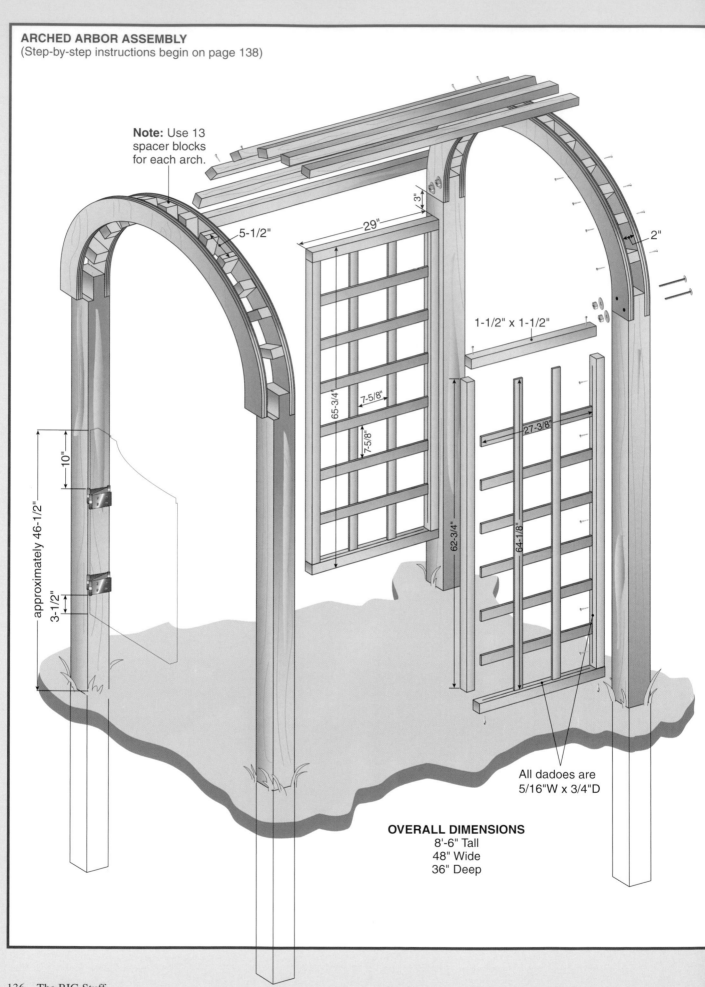

Note: Use 13 spacer blocks for each arch.

5-1/2"

3"

29"

2"

1-1/2" x 1-1/2"

65-3/4"

7-5/8"

7-5/8"

27-3/8"

62-3/4"

64-1/8"

10"

3-1/2"

approximately 46-1/2"

All dadoes are 5/16"W x 3/4"D

OVERALL DIMENSIONS
8'-6" Tall
48" Wide
36" Deep

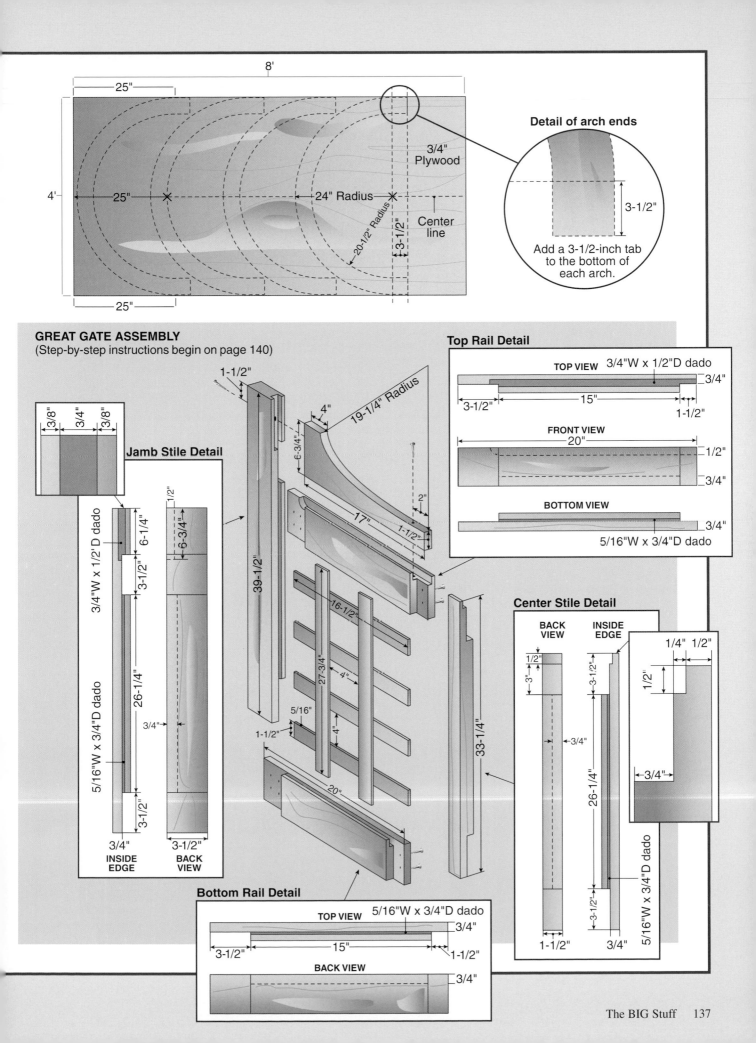

8'

25"

25"

4'

25"

25"

24" Radius

20-1/2" Radius

3-1/2"

3/4" Plywood

Center line

Detail of arch ends

3-1/2"

Add a 3-1/2-inch tab to the bottom of each arch.

GREAT GATE ASSEMBLY
(Step-by-step instructions begin on page 140)

1-1/2"

4"

6-3/4"

19-1/4" Radius

17"

1-1/2"

2"

39-1/2"

16-1/2"

4"

27-3/4"

4"

5/16"

1-1/2"

4"

20"

33-1/4"

Jamb Stile Detail

3/8" 3/4" 3/8"

3/4"W x 1/2" D dado

6-1/4"

3-1/2"

5/16"W x 3/4"D dado

26-1/4"

3/4"

1/2"

6-3/4"

3-1/2"

3/4"

3-1/2"

INSIDE EDGE

BACK VIEW

Top Rail Detail

TOP VIEW 3/4"W x 1/2"D dado

3/4"

3-1/2"

15"

1-1/2"

FRONT VIEW

20"

1/2"

3/4"

BOTTOM VIEW

3/4"

5/16"W x 3/4"D dado

Center Stile Detail

BACK VIEW

INSIDE EDGE

1/2"

3"

3-1/2"

1/4" 1/2"

1/2"

3/4"

3/4"

26-1/4"

3-1/2"

5/16"W x 3/4"D dado

1-1/2"

3/4"

Bottom Rail Detail

TOP VIEW 5/16"W x 3/4"D dado

3/4"

3-1/2"

15"

1-1/2"

BACK VIEW

3/4"

Here's What You'll Need...

Note: *Use pressure-treated lumber. Materials are for arbor and two gates.*

❑ One 4-foot x 8-foot sheet of 3/4-inch plywood
❑ Four 10-foot 4 x 4 posts
❑ Twelve 8-foot 2 x 4's
❑ 3 feet of 1-inch x 8-inch pine
❑ 27 inches of 1 x 2 (for "compass" in step 7)
❑ 2-1/2-inch, 2-inch and 1-5/8-inch galvanized deck screws
❑ 1-1/4-inch and 5/8-inch wire brads
❑ Eight 3/8-inch x 4-inch carriage bolts, washers and nuts
❑ Four double-action spring hinges
❑ Waterproof construction adhesive

Recommended Tools...

❑ Table saw and dado blade
❑ Saber saw
❑ Circular saw
❑ Belt sander and 60-grit sandpaper
❑ Power drill
❑ Clamps
❑ Post-hole digger
❑ 8-foot stepladder
❑ Rafter and combination squares
❑ Mallet
❑ Chisel
❑ Carpenter's level (post level optional)

Let's Build an Arbor

1. Based on 36-inch-deep post holes, cut each 4 x 4 post to 9 feet x 4 inches. (The frost line in your area may vary, so check with a local building center for recommended post-hole depths. Make adjustments as necessary.)

2. Make two rabbet cuts on one end of each post (see illustration). The rabbet cuts measure 3-1/2 inches and are 3/4 inch deep. Using a circular saw, make close crosscuts (about 1/8 inch apart) in the area to be notched. Chisel out the wood.

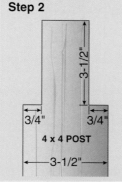

Step 2

3-1/2"

3/4"   3/4"

4 x 4 POST

3-1/2"

3. Dig four post holes 6 inches deeper than necessary in the desired location. The spacing across the front holes (and the back holes) should be 44-1/2 inches center to center. From front to back, the holes should be 32-1/2 inches center to center.

4. Add 6 inches of crushed stone to the bottom of each hole. Tamp well. Insert posts, making sure the rabbets are facing inward and outward as pictured in the plan on page 136.

5. Make sure the tops of the posts are level with each other. *This is important.* We suggest laying a straight 2 x

4 and a level across the tops of two posts at a time to check this. Also check square corner to corner. You'll need a few extra helpers to hold the 4 x 4's straight in the holes while you're on a ladder checking the level.

6. Double-check spacing between all four posts once more and adjust if needed before backfilling the holes. Use a carpenter's or post level to make sure each 4 x 4 stands straight.

7. Make a large "compass" to draw the arches. To do this, you'll need a 27-inch-long 1 x 2.

Drive a 1-5/8-inch deck screw through the board about an inch from one end so it extends 3/8 inch through the back of the board. This will be the compass point.

From that point, measure and mark the board at exactly 20-1/2 inches and 24 inches. Insert a screw at the 24-inch mark so it also extends 3/8 inch through the back of the board. Check the measurement again for accuracy—it's important!

8. Draw a center line down the length of the plywood. Position your pivot point 25 inches from one end of the plywood along the center line (punch this mark with an awl).

From the same end of the plywood, measure 25 inches from each corner. Rotate the compass between these points to draw the outer edge of the arch. The point of your screw will scratch the surface of the plywood to make a cutting line. (See illustration at the top of page 137.)

9. Reposition the outer screw at the 20-1/2-inch mark. Double-check this measurement for accuracy. Draw a second line to make the inner edge of the arch.

10. Draw 3-1/2-inch "tabs" coming off each end of the arch (see detail drawing on top of page 137). The tabs will bolt to the tops of the posts (see step 21 photo at far right).

11. Make three more identical arches, laying them out as shown in the board diagram on page 137.

12. Cut out the arches with a saber saw. Clamp them together in pairs, then shape and sand them with a belt sander with 60-grit sandpaper.

13. From an 8-foot 2 x 4, cut 26 arch spacers, each 2 inches long.

14. Align one pair of arches, making sure the line you drew down the center of the plywood in step 8 is facing up on both arches. Center one arch spacer on those lines.

Step 14: Align one pair of arches. Center a spacer at the top, then attach remaining spacers along the arches.

This will be the top center of each arch. (Use spacers to help support the outer ends of the arch as you do this.) Fasten it in place with two 1-5/8-inch deck screws from each side of the arch.

Position the remaining 12 spacers (six to each side of the centered one) 6 inches apart on center (at the top) before fastening.

15. Make lattice frames for the sides of the arbor from 8-foot 2 x 4's. Trim off rounded edges, removing as little wood as possible, then rip the boards in half. (We don't recommend buying 2 x 2's for the frames. They're often warped. It's important that these frames are straight.)

From these boards, cut four pieces 62-3/4 inches long and four pieces 29 inches long.

Steps 16 and 17

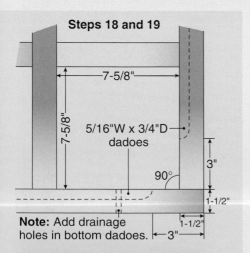

16. Using a scrap piece of 2 x 2, set up your table saw and dado blade to make a 5/16-inch-wide and 3/4-inch-deep dado. Position the dado as shown at left so *one edge* of it cuts along the *center* of the 2 x 2. (These dadoes are not centered to accommodate the offsetting lattice pieces that will be assembled in step 19.)

17. The dadoes should start and finish 3 inches from the ends of each lattice frame piece (see illustrations above and below). To help do this, place marks on the saw's fence indicating where to start and stop the dado cuts on your boards. Cut the dadoes in all lattice frame pieces the same way, using push sticks for safety. *Turn the saw off and let the blade come to a stop before removing each finished piece.*

Steps 18 and 19

7-5/8"
7-5/8"
5/16"W x 3/4"D dadoes
90°
3"
1-1/2"
1-1/2"
3"

Note: Add drainage holes in bottom dadoes.

18. Assemble the lattice frame using a rafter square, waterproof construction adhesive and 2-1/2-inch galvanized deck screws.

The dadoes should be oriented the same way on the top and bottom, and the opposite direction on the sides to offset your vertical and horizontal slats (see photo at left).

19. Cut slats for the lattice frames. Trim the rounded edges off two 8-foot 2 x 4's. Rip both boards into 5/16-inch-wide strips. (This will create lots of dust, so wear a face mask.) Cut four slats to 64-1/8 inches long and 12 slats to 27-3/8 inches long.

Insert the slats into the dado grooves on the lattice frame. Position the slats as shown in the illustration at bottom left. They will form 7-5/8-inch squares.

When all slats are in place, spread them apart gently where they intersect and apply waterproof construction adhesive. Nail each intersecting point together with a 5/8-inch wire brad. (For nailing, support the slats underneath with a scrap board.) If the brads come through a bit on the other side, nail them slightly on an angle.

20. Center lattices between the front and back arbor posts. Position them 3 inches below the bottoms of the rabbets and level. Fasten with 2-1/2-inch deck screws every 12 inches, predrilling the holes. The vertical strips of each lattice frame face outside as pictured in the plan on page 136.

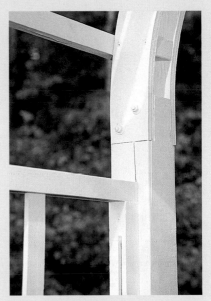

21. Attach the arches to the posts with two 4-inch carriage bolts placed diagonally on each post (see photo at right). The ends of the arches will fit into the rabbets at the tops of the posts.

Step 21: The tabs of each arch fit into the rabbets cut in the 4 x 4 posts. Attach with carriage bolts as shown.

22. Trim the rounded edges off four 8-foot 2 x 4's and rip them in half to make the stringers. Cut 13 stringers, each 46 inches long. (Note: Extra material from this step can be used to make the gate slats—step 4 in the "Great Gate" project on page 140.)

Attach the top stringer first, leaving a 5-inch overhang on each end of the arbor. Fasten it to the 2 x 4 *spacers* (not the plywood) with one 2-1/2-inch deck screw on each spacer. Attach the rest of the stringers the same way.

The arbor is finished—take a break (and a photo or two). If you want a gated arbor, continue on…

(Arbor gate instructions on next page)

Step 22: Looking up at the arch, one stringer is connected to each arch spacer. There are 13 stringers on the arbor.

How to Make a Great Gate

1. Cut the gate pieces from two 8-foot 2 x 4's. You'll need two jamb stiles 39-1/2 inches long and four top and bottom rails 20 inches long. (See labeled parts on page 137.)

2. For the center stiles, rip an 8-foot 2 x 4 to 2 inches wide, then cut two pieces 33-1/4 inches long.

3. Make dado and rabbet cuts following the measurements in the detailed diagram on page 137. This is the most difficult part of this project. So take your time, study the diagrams and measure carefully.

4. Rip 5/16-inch slats from 2 x 2 material left over from cutting the arbor stringers (step 22 from the arbor project). Cut four pieces that are 27-3/4 inches long and eight that are 16-1/2 inches long.

5. To assemble each gate, dry-fit the entire assembly (see photo at right). Start with the jamb stile and top and bottom rails. Place the horizontal and vertical slats in approximate position between the dadoes (they'll be spaced properly later). Add the center stile to the dry assembly.

6. Square the gate, add construction adhesive at each lap joint and fasten together with one 1-5/8-deck screw in each joint. Check square again before adding three more screws to each joint.

7. Position the slats as shown in the plan on page 137. They'll form 4-inch squares. Nail only the ends of the slats in place with 1-1/4-inch wire brads.

8. Make the decorative gate arch from a 3-foot piece of 1-inch x 8-inch board ripped to 6-3/4 inches wide. Cut two boards 17 inches long. Beginning 1-1/2 inches up from a bottom corner, draw an arc with a 19-1/4-inch radius. This should exit the board 4 inches from the other end, at the top of the board.

Cut the arch with a saber saw and sand smooth. Repeat this step for the second gate arch.

9. Dry-fit the arch into the top of the gate. If you're happy with the fit, add waterproof construction adhesive in both dadoes.

Put the gate arch in place and fasten with a 2-1/2-inch deck screw through the top edge of the arch near the center stile. Locate this screw about 2 inches in from the outside edge of the center stile. Predrill and countersink the hole.

From the hinge edge of the gate, drill a 3/8-inch hole with a spade bit 1-1/2 inches from the top of the stile. Drill 2-1/2 inches deep. Fasten the arch piece through this hole with a 2-1/2-inch deck screw. Attach the second gate arch the same way.

10. Wait a couple of weeks for the arbor to settle into place before hanging the gates with double-acting spring hinges. (If you hang the gates too soon, they can be thrown out of alignment if the arbor settles.) Locate the bottom hinge 3-1/2 inches above the bottom of the gate. Space the top hinge 10 inches below the top of the jamb stile. Hang gates so the top of the jamb stile is about 46-1/2 inches from the ground.

Because you've used pressure-treated wood, give it a year to completely dry before staining or painting. But don't wait that long to take a photo of your finished project—it's picture perfect as is!

Step 5: Dry-fit the entire gate assembly starting with the jamb stile. Once all pieces are in place, square and secure the joints. The gate is held onto the arbor with double-acting spring hinges (at right).

PERFECT POND. You don't have to break the bank for a pond this beautiful. Peter Loomans of Milwaukee, Wisconsin built this formal water garden from mostly recycled materials.

'Pool' Your Talents with a Formal Water Garden

Planning and preparation are the keys to this pond. When you're finished, you'll be able to call yourself a "jack-of-all-trades".

WHEN staff artist Peter Loomans decided to build a pond in his Milwaukee, Wisconsin backyard, he had a list of things he wanted to accomplish.

First, the water garden had to "fit" his long, narrow lot. In other words, it had to blend in, in both style and scale. (Peter's house is located in one of the city's oldest neighborhoods.)

Secondly, it had to attract birds and be suitable for raising fish as well.

Lastly, he wanted to build the pond on a budget. So Peter used recycled materials whenever possible.

Those specific requirements helped shape the beautiful semicircular pond pictured above.

The arched shape of the pond gives it a formal feel, and it matches window tops found in many of the older homes

in the area. (It's also the perfect complement to the arched arbor on page 135.) And the "Cream-City bricks" used to edge the pond match Peter's house, as well as many other early-Milwaukee buildings.

"One thing I learned from past experience (this is Peter's third pond) is that proper planning up front is very important," he says. "Once the thing is built, it is very hard to change, so take your time and really think it through."

Of course, we realize that any backyard pond *you* design will have its own specific requirements and individual styling. But the basics of building a pond like this one will be similar, no matter where you live.

So take a few tips from Peter. Soon, the trickling of water may fill your backyard with serenity, too.

(Step-by-step instructions begin on next page)

SUCCESSFUL SETTING. Dave Alexander (above) of Zanesville, Ohio built this natural-looking pond as a 50th wedding anniversary gift for his parents, Bill and Ruth. The pond is in an ideal location—it gets plenty of sun, is in a level area and is a focal point for their backyard.

The Ticket to a Perfect Pond

FINDING A SUITABLE location for a backyard pond is the most important step in building a successful water garden. Here are some important things to think about before settling on a site:

• First and foremost—choose a level area.

• Sun is required for water plants and fish. Water lilies need at least 6 hours of sunlight to bloom, and water that's 18 to 24 inches deep.

• If fish will remain in the pond during winter, it needs to be dug deep enough (below the frost line) to provide an ice-free area for them.

• Place the pond in view of a picture window, patio, deck, walkway or wherever your family spends a lot of time so you can enjoy it.

• If attracting birds to it is a priority, place the pond near shrubs that provide protection from predators. Also provide a shallow area for birds to bathe and drink.

• If your water garden will be used as a reflecting pool, locate it near a garden or statue you'd like to highlight.

• *Don't* place ponds in low areas. They'll collect storm runoff.

• *Avoid* placing ponds directly below trees. You'll have to constantly remove debris and leaves.

Time to Make a Splash

1. Find a great location (see suggestions below left) and select edging materials—bricks, natural rock, paver bricks, patio block, etc.—that complement your house and landscape.

2. Begin with a "dry run" of the pond's layout. Use a garden hose or clothesline to determine the shape of the pond. This is a handy way to do it because you can quickly try several layouts. If you don't like one, just move the hose or rope into a new shape.

3. Lay the edging material around the hose or rope. This gives you a chance to "fine-tune" the project *before* doing any digging.

Peter recommends leaving your "dry pond" in place for at least 1 week. This will give you plenty of time to make adjustments, check it from all viewing angles and change it if necessary. It will also kill the grass below the edging, making a clear border for you to work within.

4. Remove the edging material before digging the pond. Peter suggests stacking the bricks or stones in a sequential order so you can relay them in the same position after the liner is installed (step 12). This will save time (see photo below).

Step 4: Peter suggests laying out the edging stones before digging your pond. Once you're happy with the "dry pond", remove the bricks or stones, keeping them in a logical order so they can later be replaced in the proper sequence.

5. Time to begin digging—but first be sure to call your local utilities to ensure you don't hit buried wire, cable and pipe.

The style of pond you're building will determine how you'll approach this step. If you want an informal pond, simply dig a hole with sloping edges to about 3 to 4 feet deep in the middle. Or, you can purchase a rigid pre-formed plastic pond liner and dig to fit.

Because Peter's pond is formal and edged with mortared brick, he first built a solid 8-inch-wide x 6-

(Continued on page 144)

Here's What You'll Need...

❏ Bricks or edging stones
❏ Heavy-duty pond liner (about 30 to 45 mil thick) or a preformed plastic pond liner
❏ Liner pad, newspaper or sand (if needed)
❏ Submersible pump
❏ Fountainhead
❏ Black vinyl hose (to attach fountainhead to pump)
❏ Properly installed GFI outlet

Recommended Tools...

❏ Level
❏ Shovel
❏ Wheelbarrow
❏ Mason's trowel
❏ Wire brush

Additional Items Needed to Build Peter's Pond...

❏ One 2-foot x 8-foot sheet of 1/4-inch lauan veneer, plywood or wood paneling (for curved concrete forms)
❏ One 8-foot 2-inch x 8-inch board (for straight side of concrete form)
❏ 2-1/2-inch and 1-5/8-inch deck screws
❏ 1/2-inch copper pipe and elbows
❏ Silicone seal
❏ Bags of concrete without aggregate
❏ Mortar mix
❏ Vinyl mastic

BELOW THE SURFACE. This cross section of Peter's formal garden pond reveals some secrets below water level. He laid a concrete form around the entire pool area before digging its depth (notice the pump is in the deepest part). Then he glued the liner to the concrete form with vinyl mastic. He mortared brick on top of the concrete form and finished it off with a limestone fountainhead.

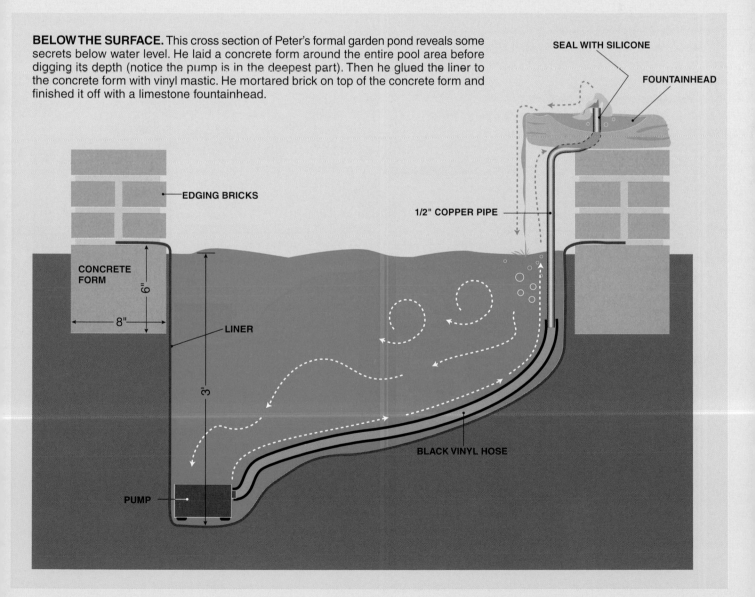

SEAL WITH SILICONE
FOUNTAINHEAD
EDGING BRICKS
1/2" COPPER PIPE
CONCRETE FORM
6"
8"
LINER
3'
BLACK VINYL HOSE
PUMP

inch-deep cement foundation for the bricks to sit on. Without a solid foundation, the mortar would crack as the soil shifts from winter frost.

If laying your pond's edging material in mortar, see steps 6 to 8 to build a concrete foundation. If you're simply stacking materials around the pond's edge, skip to step 9.

Note: No matter what type of pond you choose, be sure the top edge remains level as you dig! Otherwise, like a tipped glass, the water will run out or look uneven. To check that the edge of the pond is level, lay a long straight 2 x 4 across it (on edge) and place a level on top of the board.

6. To make a cement foundation to support the bricks (see photos), remove 6 inches of soil from the entire pond area. Build a concrete form 8 inches wide.

Since the soil Peter was working with was high in clay content, it was firm enough to use as the outside form. All he needed to do was make an inside form 8 inches from the pond's edge. If your soil is not firm enough to support the concrete, you may need to build a form for the outside edges, too.

To make a curved form that can be bent to match the pond's arch, Peter used 1/4-inch lauan veneer, but plywood or wood paneling will work well, too. Peter ripped the veneer into 8-inch x 8-foot pieces. For a form on the straight side, Peter used an 8 foot 2-inch x 8-inch board standing on edge.

Here are a few more helpful tips for building the form:

• Cut 16-inch wooden stakes from scrap 2 x 2's or 2 x 4's.

• Hammer the stakes into the ground about 8 inches from the pond's edge (consider the thickness of the material you're using for the form and make adjustments) and about 12 inches apart.

• Attach the veneer or 2-inch x 8-inch board to the wood stakes using 1-5/8-inch deck screws. Predrill the holes so the wood doesn't split.

7. Mix and pour the concrete. It's a good idea to have extra bags on hand because you'll want to fill the entire form at one time. (This is not a good time for an extra trip to the hardware store!) Mix and pour the concrete according to the label directions. (Peter mixed it in a wheelbarrow.)

8. Let the concrete completely set before removing the forms.

9. Dig out the remainder of the pond (see photo at top right). Be sure not to undercut the concrete, because you don't want to disturb the soil below it.

As you dig, strive to maintain a smooth and even bottom surface. You don't want anything poking through the bottom of your pond liner.

If it's difficult to get a smooth surface, Peter recommends purchasing a liner pad to use between the dirt and pond liner. Pads are available at many garden centers, or you can make your own using a thick layer of newspaper (at least 1/4 inch thick) or sand (if the pond doesn't have a steep slope).

Step 9: After the concrete set, Peter finished digging the full depth of his pond, being careful not to disturb the soil below the concrete. The deepest part of the pond is 3 feet.

Step 10: Spread the liner over the entire pond. Fold at the curves and corners, keeping it as smooth as possible as it fills with water.

10. Install the pond liner. (Peter's is red because it blends into the brick when the pond is filled with water.) Vinyl pond liners are available at garden centers and home improvement stores. Make sure yours is heavy duty (about 30 to 45 mil thick).

Lay the liner over the entire pond and fold it at the curves and in the corners, trying to keep it as smooth as possible. Add water to help the liner settle into place (see photo above). You may need to continue to smooth the liner and fold it as the pond fills.

11. Trim away the excess vinyl liner around the pond's edges when it's filled with water. Leave about 4 inches beyond the top if you laid a concrete foundation, or 12 inches if laying loose edging material.

12. Lay your edging material on top of the liner. If mortaring these materials in place as Peter did, see steps 13 to 15. If the edging is loosely laid on top of the pond liner, skip to step 16.

13. Glue the excess liner to the top of the foundation with vinyl mastic. Apply the adhesive with a wide putty knife, place the liner on top and hold it in place with bricks until the glue dries (see photo at right).

14. Mortar the bricks in place following manufacturer directions (see photo below). Relay your bricks in reverse order from the way you removed them in step 4.

Peter says the most important thing to remember is to mix the mortar to the proper consistency. If it's too wet, it won't hold; if it's too dry, it will crumble.

Old porous bricks, like the ones Peter used, should be wet when laying them. Soak the bricks in a bucket or in the pond first. Otherwise, they'll pull moisture from the mortar.

Step 13: Glue the top edge of the liner to the concrete foundation with vinyl mastic. Place bricks on top of the liner until the adhesive dries.

15. After all the bricks are in place and the mortar has hardened, clean the excess mortar from the joints with a wire brush.

16. A fountainhead is not necessary, but it will circulate the water, provide visual interest and add the tranquil sound of running water to your backyard.

Peter found an 18-inch-square piece of limestone from a building that was razed in his area. He chiseled a bowl into it and drilled a hole (using a carbide bit) large enough for 1/2-inch copper tubing.

He then set the tube above the water level in the bowl and sealed around it with silicone. This keeps the fountainhead filled with water, which serves as an excellent birdbath, even when the pump is not running.

There are a variety of commercially sold fountainheads to choose from, or you can make your own like Peter did. You can even design your own waterfall from extra edging material.

17. Drain and clean the pond and install a small pump, which is available at most garden centers and home improvement stores. Place the pump in the deepest part of the pond and connect it to the fountainhead with a black vinyl hose (see illustration on page 143).

The pump should be plugged into a properly installed GFI outlet. Check your local building code and have a certified electrician install an outlet near the pond.

18. Refill the pond with water. Wait about a week before adding water plants and fish.

If properly balanced (this means it has good circulation, plenty of water plants and the appropriate number of fish), a water garden will basically maintain itself.

This will be the third summer since Peter has installed his pond. He'll be the first to admit it was a lot of work. But he adds, "It's been worth it…and I feel great knowing I did it myself."

Step 14 and Step 17: Mortar the bricks in place. A straight board across the pond and a level will help keep the front and back bricks even. The finishing touch is a fountainhead. Peter used an 18-inch piece of limestone. He chiseled out a bowl in the stone to create a birdbath.

Put This Well at the Top of Your Wish List

Looking for a nostalgic decoration for your yard or garden? This well could be exactly what you're wishing for.

YEARS AGO, most rural homes relied on wells for their water supply. Many were topped with hand pumps, but the more decorative wells used a bucket system to draw water.

Such wells are part of a bygone era, but judging by the number of wishing-well lawn decorations we've seen, their charm is still *well* appreciated.

Now you can bring a little of that old-fashioned appeal to your own home. And if you have unsightly pipes or other eyesores in your yard, this well is the perfect way to hide them—just cut a hole in the plywood base and place on top.

The well was designed by Ada Mae Allen, who displays the original in her front yard in Cut Bank, Montana. Ada Mae painted her well to match the exterior of her house. We treated our version with a coat of protective deck stain.

No matter how you decorate yours, it's sure to be everything you wished for.

Here's What You'll Need...

- ❑ Fifteen 8-foot 2 x 4's
- ❑ Two 6-foot 2-inch x 6-inch boards
- ❑ 18 feet of 1-inch x 6-inch No. 2 pine
- ❑ One 4-foot x 8-foot sheet of 1/2-inch plywood
- ❑ One 2-foot x 8-foot sheet of decorative exterior paneling (optional) or plywood with 3/8-inch dadoed grooves
- ❑ 20 inches of a 1 x 2 (for "compass" in step 3)
- ❑ One 1-1/4-inch x 4-foot dowel
- ❑ 2-1/2-inch (we recommend a 5-pound box of these), 1-5/8-inch, 1-1/4-inch and 1-inch galvanized deck screws
- ❑ 2-1/2-inch, 2-inch and 1-1/4-inch galvanized finishing nails
- ❑ One 1-1/2-inch round-head screw and washer
- ❑ Waterproof construction adhesive
- ❑ Waterproof carpenter's glue
- ❑ Glue stick
- ❑ 6 feet of 1/2-inch rope (optional)
- ❑ 12-inch-diameter wooden planter (optional)
- ❑ Exterior stain

If You Want a Cedar Shake Roof...
(See separate instructions on page 150)

- ❑ One bundle of cedar shingles
- ❑ One 3-foot piece of 4-inch or 6-inch cedar siding
- ❑ Roofing paper
- ❑ 1-1/4-inch small-head shingle nails
- ❑ Foam insulation board (optional)

Recommended Tools...

- ❑ Miter box
- ❑ Saber saw
- ❑ Power drill
- ❑ Strap clamp

Make a Wish Come True

1. You'll need 156 6-inch blocks (they look like bricks when you're finished) cut from 8-foot 2 x 4's to make the well's base. It's a good idea to cut some extra blocks because a few may split as you're building.

To ensure that each piece is the same length, set up a "stop block" on your table saw or miter box (see "Workshop Wisdom" on page 148). Cut one piece, then double-check the length to make sure it measures 6 inches long before cutting the rest of the blocks. Periodically measure your blocks to make sure they're uniform in size. There should be enough extra material to eliminate any large knotholes before cutting the next block.

Set aside 12 blocks to use for the bottom layer.

2. Drill two pilot holes in each remaining block following the diagram below. This is an option, but we recommend predrilling so you don't split the blocks.

3. Cut out a 30-inch circular base from 1/2-inch plywood. This base provides a solid foundation for the wooden blocks. (If you're going to cover a pipe with the wishing well, it's best to cut a hole in the plywood now. It'll be too heavy to do it after the well is built.)

To do this, you'll need to make a compass. You can use a "string compass", but for accuracy we recommend making one from a 20-inch-long 1 x 2.

Drive a 1-5/8-inch deck screw through the board about

an inch from one end so that it extends 3/8 inch through the backside of the board. This will be the compass point.

From that point, measure and mark the stick exactly 15 inches. Insert a screw at that point so it extends 3/8 inch through the backside of the board.

Locate the circle's center point on the plywood, mark with an awl and draw a circle. The point of the far screw will scratch the surface of the plywood, making a cutting line. Cut along the guideline with a saber saw.

4. Stain the blocks as desired. Stain all but one side at a time. The unfinished side can rest on paper while the other sides dry. When dry, stain the unfinished side.

5. Spread a ring of carpenter's glue (only for a temporary hold) around the edge of the plywood base. Lay out the 12 wood blocks set aside in step 1 around the base, with the inner edges touching. Allow the glue to dry for 30 minutes to an hour. Flip the base upside down and fasten each block with two 1-5/8-inch deck screws.

6. Turn the base upright. Stagger a second layer of blocks over the first layer so each one bridges two pieces below it. Make sure the predrilled holes made in step 2 are *to the outside* (like the top block pictured in the illustration at left). Attach with 2-1/2-inch deck screws, driving the screws flush with or just below the surface. This way the next layer will sit flat.

Position the third row of blocks so the predrilled holes are *to the inside*. That way you won't run into screws already in place.

Continue building up the "bricks" until you have a total of 13 layers (see photo on next page). *Don't forget to alternate the position of the screws for each new row.*

7. Make the well rim from two 6-foot 2-inch x 6-inch boards. Cut 12 9-inch pieces with opposing 15° angles on both ends. (These angle cuts must be accurate for all boards to meet properly.) Set up a stop block to make sure the pieces are cut to uniform lengths. That way the pieces will meet without gaps.

(Continued on next page)

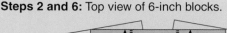

Steps 2 and 6: Top view of 6-inch blocks.

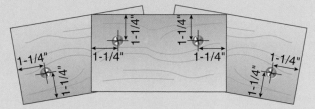

1-1/4" 1-1/4" 1-1/4" 1-1/4" 1-1/4" 1-1/4" 1-1/4" 1-1/4"

WHEN CUTTING multiple pieces to the same length, you can be more accurate and efficient by setting up a "stop block" on your table saw or miter box fence.

A stop block provides a consistent guide for cutting each piece. This ensures that every piece cut will measure exactly the same, greatly improving the accuracy of your project. After you cut the first piece, you won't have to measure the rest. (Just be sure to double-check the first cut piece to make sure it's measured correctly. Otherwise, you'll end up with a lot of extra firewood.)

To create a stop block for cross-cutting on a table saw or power miter box, simply clamp a scrap board against a saw fence at the position you want every board measured to (see photos at right). Make sure the clamps aren't in the way of the boards you're cutting. (Never use a table saw fence as a stop block. This will cause dangerous "kickbacks".)

8. Lay the rim pieces in a circle on the floor and hold them together by placing a strap clamp around them. If you're happy with the fit, loosen the clamp and glue them together (clamp again until dry). When dry, set the rim on top of the final layer of wood blocks with the clamp attached (see photo below right) and center on top of the well. Fasten each piece with 2-1/2-inch deck screws, drilling pilot holes first.

9. Cut two 58-inch roof supports from two 8-foot 2 x 4's. At one end, cut two angles (remove 30° on each cut) to form a 120° peak.

10. With the bottom end of each 2 x 4 resting on the plywood base, square them (use a rafter square) perpendicular to the well rim. Attach each support—one on each side—to the well's interior using three 2-1/2-inch deck screws.

11. Cut two side panels from 1/2-inch plywood. (See dimensions of side panels at the bottom of next page.) For a decorative look, you can use scrap pieces of exterior plywood paneling as we have, or use a dado blade to cut 3/8-inch grooves into plywood. Another option is to glue and tack wood strips onto the plywood for a planking effect.

Step 6

12. Center and square each side panel to the outside of the roof supports. Clamp one panel in place, allowing just enough "play" for you to square it. When square, tighten the clamp and attach it to the roof support with 1-5/8-inch deck screws. Attach the other side panel the same way.

13. Cut four roof beams from two 8-foot 2 x 4's and the leftover material from the 2 x 4 roof supports. To determine the length of the beams, measure the distance between the outer edges of the roof supports at the top of the well rim.

Cut one piece to this length and temporarily clamp it to the roof supports. If it fits well, cut three more pieces of the same length or make adjustments.

14. Attach two of the roof beams to the roof supports. Locate these beams 1 inch below the bottom of each peak. Drill pilot holes and attach with 2-1/2-inch deck screws.

Step 8

15. Attach the remaining two beams near the lower edge of the side panels. Position so the edge of the 2 x 4's follow the angle of the roof (see photo and plan at right for exact position). Attach them to the side panels with two 1-5/8-inch deck screws at each end.

16. Paint or stain the roof beams, supports and side panels before the roof is attached. The rest of the paint or stain job can be finished when the well is built.

Steps 12 to 15

17. Cut roof covering from a sheet of 1/2-inch plywood. One piece should measure 19-1/2 inches x 33 inches and a second piece should be 20

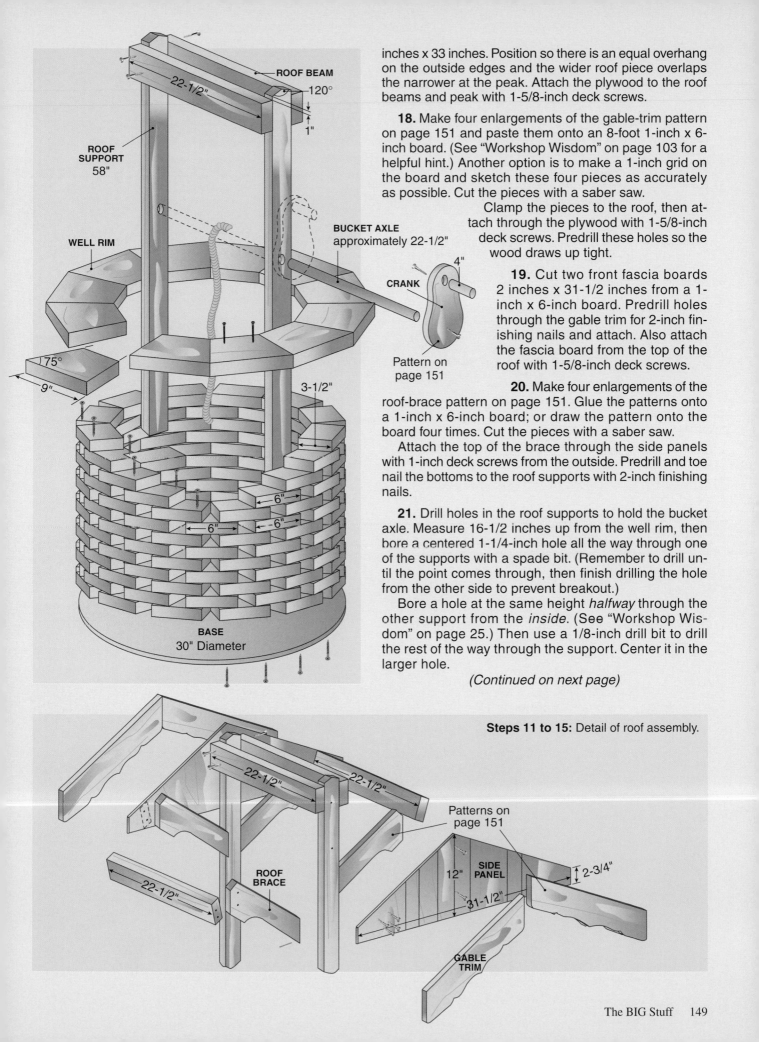

ROOF BEAM

22-1/2"

120°

1"

ROOF SUPPORT 58"

WELL RIM

BUCKET AXLE approximately 22-1/2"

CRANK

4"

Pattern on page 151

75°

9"

3-1/2"

6"

6"

6"

BASE 30" Diameter

inches x 33 inches. Position so there is an equal overhang on the outside edges and the wider roof piece overlaps the narrower at the peak. Attach the plywood to the roof beams and peak with 1-5/8-inch deck screws.

18. Make four enlargements of the gable-trim pattern on page 151 and paste them onto an 8-foot 1-inch x 6-inch board. (See "Workshop Wisdom" on page 103 for a helpful hint.) Another option is to make a 1-inch grid on the board and sketch these four pieces as accurately as possible. Cut the pieces with a saber saw.

Clamp the pieces to the roof, then attach through the plywood with 1-5/8-inch deck screws. Predrill these holes so the wood draws up tight.

19. Cut two front fascia boards 2 inches x 31-1/2 inches from a 1-inch x 6-inch board. Predrill holes through the gable trim for 2-inch finishing nails and attach. Also attach the fascia board from the top of the roof with 1-5/8-inch deck screws.

20. Make four enlargements of the roof-brace pattern on page 151. Glue the patterns onto a 1-inch x 6-inch board; or draw the pattern onto the board four times. Cut the pieces with a saber saw.

Attach the top of the brace through the side panels with 1-inch deck screws from the outside. Predrill and toe nail the bottoms to the roof supports with 2-inch finishing nails.

21. Drill holes in the roof supports to hold the bucket axle. Measure 16-1/2 inches up from the well rim, then bore a centered 1-1/4-inch hole all the way through one of the supports with a spade bit. (Remember to drill until the point comes through, then finish drilling the hole from the other side to prevent breakout.)

Bore a hole at the same height *halfway* through the other support from the *inside*. (See "Workshop Wisdom" on page 25.) Then use a 1/8-inch drill bit to drill the rest of the way through the support. Center it in the larger hole.

(Continued on next page)

Steps 11 to 15: Detail of roof assembly.

22-1/2"

22-1/2"

Patterns on page 151

22-1/2"

ROOF BRACE

12"

SIDE PANEL

31-1/2"

2-3/4"

GABLE TRIM

The BIG Stuff   149

Top It Off with a Cedar Shake Roof

TO GIVE YOUR WELL that old-fashioned touch, you may want finish the roof with cedar shakes. It takes a little time and planning, but we think you'll be pleased with the authentic look.

You'll need a full bundle of shingles to complete the roof. Space the shingles 1/2 inch apart.

1. Staple one piece of roofing paper over both roof sections, overlapping the peak. Roofing paper is sold only in large rolls, and you'll only need a little. If you don't have a roll on hand, check with a friend or neighbor. Odds are someone you know would be happy to get rid of some.

2. Cut the shingles for the first layer to 9 inches long, cutting away the thickest part of the shingle. Lay out the shingles flush with the edges of the roof and nail them in place with 1-1/4-inch small-head shingle nails.

3. Place a second layer of singles over the bottom row, using them at their full 16-inch length. These shingles should overhang the roof edge by 2 inches, and overlap the gaps on the first layer by at least 1 inch. Nail the shingles in place.

Step 2: The first layer of shingles is covered by the second layer, which overhangs the edge of the roof by 2 inches.

4. The third layer of shingles is also used at full length. Place them over the second layer, again overlapping the gaps. Leave 5 inches of the previous layer exposed and nail in place.

5. Cut the fourth and fifth layers of singles to 12 inches and 7 inches, respectively, *this time cutting away the thin part of the shingles*. Continue layering and nailing the rows until you reach the peak.

6. Shingle the other side of the roof repeating steps 2 through 5.

7. Cut a roof cap from a 3-foot piece of 4-inch or 6-inch cedar siding. Rip one piece 2-3/8 inches wide and a second piece 2 inches wide, using the *thick edge* of the siding.

8. Measure the width of the top layer of shingles and cut each roof cap to that length.

9. Predrill holes for shingle nails and attach with the wider piece overlapping the narrow one. Use construction adhesive on each piece.

Shingle nails will protrude through the underside of the roof. If you want to cover the exposed points, cut a piece of foam insulation board to size and glue it under the roof with construction adhesive.

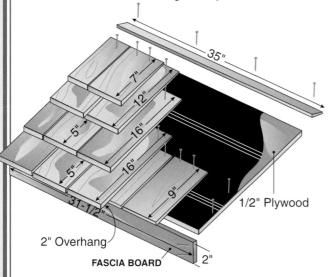

22. Enlarge the crank pattern. Glue or sketch the pattern onto a scrap piece of 1-inch x 6-inch board and cut it out with a saber saw.

23. Insert the 1-1/4-inch x 4-foot dowel through the holes in the roof supports (this will become the bucket axle). Mark the length of the dowel so that it extends beyond the roof support by about 1/2 inch, then remove it and cut.

24. Install the bucket axle. Center and drill a pilot hole into each end of the dowel.

Attach the dowel with a 1-1/2-inch round-head screw with a washer through the roof support with the 1/8-inch

hole. Don't overtighten or the axle will not turn.

Drill a pilot hole through the crank and attach it to the other end of the axle with a 1-5/8-inch deck screw. Cut a 4-inch piece of dowel for the handle and attach it to the crank the same way.

25. Finish staining. Touch up any spots that need it.

26. If you decide to shingle the roof with cedar shakes as we have, see the article above.

27. Wrap 1/2-inch rope around the bucket axle and attach to a wooden flower planter for display. That's it—now you deserve to well up with pride!

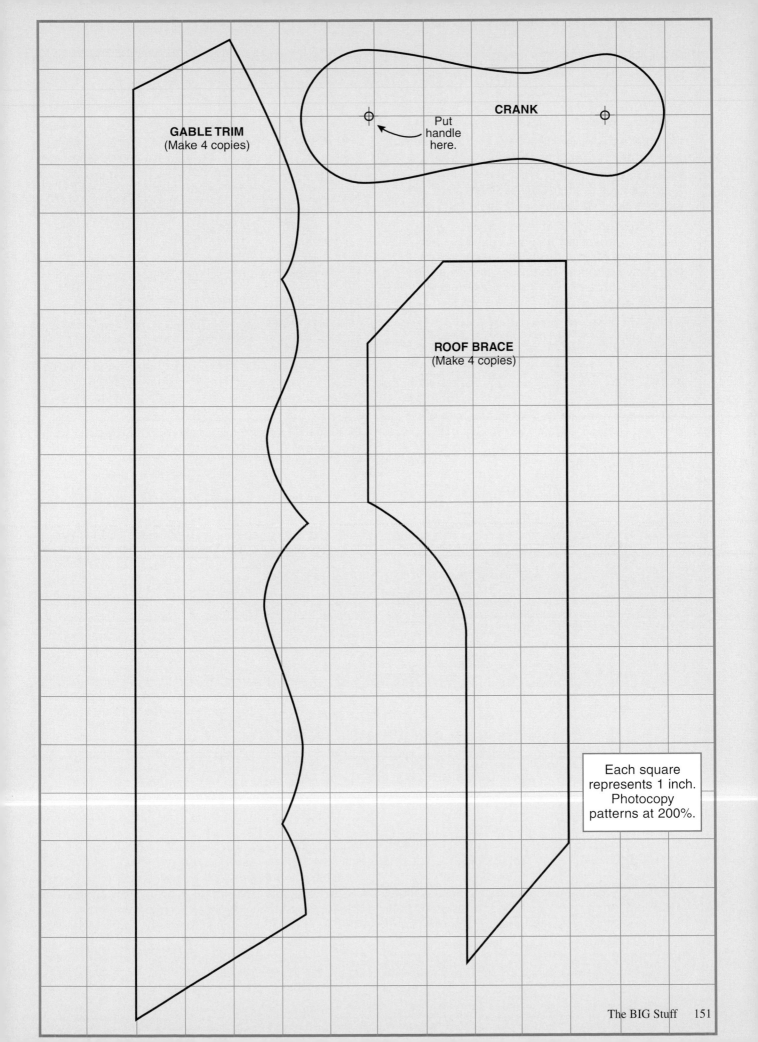

GABLE TRIM
(Make 4 copies)

CRANK

Put handle here.

ROOF BRACE
(Make 4 copies)

Each square represents 1 inch. Photocopy patterns at 200%.

It's a Picnic Table...
No, It's Benches...

With the twist of a wrist, you can transform a pair of sturdy benches into one great picnic table.

DO YOU NEED more room on your patio or deck? Are you tired of trying to move a picnic table that's just too heavy? Would you love to complete two projects for the time and expense of one?

If so, this simple plan may offer some welcome help. It'll enable you to make a set of attractive benches, which can become a full-size picnic table faster than you can say, "Superplan".

Submitted by Herman Hoffman of Michigan Center, Michigan, this one project gives you the best of both worlds—comfortable sturdy benches and the fun of backyard picnics.

"I came up with this design because our regular picnic table was too heavy to move around when I mowed

the grass," Herman says. "Plus, I wanted some benches, too. So I combined the two and developed this one practical project."

Herman recommends using 1-inch x 4-inch boards for the bench and tabletop rather than 2 x 4's. This keeps the project light enough for two people to easily move it anywhere in the backyard. Because you're only carrying half the table at a time, it's a lot less awkward, too.

We made this table out of pressure-treated wood. In this case, build the project as soon as you get the materials because 1-inch-thick wood will warp as it dries. When fastened into position, it can't warp.

Once you're finished building it, have a seat, or even lunch. The choice is yours.

TWO FOR ONE. By removing just a few wing nuts and bolts, a pair of garden benches like the one shown at left can change into a full-size lightweight picnic table (above). Insert the bolts—and you're ready for lunch.

Let's Get This Project Off the Table!

Note: *Step-by-step instructions are for building complete picnic table/two benches.*

1. Cut pieces according to the cutting list on page 155. Double-check all measurements before cutting multiple pieces. Remember: "Measure twice, cut once!"

2. Lay out the legs (A) and horizontal connectors (C and D) on the floor or workbench. The lower horizontal connector should be positioned 5-1/4 inches from the bottoms of the legs, and the upper connector should be flush to the tops of the legs.

Drill two 1/4-inch holes at each joint for 3-1/2-inch carriage bolts. (*Helpful hint:* clamp the pieces before drilling.) The heads of the bolts face outside.

Assemble a second frame identical to the first one,

Here's What You'll Need...

Note: *Use pressure-treated lumber. Materials are for complete picnic table/two benches.*

- ❑ Eighteen 6-foot 1-inch x 4-inch boards
- ❑ Five 8-foot 2 x 4's
- ❑ One 6-foot 2-inch x 6-inch board
- ❑ Sixty 1/4-inch x 3-1/2-inch carriage bolts, nuts and washers
- ❑ Eight 1/4-inch wing nuts
- ❑ Forty-four acorn nuts
- ❑ 2-inch and 2-1/2-inch galvanized deck screws

Recommended Tools...

- ❑ Miter box or table saw
- ❑ Rafter square
- ❑ Power drill
- ❑ Combination square

---

then build two more with the horizontal connectors located on the opposite side of the legs.

3. Drill a pivot hole through each main top support (F) and main vertical support (B). Locate each hole as indicated in the diagram for pieces at the bottom of page 155.

It's important to locate the pivot holes in the same position on each piece—accuracy is important so the pieces move properly. Drill a perpendicular 1/4-inch hole through the boards. (Use a drill press or see "Workshop Wisdom" on page 49 for a helpful tip.)

4. Bolt each main vertical support to the leg frames made in step 2. The support should be parallel to the front legs. To help position them, use a scrap 2 x 4 (at least 12 inches long) as pictured at the top of page 155. This will space the supports 3-1/2 inches from the front legs and also ensure the two pieces are parallel. The bottom of the main vertical supports should be flush with the bottoms of the lower horizontal connectors. Drill two 1/4-inch holes through the main vertical support and

(Continued on page 155)

Step 2: Assemble the horizontal connectors to the front and back legs. Clamp them together as pictured and fasten with carriage bolts. Note that you will make two leg frames as pictured, and a second pair with the horizontal connectors on top of the legs. Use one assembly of each per bench as shown in the plan on next page.

PICNIC TABLE AND BENCH ASSEMBLY (Make two for a complete table.)

Note: Cut all pieces by following the cutting list and board diagrams on page 155. Dimensions of fully assembled pieces are on page 156.

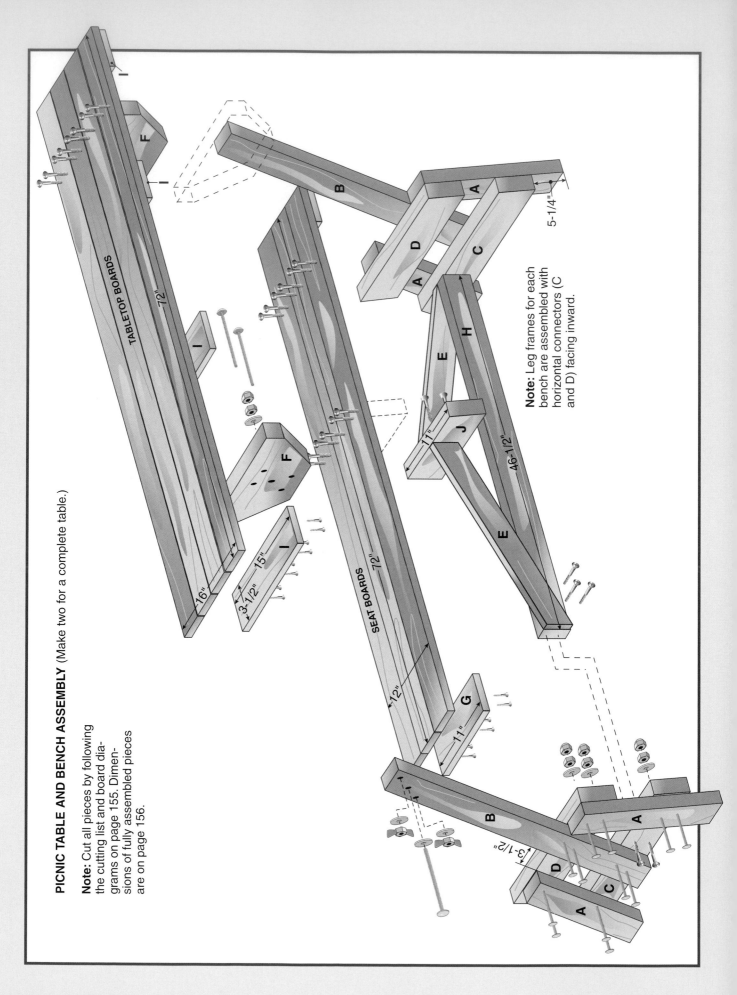

TABLETOP BOARDS

72"

SEAT BOARDS

72"

Note: Leg frames for each bench are assembled with horizontal connectors (C and D) facing inward.

5-1/4"

12"

11"

11"

16"

15"

3-1/2"

46-1/2"

3-1/2"

A B C D E F G H I J

Step 4: Use a scrap 2 x 4 to quickly and accurately align the main vertical support (B) parallel to the front legs (A).

each horizontal connector. Fasten with carriage bolts.

5. Connect each main top support and main vertical support with a carriage bolt through the pivot holes. Tighten the bolts enough to hold the tabletops horizontal.

6. Recruit a helper who can hold two assembled frames upright as you begin to attach the seat boards. Set a combination square to 10 inches to help position the leg frames 10 inches in from the ends of the seat boards.

7. Attach one 6-foot 1-inch x 4-inch seat board positioned *against* the main vertical supports with 2-inch deck screws. (Make sure the horizontal connectors of each leg assembly face inward as shown in the plan at left.) Drive them in just enough to hold the board in place so you can square the frames to the seat boards.

Add a second seat board overhanging the front edge 1/2 inch, squaring the legs as you continue. Attach the third seat board spaced evenly between them. Now drive the screws home. Repeat this step for the second bench and thank your helper.

8. Attach the 6-foot 1-inch x 4-inch tabletop boards to the main top support with 2-inch deck screws. Center the boards on the supports and overhang the front and back of the support 1/2 inch. Evenly space and attach two boards between them. Repeat this step for the second bench.

9. Attach the seat brace anchor (J) to the seat boards with 2-1/2-inch deck screws. Position it vertically and centered on the underside of the seat, then fasten it from the top side. Repeat for the other bench.

10. Attach the 2 x 4 seat braces (H) that connect the two leg frames. Center this piece on the lower horizontal connectors and fasten with 2-1/2-inch deck screws from the outsides of the frames.

11. Attach two 1-inch x 4-inch angle seat braces (E) to each seat brace anchor and the horizontal 2 x 4 installed in the previous two steps. One brace attaches to the front of the 2 x 4 and the other should be fastened to the back.

12. Attach the four 15-inch-long tabletop supports (I)

(Continued on next page)

Here's a Cutting List to Help...

Note: *This list includes the pieces needed to make complete picnic table/two benches.*

From five 8-foot 2 x 4's, cut:

- Eight legs, 20 inches long (cut parallel angles on each end) (A)
- Four main vertical supports, 28 inches long (cut parallel angles on the ends) (B)
- Four lower horizontal connectors, 26 inches long (cut opposing angles on the ends) (C)
- Four upper horizontal connectors, 21-1/2 inches long (cut angles on one end) (D)
- Two seat brace anchors, 11 inches long (J)
- Two seat braces, 46-1/2 inches long (H)

From one 6-foot 2-inch x 6-inch board, cut:

- Four main top supports, 15 inches long (cut to dimensions shown below) (F)

From four 6-foot 1-inch x 4-inch boards, cut:

- Four seat braces, 24 inches long (cut parallel angles on each end) (E)
- Four seat supports, 11 inches long (G)
- Eight tabletop supports, 15 inches long (I)

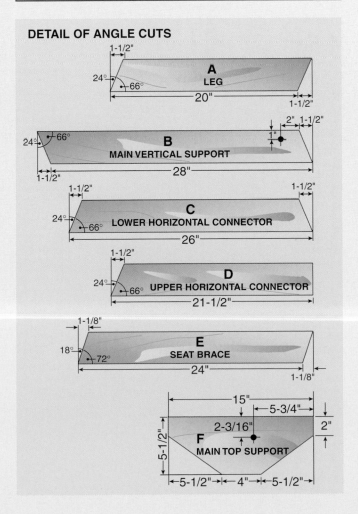

DETAIL OF ANGLE CUTS

Step 14: The same holes are used in the main vertical support for the bench and picnic table positions.

(see where to position them below). Fasten from the bottom side of the table with 1-5/8-inch deck screws. Clamping the braces to the tabletop will help the screws draw tight. (See "Workshop Wisdom" below for a helpful hint.)

13. Position each bench in the "table" position so the top rests firmly on the main vertical support (it should be parallel to the seat). Hold the table firmly in place and clamp it in this position. Then drill two 1/4-inch holes through the main vertical and main top supports.

14. Pivot the tabletops to the "bench" position. When the seat backs rest firmly against the main vertical supports, hold or clamp in position. Using the same 1/4-inch holes just made in the main vertical supports as a guide (see photo at right), drill again. Use 1/4-inch x 3-1/2-inch bolts, washers and wing nuts to secure the seat back or tabletops in position.

15. Sand all rough corners and edges. Cap bolts on the horizontal connectors with acorn nuts. Your guests wearing shorts will appreciate it, and so will you!

Now the dilemma: Should you first use it as a picnic table or as benches? Why not sit down and think about it?

Workshop Wisdom
Want Deck Screws to Pull Tight?

A FREQUENT PROBLEM when using deck screws (without predrilling) is that the second board often pushes away from the first board before the threads begin to bite. Then, when the screw is all the way in, there is a noticeable gap between the boards.

Simply clamp the pieces together first, or back the screw out of the second board, then apply pressure and tighten again.

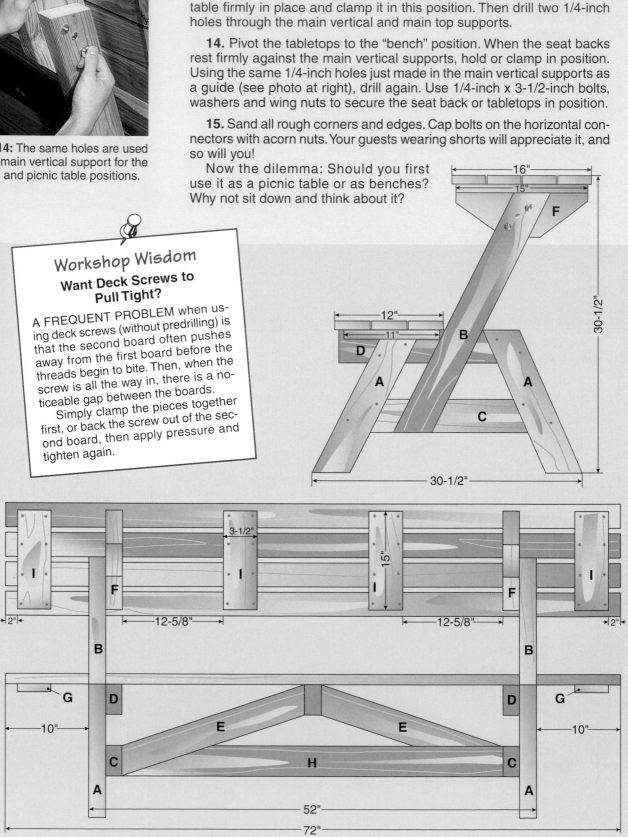

Small Garden Shed Is Big On Ideas

Need extra space for your garden supplies? Build this handy shed. It's like having an outdoor closet.

IF YOU NEED some extra space in the garage and a handy place to store your gardening supplies, perhaps this small garden shed is the answer. It's like having a storage closet near the garden—exactly where you could use it!

For a shed only 2-feet square, you can pack a lot into its efficient cavity. There are shelves for supplies, a special notch for holding long-handled tools and wire racks that hold a bevy of additional goods.

We built this shed from solid cedar. It's a little more expensive than cedar paneling, but is much sturdier, allowing the shed to be built without any vertical framing (except for around the door). This not only makes it easier and faster to build, it also provides maximum storage space inside.

This project may look somewhat intimidating at first, but if you take it one section at a time, it's fairly easy to build. Once you get used to having the extra space this simple shed provides, you may just find yourself building another—for the other side of the house.

(Step-by-step instructions begin on next page)

Here's What You'll Need...

- ❑ Twelve 8-foot 1-inch x 6-inch tongue-in-groove cedar boards
- ❑ Twelve 6-foot 1-inch x 6-inch tongue-in-groove cedar boards
- ❑ One 4-foot x 8-foot sheet of 1/2-inch plywood
- ❑ Two 8-foot 2 x 2's
- ❑ Two pressure-treated 8-foot 2 x 4's
- ❑ Two 6-foot 2 x 4's
- ❑ 3-inch, 2-1/2-inch and 1-5/8-inch galvanized deck screws
- ❑ 2-inch finishing nails
- ❑ 3 feet of flashing (for the roof)
- ❑ Two bundles of cedar shingles (optional)
- ❑ 1-1/4-inch small-head shingle nails
- ❑ One door latch
- ❑ Two galvanized hinges
- ❑ Wire shelving (optional)
- ❑ Waterproof construction adhesive

Recommended Tools...

- ❑ Table saw
- ❑ Circular saw
- ❑ Rafter square
- ❑ Stapler
- ❑ Utility knife
- ❑ Block plane

Shed Some Light on This Project

1. Begin by making two identical 23-inch-square frames from pressure-treated 2 x 4's for the base and roof support. Cut four pieces 23 inches long (front and back pieces) and four 20 inches long (side pieces).

2. Assemble the frames, placing the 2 x 4's on edge. Drill pilot holes through the front and back pieces and fasten with 3-inch deck screws (see photo above).

3. Cut two 23-inch-square pieces of 1/2-inch plywood. Attach one plywood square to the *bottom* of one frame with 1-5/8-inch deck screws. This will become the base of the shed. Place the other piece aside until the final step, when the floor is filled with ballast.

4. Cut four rafter pieces 17-1/8 inches long from 2 x 2's with opposing 45° angles on the ends. Attach them to the roof frame and at the peak so they form a 90° angle. The bottom ends of the rafters should overhang the sides (see photo below left) by the same thickness as the tongue-and-groove cedar. (Be sure to measure the thickness of the lumber because milled cedar can vary in thickness.)

5. Connect the two rafters at the peak using a 2 x 2 between them. Rotate the 2 x 2 so it lines up with the 90°

Steps 4 and 5: The rafter pieces are made from 2 x 2's and form a 90° peak at the top of the shed (above right). The bottom end of the rafters (above left) overhang the top frame by the thickness of the cedar you are using.

roof peak (see photo bottom right). Attach with construction adhesive and 3-inch deck screws. Be sure to drill pilot holes so the 2 x 2's don't split.

6. Make four feet for the shed to sit on by cutting 3-1/2-inch-square pieces from pressure-treated 2 x 4's. Predrill each piece and fasten one flush with each corner of the shed's base using 2-1/2-inch deck screws.

Adding the Sides and Back

7. Connect the roof and base frames using 6-foot tongue-and-groove cedar boards on each side. To do this, follow steps 7a to 7d:

7a. Lay the roof frame and the base frame on the floor so one *side* is facing up. Space them approximately 6 feet apart from the top of the roof frame to the bottom of the base frame.

7b. Fit five of the cedar boards together on a flat surface. Square the top edge with a rafter square. Tap them together to make sure the tongue and grooves are thoroughly seated. Nail the boards together with a temporary strip near both ends with finishing nails to hold them tightly together.

DOOR JAMB

Step 7c: The cedar sides of the shed will fit under the rafter overhangs. The sides should also overhang the roof and base frames (as pictured above) by the thickness of the cedar. The door jamb (pictured in lower right of the photo) will not be screwed in place until step 10.

7c. Position the frames to fit snugly under the gable overhang. Make sure the boards also equally overhang both sides of the frames and extend past the bottom of the base frame by 1/2 inch. Using a scrap piece of tongue-and-groove cedar, mark its thickness along the underside of each end cedar board to represent the *front* and *rear* siding. (The width of the side should be 23 inches plus *twice* the thickness of the cedar you're using. See photo above.)

7d. Remove the two *outside* cedar boards and rip along the lines you drew in the previous step. This will remove the tongue from one board and the groove from the other. Put the boards back in place. Check position once more, then apply construction adhesive to the top and bottom frames, then fasten the side boards in place with 1-5/8-inch deck screws. Position screws within 1-3/4 inches of the top and bottom edges of the boards. They'll be

BEFORE USING SCREWS close to the edge of boards, it's a good idea to test a couple on scrap board positioned the same distance from the edge. If the scrap board splits, you'll know to predrill holes on the boards you're working with.

covered by finish molding later. (See "Workshop Wisdom" at left for a helpful hint.)

8. With a helper, turn the shed over to the opposite side and repeat step 7 to attach the second side wall. Continue to square the pieces as you build.

9. Fit five 8-foot 1-inch x 6-inch tongue-and-groove boards together snugly for the back. Locate the center point on the middle board. From that point, draw two 45° angles to follow the roof line. Cut the angles with a circular saw and place the boards in position on the back of the shed. Mark the outside edges—you'll rip the boards at these

Step 9: Center the middle board on the back wall at the peak. Cut the boards at 45° to follow the angle of the peak. Notice that the side wall in lower right of photo overhangs the outermost back board. The outermost tongue and groove are trimmed off to fit between the side walls.

marks, cuttings off one tongue and one groove. Put them back in position, apply construction adhesive and fasten the boards in place with 1-5/8-inch deck screws (see photo above).

Moving on to the Front

10. Measure and cut two *straight* 6-foot 2 x 4's for the door jamb. Toe-nail them in place (you can do this with 3-inch nails or deck screws), positioning the *inside* edge 4-3/8 inches in from each side.

Before you drive the nails home, make sure the jambs are square at the top and bottom. Also measure the opening at the top and bottom—it should be 14-1/4 inches. Adjust if necessary before securing them.

11. Cut and attach the end cedar boards to the front of the shed using two 8-foot cedar boards. Rip the tongue and grooves off *both edges* of both pieces, making sure they're cut to the same width. Before fastening, draw a line on the boards along the top of the gables and cut at a 45° angle (see photo on page 162 at top left). Apply construction adhesive and fasten the boards to the roof

and base frames, as well as the rafters, with 1-5/8-inch deck screws. Place the screws within 1-3/4 inches of the ends so that moldings will cover them.

12. Make the door from three *straight* 8-foot cedar boards. Rough cut each board to 70 inches long. Save the cutoffs from these boards—they will be used later (in step 15) to trim above the door. (Mark each board so you can match them to the same board later.)

Fit the door boards together snugly and hold the pieces together at the top and bottom with 1/2-inch plywood straps measuring 5-1/2 inches x 12-1/2 inches.

After joining the boards together, trim off the tongue from one edge and the groove from the other on your table saw. (When cutting something this long, make sure you have a helper or a roller stand, table, sawhorse, etc. on the other side of the saw to help support the piece as it passes the blade.) The final width of the door should measure 14 inches.

13. Trim the door to its final length of 65-3/8 inches.

To do this, lay the shed on its back. Square the top and bottom of the door, trimming it off 2 inches above and below the plywood straps. Place the door onto the shed so it overlaps the roof frame 1/2 inch. The bottom of the door should overlap the base frame by 1 inch. Save the pieces trimmed off the bottom for step 16.

Set the door in place and do any final fitting.

14. Attach the door to the shed. To do this, position the door with a 1/8-inch gap on the hinge side. Tack in place with two or three *small* finishing nails.

Lay out the hinges about 5 inches from the top and bottom of the door. (Position them so they screw into the plywood straps on the inside of the door.) Mark the centers of the hinge holes with an awl and predrill them to the size indicated by the hinge manufacturer's instructions. If hole size is not specified, test pilot holes on a scrap piece of cedar until you find the best size.

(Instructions continued on page 162)

Step 12

DOOR STRAP
2"
5-1/2"
12-1/2"
1/2" PLYWOOD

INSIDE OF DOOR

14"

65-3/8"

12-1/2"
5-1/2"
2"

GARDEN SHED ASSEMBLY, ILLUSTRATION NO. 1

Roof and base frames (steps 1 to 3), rafters (steps 4 to 5), side walls (step 7 to 8), door jamb (step 10), door stops (step 22), side trim (steps 23 to 28) and inside shelf (step 29).

OVERALL DIMENSIONS
86-1/2" Tall
24-3/4" Wide
24-3/4" Deep

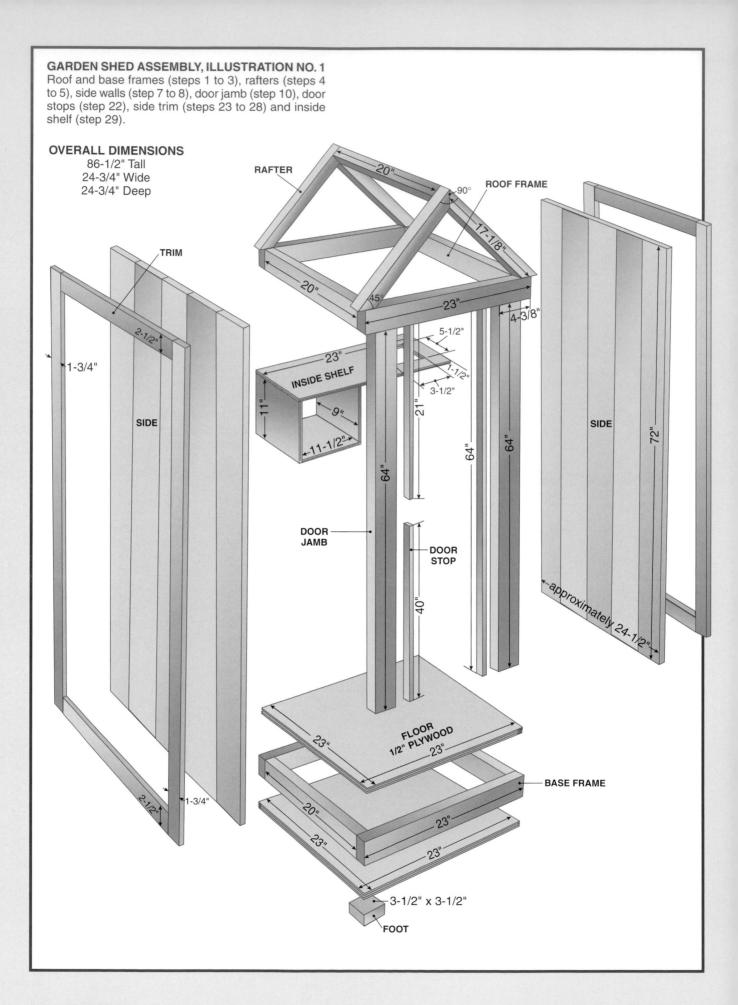

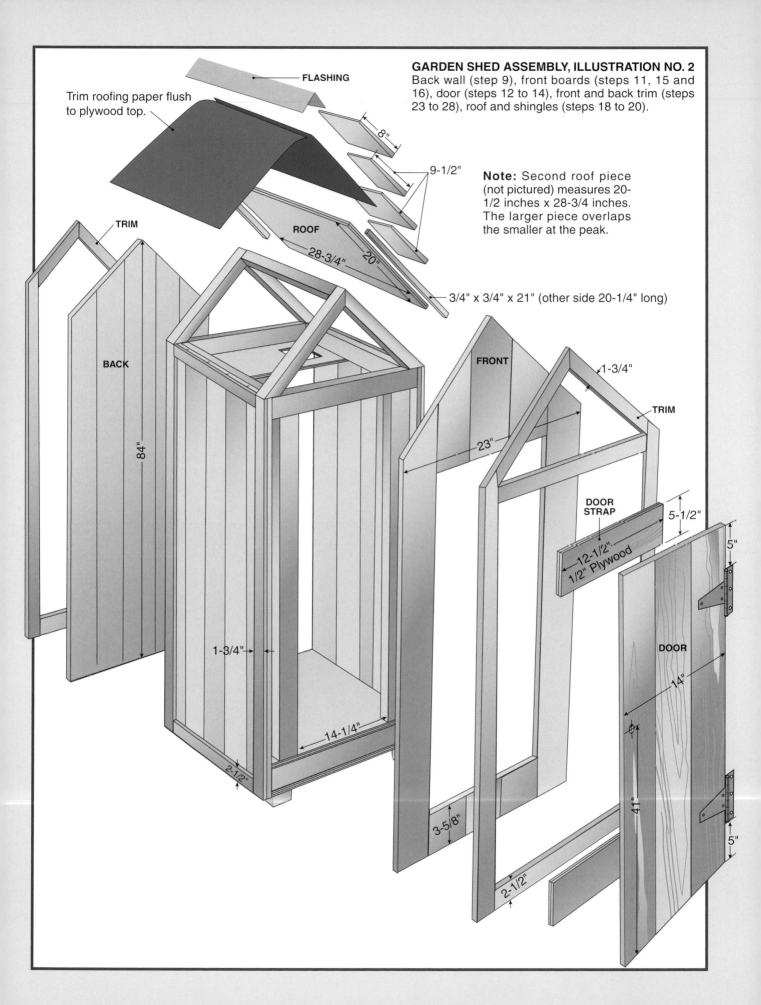

GARDEN SHED ASSEMBLY, ILLUSTRATION NO. 2
Back wall (step 9), front boards (steps 11, 15 and 16), door (steps 12 to 14), front and back trim (steps 23 to 28), roof and shingles (steps 18 to 20).

FLASHING

Trim roofing paper flush to plywood top.

Note: Second roof piece (not pictured) measures 20-1/2 inches x 28-3/4 inches. The larger piece overlaps the smaller at the peak.

TRIM

ROOF

8"

9-1/2"

28-3/4"

20"

3/4" x 3/4" x 21" (other side 20-1/4" long)

BACK

84"

FRONT

23"

1-3/4"

TRIM

DOOR STRAP

12-1/2"

1/2" Plywood

5-1/2"

5"

1-3/4"

14-1/4"

2-1/2"

DOOR

14"

41"

3-5/8"

2-1/2"

5"

Step 15b: Remove the tongue and groove from the boards surrounding the door. Also remove the tongue or groove only on the side of the cedar pieces that abut them above the door.

15. Cover the rafter frame above the door with the cedar cutoffs that were saved in step 12. To do this, follow steps 15a to 15d:

15a. Line up the cutoffs with the door boards they match. (That's why we marked them earlier.)

15b. Because the tongue and groove were trimmed off the edge cedar boards in step 11, you'll need to also trim the tongue or groove off the side of the cedar pieces that will abut them so they will align with the door boards below (see photo above).

Plane a bevel on the pieces that the tongues and grooves were removed from to replace the "V" groove that was cut off.

15c. Cut 45° angles so the boards fit the shed's peak, then "dry-fit" (that means test the pieces for fit before gluing them). The grooves should align with the grooves on the door boards.

15d. Glue along the tops and bottoms of the boards and attach them to the roof frame and rafters with 1-5/8-inch deck screws. (Also apply adhesive on the edge where the tongue or groove was removed.) Position the screws so they will be covered by a 1-3/4-inch molding.

16. Attach the small cutoffs leftover from step 13 below the door. Line the bottoms of the pieces up with the bottoms of the side walls. Mark the pieces allowing for a 1/4-inch gap below the bottom of the door then trim each piece to length.

Again, you will have to trim the tongue or groove off the outermost pieces as in step 15b and add a bevel.

Because these are small pieces, be sure to use construction adhesive and 1-5/8-inch deck screws to hold them in place. Predrill holes so the cedar doesn't split.

Put a Roof Overhead

17. Find a helper and stand the shed upright.

18. Cut two pieces of 1/2-inch-thick plywood for the roof. One piece should measure 20 inches x 28-3/4 inches and the other 20-1/2 inches x 28-3/4 inches. The wider piece will overlap the narrower.

19. Position the narrower roof piece so it is flush with the peak and overhangs the front and back of the shed by 2 inches. Clamp it in position and screw it to the rafters with 1-5/8-inch deck screws.

Position the wider roof section so it overlaps the narrower piece at the peak and attach it with 1-5/8-inch deck screws.

20. Shingle the roof with cedar shakes to give the shed more character. However, if you're like most of us who have a bundle of leftover shingles laying around that match the roof on your house, this is a chance to use some of them up.

If you'd like a cedar shake roof, you'll need two bundles. Directions for laying a shake roof are on page 150. Take into account these few specifics for this project:

• The bottom three rows of shingles will measure 9-1/2 inches long, and the top row will be 8 inches long. Cut all the excess material off the thin end of the shingles.

• You'll need eight shingles for the roof cap that are 4 inches wide and 10-1/2 inches long. *Put them aside before starting, along with a couple extras.*

• Place flashing along the peak of the roof to seal it. This is attached with shingling nails before the roof cap is attached. Make sure the flashing does not hang out below the cap.

• The bottom row of shingles should overlap the roof edge by 2 inches. In this project, we start with only a single row of shingles on the bottom.

• Construction adhesive will help hold the cap shingles in place.

Step 20: Place aluminum flashing along the peak of the roof.

The Finishing Details

21. A variety of catches and handles can be used with this project. Follow the manufacturer's directions to install the door handle.

If you're using a latch like ours, make sure the hole for it is large enough. If it's too small and rubs even a little, it will not work properly.

22. From a 6-foot piece of cedar, rip two strips 3/4 inch wide for door stops. Cut one stop into two pieces, attaching it above and below the door catch (as shown in the plan) using construction adhesive and 1-1/2-inch finishing nails. (This will provide a good weather seal.)

Be sure the stop is set back about 1/16 inch or more

to allow for expansion with weather. Don't drive the nails in the stop until you try the door and it operates well. Add a second door stop to the hinge side using the same method.

23. Use leftover tongue-and-groove cedar to make the finish trim. Saw off the tongue and grooves and rip a board 2-1/2 inches wide for horizontal trim and 1-3/4 inches wide for the vertical moldings. (Note: We resawed these pieces to approximately 5-1/6 inch thick on a table saw to get more trim from one board. You can use it at full thickness.)

24. Attach 1-3/4-inch molding to cover the vertical joints between the front and side walls. Cut the trim pieces 45° at the top to fit the roofline. Attach all trim with construction adhesive and 1-1/2-inch finishing nails, setting the heads. The trim will help seal out the weather.

Repeat this step on the back of the shed, then trim the sides so they overlap the front and back trim boards.

25. Continue adding 1-3/4-inch trim along the roof peak on the front and back sides, cutting the ends at 45° angles (see photo below). Trim the back of the shed first (it's better to practice here), then the sides and front.

26. Trim around the bottom of the shed and above the door with 2-1/2-inch molding. Cut these pieces to fit between the corner moldings.

ALMOST FINISHED. The front cedar pieces above the door were marked and saved from step 12. They are placed above the same boards from which they were trimmed off. Also notice how the roof cap and trim boards are placed.

27. Attach trim on each side below the roof eaves, making sure the bottom edge of the molding is aligned with the piece over the door. Rip the piece down to size if necessary.

28. Rip 3/4-inch-square cedar trim pieces to attach to the plywood edge of the roof. Fasten them to the plywood with construction adhesive and 1-1/2-inch finishing nails.

29. Finish the inside of the shed with shelving.

Make the back shelving unit on a workbench, using 1/2-inch plywood. Measure the inside of the shed from wall to wall and cut the plywood to length. Then trim the piece 9 inches deep.

Cut a 3-1/2-inch x 5-1/2-inch rectangular hole in the far right end to accommodate long-handled tools (see

Step 29: This two-level shelving unit is plenty handy. You can use it to store garden supplies as well as to keep your long-handled tools in place when you open the door. Just slip the ends of the handles through the notch on the right.

photo above and refer to plan on page 160 for dimensions.)

The 11-1/2-inch x 9-inch lower shelf will be mounted to side boards measuring 11 inches x 9 inches. Assemble the shelving unit with carpenter's glue and 1-1/2-inch finishing nails (as pictured above).

Fasten the shelf unit to the bottom of the roof frame as pictured below with 1-5/8-inch deck screws.

30. Add wire shelving to the shed and door as needed.

31. Move the shed to its final location. Fill the bottom frame with stone, sand, leftover bricks, etc. for ballast. This will help keep it upright in windy areas.

Cover the ballast with the second 23-inch-square piece of plywood cut in step 3. This will be the inside floor. Screw it to the base frame using 1-5/8-inch deck screws.

Congratulations! Take a well-deserved break before you begin cleaning out the garage.

ADDITIONAL STORAGE. Attach the plywood shelving unit to the underside of the roof frame. We've added more shelving to the shed and door by purchasing premade wire racks and shelves from the local hardware store.

Redwood Water-Pump Pond Will Soothe the Senses

The calming sound of running water can turn your patio or deck into a haven of tranquillity.

ADD THE SOUND of running water to your backyard and you'll discover why so many gardeners find the gentle trickling adds a soothing dimension to their hobby.

There are other benefits, too. Moving water will attract birds to your yard, and you'll have the option of stocking your own small fish pond, or experimenting with a few aquatic plants as well.

This attractive water-pump pond is the perfect starter pond and just the right addition for a small nook. Because it's portable, it can be moved to a new location year after year. Just unplug it, drain the tub and move it to the desired location.

We opted for an antique cast-iron pitcher pump to give our pond rustic charm, but a new one would work just

as well. Buying, sandblasting and repainting our antique pump cost about $50—the entire project totaled over $250. So if you take this one on, consider it an investment.

If you can't find an antique pump, new ones are available at most hardware stores for about the same price. You'll have to remove some of the inside working parts before mounting the pump to the pond though.

While this looks like a simple project, it should be built with care. If you want your investment to last a long time, the joints must be tight, and the wood has to be protected with a redwood preservative to ensure its rich, red color lasts for years.

With some attention to detail, this delightful project will provide years of enjoyment and relaxation.

Let's Have a Pool-Building Party!

1. Begin constructing a framework to support the tub by cutting these pieces from pressure-treated 8-foot 2 x 4's (the letter after each piece corresponds with labeled parts on the next page):

- Four corner pieces, 9-1/2 inches long (A)
- Four end pieces, 20-3/4 inches long (B)
- Four side pieces, 36-1/2 inches long (C)
- Four support feet, 3-1/2 inches square (D)
- Four tub supports, 27-3/4 inches long (E)

2. Attach the 2 x 4 side and end pieces to the vertical corner pieces using 2-1/2-inch deck screws, squaring as you go. These will have to be "toe nailed" to the corner 2 x 4's, so predrill the holes at an angle. The side and end pieces should be flush with the top and bottom of the corner pieces (see photo below).

3. Turn the framework upside down and fasten a support foot in each corner with 2-1/2-inch deck screws. These will keep the redwood from sitting on the ground, protecting it from continuous moisture.

4. Space the four tub supports evenly across the *underside* of the frame and attach to the bottom of the frame with 2-1/2-inch deck screws (see photo below left).

5. From three 8-foot 1-inch x 12-inch redwood boards, cut the exterior redwood pieces following the board layouts on page 166.

6. Cut a small notch at the bottom center of *one* vertical end piece for the pump's electric cord to pass through.

7. Position the vertical end pieces flush with the top and sides of the frame, clamp in position and fasten in place from the *inside* of the frame with 2-inch deck screws. Drill pilot holes slightly larger than the screws' diameter through the 2 x 4 frame. This will pull the redwood tight to the frame.

8. Clamp the vertical side pieces in position so they're flush with the top of the frame and the end boards. Attach as in the previous step.

9. To finish off the corners of the redwood box, you may want to make four caps to protect them.

Cut these pieces from a redwood 2 x 4. Rip the board to a width of 2-1/2 inches. Then remove an area measuring 1 inch x 2 inches from the length of the board. (See the dimensions of piece L on the next page.) You can do this on a table saw with just two cuts, creating a rabbet with your saw blade. The growth rings on the corner boards should face inward. Double-check this before cutting the rabbets. Each cap measures 10-7/8 inches long.

10. Glue the corner caps in place with a small amount

(Continued on page 167)

Step 2: The 2 x 4 framework for the pond cabinet is attached to vertical corner pieces (A). End (B) and side (C) pieces are attached to the corner in "toe-nail" fashion.

Steps 3 and 4: Support feet (D) and tub supports (E) are attached to the underside of the framework as pictured.

Here's What You'll Need...

- ❑ Five pressure-treated 8-foot 2 x 4's
- ❑ One redwood 4-foot 2 x 4
- ❑ Three 8-foot 1-inch x 12-inch redwood boards
- ❑ 2-1/2-inch and 2-inch galvanized deck screws
- ❑ 1-3/4-inch, 1-1/2-inch, 1-inch and 1/2-inch brass flat-head screws
- ❑ Small pieces of scrap 3/8-inch plywood (or biscuits and a biscuit jointer)
- ❑ Waterproof construction adhesive
- ❑ Waterproof carpenter's glue
- ❑ One 24-inch x 36-inch x 8-inch-deep plastic tub
- ❑ Cast-iron pitcher pump
- ❑ PVC cap or flat piece of plastic that fits inside the pump's housing
- ❑ Silicone sealant caulk
- ❑ Submersible pump (one that pumps about 60 gallons per hour)
- ❑ 2-foot black vinyl hose (to fit submersible pump)
- ❑ Redwood preservative

Recommended Tools...

- ❑ Table saw
- ❑ Power drill
- ❑ Countersink bit
- ❑ 4-inch clamps
- ❑ Pipe clamps (48-inch capacity)

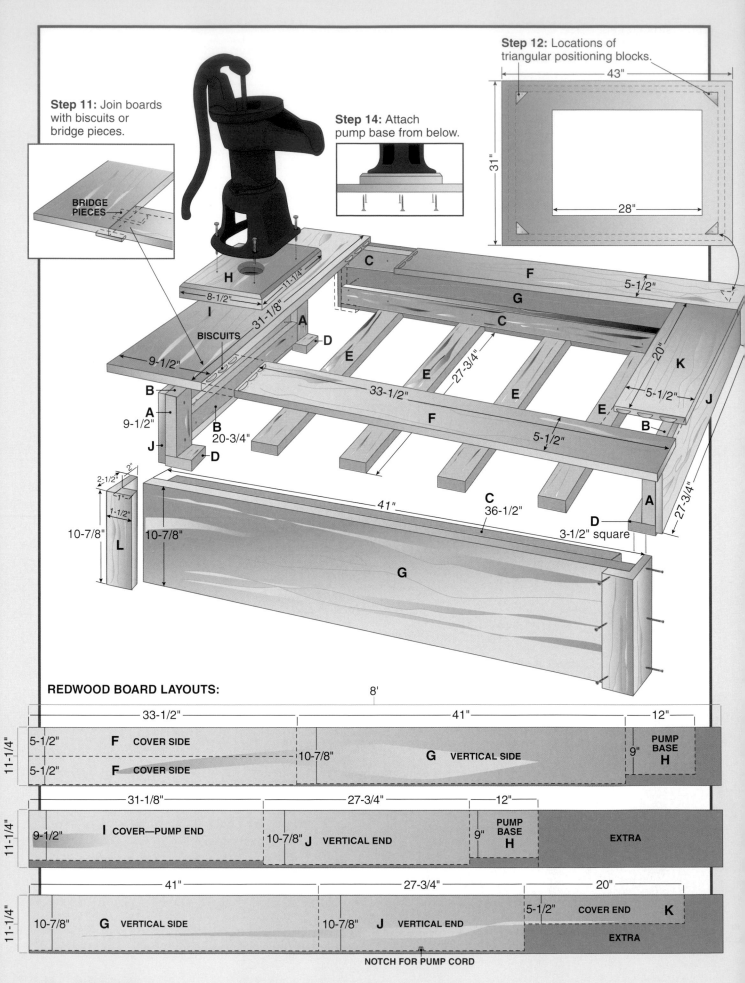

Step 11: Join boards with biscuits or bridge pieces.

BRIDGE PIECES

BISCUITS

Step 14: Attach pump base from below.

Step 12: Locations of triangular positioning blocks.

43"

31"

28"

H

8-1/2"

11-1/4"

I

31-1/8"

C

F

G

C

5-1/2"

9-1/2"

A

D

B

E

E

E

27-3/4"

K

20"

5-1/2"

A

9-1/2"

B

B

33-1/2"

F

E

B

J

J

D

20-3/4"

5-1/2"

A

27-3/4"

2"

2-1/2"

1"

1-1/2"

10-7/8"

L

10-7/8"

41"

C

36-1/2"

G

D

3-1/2" square

REDWOOD BOARD LAYOUTS:

8'

33-1/2"

41"

12"

11-1/4"

5-1/2" **F** COVER SIDE

10-7/8" **G** VERTICAL SIDE

9" **PUMP BASE H**

5-1/2" **F** COVER SIDE

31-1/8"

27-3/4"

12"

11-1/4"

9-1/2" **I** COVER—PUMP END

10-7/8" **J** VERTICAL END

9" **PUMP BASE H**

EXTRA

41"

27-3/4"

20"

11-1/4"

10-7/8" **G** VERTICAL SIDE

10-7/8" **J** VERTICAL END

5-1/2" COVER END **K**

EXTRA

NOTCH FOR PUMP CORD

of construction adhesive. Place the ends of the pieces flush with the tops of the vertical end and side boards and screw them in place from the outside with 1-3/4-inch brass flat-head screws. Drill pilot holes so the wood doesn't split and countersink.

11. Assemble the pond cover, which is removable for easy access to the plastic tub and pump. To do this, you'll need pipe or bar clamps and a *flat* surface for gluing.

The pieces can be joined one of two ways (pictured in plan at left):

• You can cut slots with a biscuit jointer or slot cutter. Squeeze waterproof carpenter's glue (*not* construction adhesive) into the slots, insert biscuits, then clamp the pieces together. (The slots are cut in the exact same position on both pieces so they're level when joined.)

• Or...glue joints together with waterproof carpenter's glue and hold them tight with bar clamps. Then glue small flat pieces of 3/8-inch plywood to the bottom of each joint and screw through the plywood with 1-inch brass flat-head screws to secure.

Regardless of which method you choose, be sure to wipe away any excess glue from the redwood surface or it will ruin your finish. Check for excess glue several times as it's drying.

12. Attach triangle positioning blocks to the underside of the cover at each corner. This will hold the cover in place when set on top of the framework (see illustration above left).

Make the positioning blocks from redwood scraps. Cut out four 45° triangles—the short sides should each measure 2-1/2 inches. Don't make the fit too tight—allow about 1/4-inch "play" in both directions. Attach the positioning blocks with glue and 1/2-inch brass flat-head screws.

13. Glue the two pump base pieces together using a liberal amount of waterproof glue near the edges and where the pump hole will be located. Clamp together and allow to dry completely before cutting the base to its final size of 8-1/2 inches x 11-1/4 inches.

You may want to bevel the top edges of the pump base as we did to give it a more finished look. This can be done with a block plane, table saw or router.

14. Position the pump base on the 9-1/2-inch-wide end of the cover. Glue the base to the cover with waterproof glue and clamp. The glue should ooze from all edges to create a watertight seal. Wipe away the excess glue and check frequently as it's drying. (Clean glue by following the manufacturer's instructions.)

When the glue dries, screw the pieces together from the bottom with eight 1-1/2-inch brass flat-head screws (see illustration at left).

15. Drill a hole for the pump hose through the base and cover with a spade bit or hole saw. The opening should be slightly larger than the vinyl hose. Drill until the point starts to come through the bottom, then flip over and finish drilling from the other side. This will give you a clean hole on both sides.

Position the cover so the pump base is on the same end as the notch you cut for the electric cord in step 6.

16. Before attaching the pump, you'll need to make a water-tight chamber inside the pump housing to prevent water from flowing back down the pump. This will take a bit of creative ingenuity to modify your pump.

We cut a 4-inch flat piece of PVC from a cap that fit *inside* the pump housing (any flat plastic piece will work). Before gluing the PVC inside the pump with silicone caulk, drill a hole through the middle of the PVC the same size as the vinyl hose. The hose should stick up into the pump's chamber about an inch. Insert the hose and seal around it with silicone caulk. Then caulk the PVC into the pitcher pump's housing.

17. Attach the pitcher pump to the pump base with three 1-1/2-inch brass flat-head screws.

18. Place the submersible pump in the plastic tub and attach the vinyl hose. This will circulate the water into the pitcher pump. Because you sealed the chamber, the water will be forced to drain from the spout.

19. To preserve and prolong the redwood's rich natural color, apply a couple of coats of redwood preservative. If you're using untreated wood, apply a coat of deck stain.

20. Add water to the tub. Plug the pump into a properly installed GFI outlet and give your friends and neighbors a call. Go ahead, tell them you're relaxing by your new pool.

Detail of water-tight pump housing

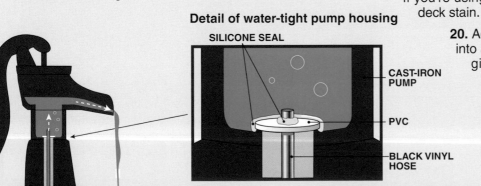

SILICONE SEAL

CAST-IRON PUMP

PVC

BLACK VINYL HOSE

A PEEK INSIDE. This cross section of the water-pump pond shows the simple inner workings of this unique water garden. The submersible pump circulates water back into the cast-iron water pump.

Roomy Storage Box Keeps Firewood and Outdoor Items Dry

Need more outdoor storage space? Try this generous-size box—it's big enough to hold firewood, outdoor furniture cushions and more.

THIS VERSATILE BOX is sturdy enough to last a lifetime, yet light enough to be easily moved when empty. It has a multitude of uses, too.

It's designed to hold firewood, but you can use it to store outdoor furniture cushions, lawn and garden supplies, sports equipment or other outdoor items. It also makes a convenient serving buffet when entertaining on the patio.

The box's removable floor makes cleanup a breeze. Foot pads keep it off the ground, which keeps your contents nice and dry.

For safety and convenience, we've included a lid support with a "lock" to hold it firmly in place. And a chain keeps the lid from falling backward.

Apply a coat of protective stain and the box can be put to use year-round.

Here's What You'll Need...

- ❏ Eight 8-foot 2 x 4's
- ❏ One 4-foot 1-inch x 4-inch board
- ❏ Two 4-foot x 8-foot sheets of 3/8-inch grooved fir paneling
- ❏ One 4-foot x 4-foot sheet of 1/2-inch plywood
- ❏ One 6-foot 2-inch x 6-inch board
- ❏ One 8-foot 1-inch x 6-inch No. 2 pine board
- ❏ 2-1/2-inch, 2-inch, 1-5/8-inch and 1-1/4-inch galvanized deck screws
- ❏ 7/8-inch No. 8 flathead brass wood screws
- ❏ 1-1/4-inch finishing nails
- ❏ 3/4-inch No. 10 and 1/2-inch No. 6 round-head screws
- ❏ One small strap (to anchor chain)
- ❏ One small flush-ring handle (optional for lifting floor)
- ❏ One 48-inch brass piano hinge
- ❏ Two heavy-duty handles
- ❏ 12 inches of light chain for lid
- ❏ Waterproof construction adhesive
- ❏ Exterior stain

Recommended Tools...

- ❏ Table saw
- ❏ Circular saw
- ❏ Miter box
- ❏ Hacksaw
- ❏ Power drill
- ❏ Countersink bit
- ❏ Rafter square
- ❏ Two bar clamps (48-inch capacity)

AT YOUR SERVICE. Besides holding firewood, gardening or other outdoor items, this sturdy wood storage box looks good enough to use as a serving buffet for outdoor entertaining.

Time to Build the Box

1. Cut pieces for the frame as described in cutting list on page 171.

2. Assemble front and back 2 x 4 frames on a workbench or other flat surface using 2-1/2-inch deck screws. Use a rafter square as you go. (It's important to assemble on a flat surface for this step so you don't build any "wobble" into the project.) Predrill the screw holes. Drive screws at an angle from the top and bottom in "toe-nailing" fashion. Clamping will help hold these pieces in place while toe nailing.

3. Fasten front and back frames to end 2 x 4's with 2-1/2-inch deck screws. Install floor supports flush to the bottom of the frame with 2-1/2-inch deck screws. Fasten the end 1-inch x 3-inch x 19-inch floor supports to the ends of the frame with 1-5/8-inch deck screws.

4. Cut side and end panels as shown on page 171 from a 4-foot x 8-foot sheet of grooved fir paneling.

Here's a hint…before you start sawing the paneling, test-cut a piece from the second sheet of paneling. (You'll cut the lid from this piece later and will have some excess material.) If you don't get a clean test cut, it's worth buying a new plywood saw blade.

Glue end panels to the framework with beads of waterproof construction adhesive, then fasten with 1-1/4-inch deck screws around the perimeter. Position screws 7/16 inch from the edge so they'll be covered by molding. After the ends are attached, fasten the side panels to overlap the ends.

5. Make the lid by rough-cutting a piece of paneling 25-1/2 inches x 49-1/2 inches. The grooves should run lengthwise—double-check this before cutting.

Turn the sheet of paneling grooved side down on a flat surface. Lay a 2-foot x 4-foot piece of 1/2-inch plywood on top of the paneling, with the rougher side facing the back of the paneling. Glue the plywood and paneling together with waterproof construction adhesive and align the pieces along one straight edge that runs parallel with the grooves. Tack the pieces together close to the edge with three or four finishing nails to keep them from sliding. Then weight the pieces down or clamp well. Allow 24 hours drying time.

Remove any glue that has seeped out of the aligned edge of the paneling and plywood, because this is the edge that will be guided by your table saw's fence as you cut the lid to size. A clean edge is needed to cut it square.

6. Cut the lid to its finished size of 23-3/4 inches x 47-7/8 inches.

7. As insurance to keep the pieces from separating later, fasten them together with 7/8-inch No. 8 flathead brass wood screws around the underside of the lid. You'll need about 30 screws, positioned about an inch from the edge and spaced 4 to 5 inches apart.

8. Rip the rest of the 8-foot 1-inch x 6-inch pine board to 2-3/8 inches for the lid moldings. Measure the lid to determine the length of the end moldings, which will fit flush with the top panel.

Attach the end moldings with waterproof construction adhesive. Clamp and allow the glue to dry before fastening with 1-1/4-inch deck screws. Predrill and countersink the screws 1/2 inch down from the top edge using a 3/32-inch drill bit. Drill 1-1/4 inches deep. Measure and space the screws evenly, about 6 inches apart.

After the end moldings are attached, cut the front and back moldings to fit and attach them the same way. Put the lid aside until step 12.

9. Cut the floor from the remaining sheet of 1/2-inch plywood. The floor will measure 18-3/4 inches x 42-7/8 inches. Attach a small flush-ring handle at one end so the floor can be lifted for cleaning.

10. Rip a lid support from a 2 x 4 scrap (or if you

have any hardwood, use it) measuring 1/4 inch thick and 1-1/8 inch wide. Cut this piece 21-1/2 inches long. *The support must be free of knots or it will break under the weight of the lid.* Fasten on one end with a 1-5/8-inch pivot screw 1-3/4 inches from the front of the box so it is flush with the top of the outside frame (predrill the hole so the support doesn't split).

Attach a 1/2-inch No. 6 round-head screw to the top end of the lid support (predrill the hole) that will contact the lid. Allow the screw to protrude from the support stick 1/4 inch, including the head. Then attach a small wood block below the support stick for it to rest on when not being used (see detailed drawing on the next page).

11. Make the box's trim *(Continued on next page)*

TRAPDOOR. The floor of the storage box is removable for easy cleaning. Just grab the small flush-ring handle and lift.

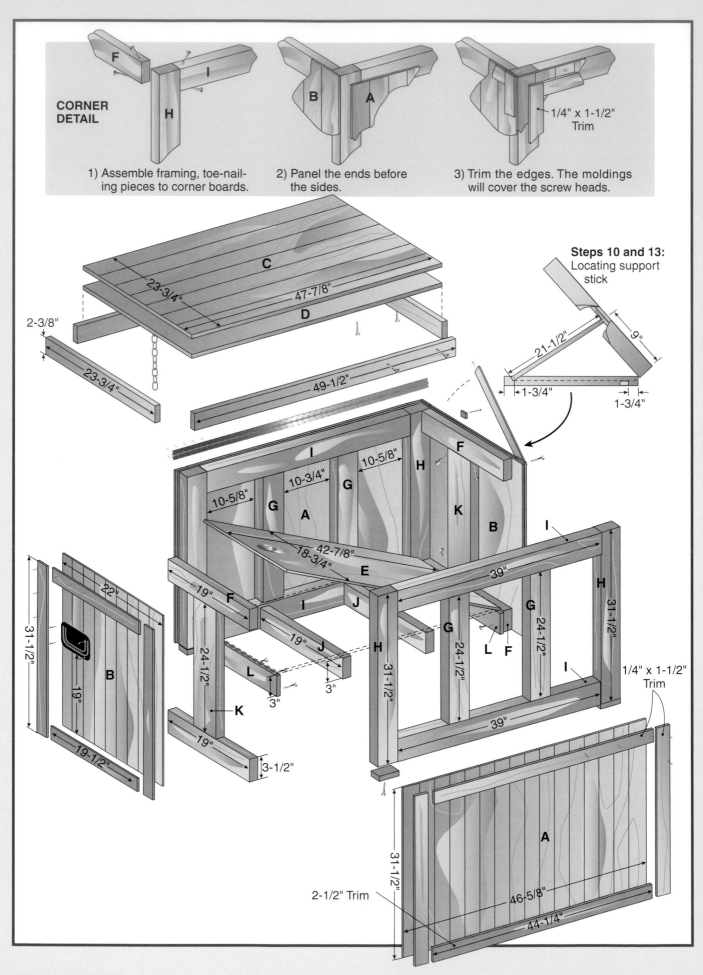

CORNER DETAIL

1) Assemble framing, toe-nailing pieces to corner boards.

2) Panel the ends before the sides.

3) Trim the edges. The moldings will cover the screw heads.

1/4" x 1-1/2" Trim

Steps 10 and 13: Locating support stick

2-3/8"

23-3/4"

23-3/4"

47-7/8"

49-1/2"

21-1/2"

9"

1-3/4"

1-3/4"

10-5/8"

10-3/4"

10-5/8"

42-7/8"

18-3/4"

19"

19"

3"

3"

39"

31-1/2"

24-1/2"

24-1/2"

31-1/2"

39"

1/4" x 1-1/2" Trim

22"

31-1/2"

19"

24-1/2"

19-1/2"

19"

3-1/2"

31-1/2"

46-5/8"

2-1/2" Trim

44-1/4"

Here's a Cutting List To Help...

From eight 2 x 4's, cut:

- Four top and bottom end frame pieces, 19 inches long (F)
- Four vertical frame pieces, 24-1/2 inches long (G)
- Four vertical corner boards, 31-1/2 inches long (H)
- Four front and back horizontal pieces, 39 inches long (I)
- Two 3-inch x 19-inch floor supports. (Cut a length of 2 x 4 to 39 inches, rip to 3 inches, then cut the 19-inch pieces.) (J)

From one 2-inch x 6-inch board, cut:

- Two vertical end pieces, 24-1/2 inches long (K)

From one 1-inch x 4-inch board, cut:

- Two end floor supports, 3 inches x 19 inches (L)

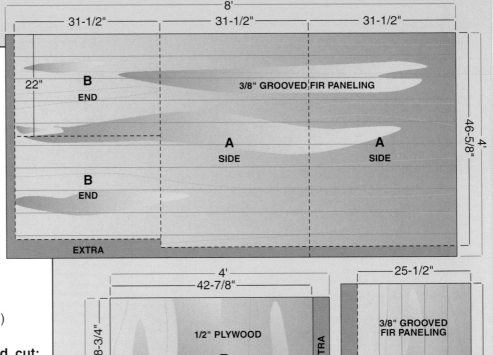

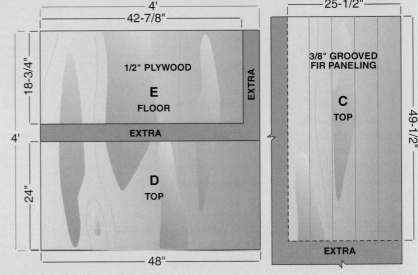

moldings from a 2 x 4. Rip three 8-foot 1/4-inch x 1-1/2-inch pieces. Cut the vertical corner moldings to fit flush with top and bottom of the box, making two pieces for each corner. One molding will overlap the other piece.

Attach the molding starting at the front corners. Fasten the vertical molding strips on the sides first with waterproof construction adhesive and 1-1/4-inch finishing nails. Don't drive the nails home until you attach front molding to overlap it. When you're happy with the position and fit, drive the nails home. Attach the back corner moldings the same way.

When all corner moldings are in place, cut the horizontal moldings to fit. Attach with waterproof construction adhesive and 1-1/4-inch finishing nails.

12. Center the lid end to end, allowing space for the support stick. Leave a 1/8-inch gap at the back and a 3/8-inch gap at the front. Cut the 48-inch brass piano hinge to 45-1/2 inches with a hacksaw. Center the hinge and screw it to the back of the box. When you're sure the lid is properly positioned, find someone to sit on it as you attach it. Recheck the position of the lid after your "sitter" is in place to make sure it didn't shift. Start the holes with an awl and fasten a *few screws*. Check to make sure the lid opens and closes properly before fastening the rest of the screws.

13. Lift the lid and use the support stick to hold it open. The support stick should meet the lid at approximately a 90° angle 9 inches from the back corner. Mark the spot where the protruding screw meets the lid. Drill a shallow hole the size of the screw head in the bottom of the lid for it to rest when the lid is open. This will basically lock the lid in the open position—a reassuring thought when you're working below it.

14. Attach a 1-foot safety chain to one end of the lid with a strong metal strap to prevent it from falling backward. Attach the other end of the chain to a back corner piece (H) with a round-head screw.

15. Fasten the end handles 19 inches from the bottom of the box. (This may vary with different handles.) The screws must attach to the 24-1/2-inch vertical end pieces to give them the strength needed to support the weight of the box when lifted.

16. Cut four 3-1/2-inch-square foot pads from a scrap of 3/4-inch wood. If you have green-treated lumber, use that; if not, you can use scrap pine, but be sure to stain all the sides of the foot pads. Predrill holes and attach to the bottom with 2-inch deck screws.

17. Stain the box to protect it from the elements and let it dry. Now you're ready to fill 'er up.

Bring the 'Swing Era' Back to Life

Whether hanging from porch rafters or mounted on a custom stand as pictured, this project will surely lull you to sleep.

MANY OF US have fond memories of a favorite porch swing. The very sight of one brings back images of a simpler era, when people had time to sit back and visit as the swing slowly creaked back and forth.

This swing is based on a design staffer Sally Chadwick shared with us. It was made by her grandfather, the late Bert Brixey of Springfield, Missouri, nearly 50 years ago. It brings back many cherished memories for her—and is sure to make new ones for you and your family.

"We never really thought of Grandpa as a craftsman, but he did come up with the design on his own," Sally says. "I haven't seen anything like it since."

Sally was the proud caretaker of her grandfather's swing for many years, and she was delighted with assistant editor Cliff Muehlenberg's updated garden swing based on photographs of the original design.

"It was a thrill to see it," Sally says. "It's a true pleasure to see a swing just like it again."

This garden swing is designed to be hung as a traditional porch swing or suspended from the sturdy free-standing frame like the one Sally's grandfather designed.

We've included separate plans for both so you can pick and choose what best suits your place.

Since our version is made from No. 2 pine, it's important to be choosy when selecting lumber. You most likely won't find any boards that are completely knot-free, but if you choose lumber with small knots, you'll have ample opportunity to cut them away. (See "Workshop Wisdom" on page 174 for a helpful hint.) The result will be a showpiece swing that looks like it was made with high-quality lumber.

Most of the screws in this project will be attached near the ends of the boards, so all holes should be predrilled and countersunk. (See "Workshop Wisdom" on page 93 for a helpful hint.) If you don't already own a combination drill bit/countersink for No. 8 screws, you might want to consider buying one for this project. The professional look it will give the finished garden swing is well worth its price (about $7).

When you're finished, friends and family will be so impressed, you just may find more people swinging on over for a visit on warm summer nights.

Garden Swing:
Here's What You'll Need...

❑ Five 8-foot 1-inch x 8-inch No. 2 pine boards

❑ One 4-foot 1-inch x 10-inch No. 2 pine board

❑ Two 8-foot 2 x 4's (as free of knots as possible)

❑ One 4-foot 2-inch x 6-inch board

❑ 2-1/2-inch, 2-inch, 1-5/8-inch and 1-1/4-inch galvanized deck screws

❑ 2-inch galvanized finishing nails

❑ Two 3/8-inch x 4-inch carriage bolts

❑ Eight 3/8-inch x 3-1/2-inch carriage bolts

❑ Four 3/8-inch x 4-inch lag bolts

❑ Four 3/8-inch x 2-1/2-inch eyebolts

❑ Twenty-four 3/8-inch washers

❑ Eighteen 3/8-inch nuts

❑ Heavy-duty chain to hang the swing (6 feet if using the freestanding frame pictured)

❑ Eight heavy-duty S hooks

Recommended Tools...

❑ Table saw
❑ Saber saw
❑ Power drill
❑ Dust mask

❑ Router/Router table
❑ Router bits (3/8-inch roundover bit)
❑ Rafter square
❑ Clamps

Let's Start Swinging
...the Hammer!

1. Examine the edges along the length of four 8-foot 1-inch x 8-inch pine boards. If they need to be cleaned up (because the edges are nicked, dirty, etc.), trim them off by ripping the boards about half the thickness of the saw blade.

2. Rip three 2-1/4-inch-wide boards from each 1-inch x 8-inch board. This will create a considerable amount of sawdust, so it's a good idea to wear a dust mask.

3. Cut the ends of the seat frame first. To do this, rip a 2 x 4 to 3 inches wide. From that board, cut two pieces 16-1/4 inches long, then cut a notch in each end as shown below.

4. From 2-1/4-inch stock, cut front and back seat supports 44 inches long. These pieces must be free of

large knots for strength. Attach them to the ends of the seat frame with 2-1/2-inch deck screws. (Remember to predrill and countersink holes throughout this project.) These supports should rest flush in the notches cut in the end pieces. Keep the frame square as you fasten the screws.

5. Cut four vertical armrest supports from a 2 x 4. Start by cutting a 48-inch-long piece, then rip to 2-3/4 inches wide. Cut into four pieces 11-3/4 inches long.

6. Attach both front armrest supports. Position them flush with the bottom of the frame and 3/4 inch from the front, which will be even with the rear edge of the notch. Square these pieces and drill two holes for 3/8-inch x 3-1/2-inch carriage bolts. Make sure these holes are staggered for strength (see photo above). Attach supports to the frame.

Step 6: Attach armrest support to seat frame with two carriage bolts. Place bolts diagonally for strength.

7. Cut two 17-1/2-inch-long backrest supports from clear 2-1/4-inch stock. Round one top corner of each piece with a saber saw. Draw a guideline with a compass or a half-pint paint can.

8. Follow the illustration below to set the backrest support at the proper angle. Position the piece measuring

(Continued on next page)

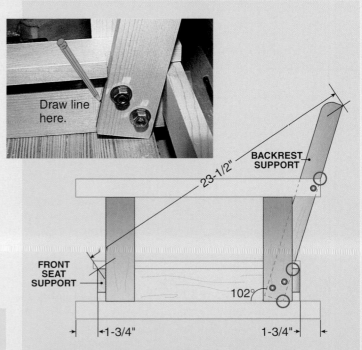

Draw line here.

23-1/2"

BACKREST SUPPORT

FRONT SEAT SUPPORT

102°

1-3/4" 1-3/4"

Step 8: The angle of the backrest support is set by measuring 23-1/2 inches from the top edge of the front seat support to the top outside corner of the backrest support. Blue shaded pieces have not been attached yet, but give an idea of how pieces will line up when finished.

Step 3

3/4"

2-1/4"   3"

16-1/4"

23-1/2 inches from the top outside corner of the front seat support to the top outside corner of the backrest support as pictured. Clamp backrest support in place. Then draw a line along the backrest support on the inside of the seat frame ends (see photo on previous page).

Place the back armrest supports in position, lining them up flush with the bottom of the frame and 3/4 inch from the back of it, which will be even with the edge of the notch. Square these pieces and clamp to the seat frame and the backrest supports. Double-check that the pieces are square and the backrest support is still sitting along the pencil line.

Drill two 3/8-inch holes through all three pieces for 3/8-

inch x 3-1/2-inch carriage bolts and attach. The holes should be staggered as in step 6.

9. Make the armrests by ripping a 2 x 4 to 3-1/4 inches wide. Cut two pieces 19 inches long from it. Round the front end of each armrest with a saber saw. Draw a semicircle with a compass, or use a pint paint can as a template.

Also round the edges of the best-looking side of each armrest with a router, using a 3/8-inch roundover bit.

Step 9: For added comfort, round front of armrest and top edges.

Attach the armrests to their supports with 2-1/2-inch deck screws (see photo above).

10. Cut fifteen seat boards 17 inches long from 2-1/4-inch stock. Eliminate knots whenever they are near the ends of the board.

11. Shape the front edge of each board using a router table with a 3/8-inch roundover bit. Choose the best-looking side of each board and rout that side only. Since you'll be routing across the ends of the boards, the wood will tend to chip at the end of

each cut. To prevent this, "back up" each board with a scrap piece as it is pushed through the router bit. Use the same scrap piece to back up the rest of the boards.

12. Notch the two outside seat boards with a hand saw or saber saw so the back ends fit between the backrest supports and back armrest supports.

13. Attach the seat boards to the frame. Predrill each board for 2-inch finishing nails. Use a drill bit (not a nail as we did in some other projects in this book) slightly smaller than the finishing nails for a tight fit.

Position the two notched outside boards first, then space the remaining boards 3/4 inch apart between them. Use another seat board on edge as a spacer to quickly determine the gap between the boards (see photo below). Square each board to the front seat support and tack them lightly in place. Don't drive the nails "home" until all the boards are in place and you've made sure they're square and properly spaced. Finish nailing so the heads are *flush* with the surface. *Don't countersink* or the holes made from it will collect water.

Step 13: Use a loose seat board to measure 3/4-inch space between the other seat boards. Don't drive nails home until all boards are evenly spaced.

Step 14: The armrest attaches to the armrest supports and backrest supports. Notice how the washer and nut at the back edge of the armrest sits inside a predrilled hole.

14. Bore a hole 3/8 inch deep with a 7/8-inch spade bit in the side of each armrest. Center this hole 7/8 inch from the back of each armrest. (See "Workshop Wisdom" on page 25 for a helpful hint.) Then finish drilling hole with a 3/8-inch drill bit, boring through the armrest and backrest support on both sides of the swing. Secure the pieces with 3/8-inch x 4-inch carriage bolts. The 3/8-

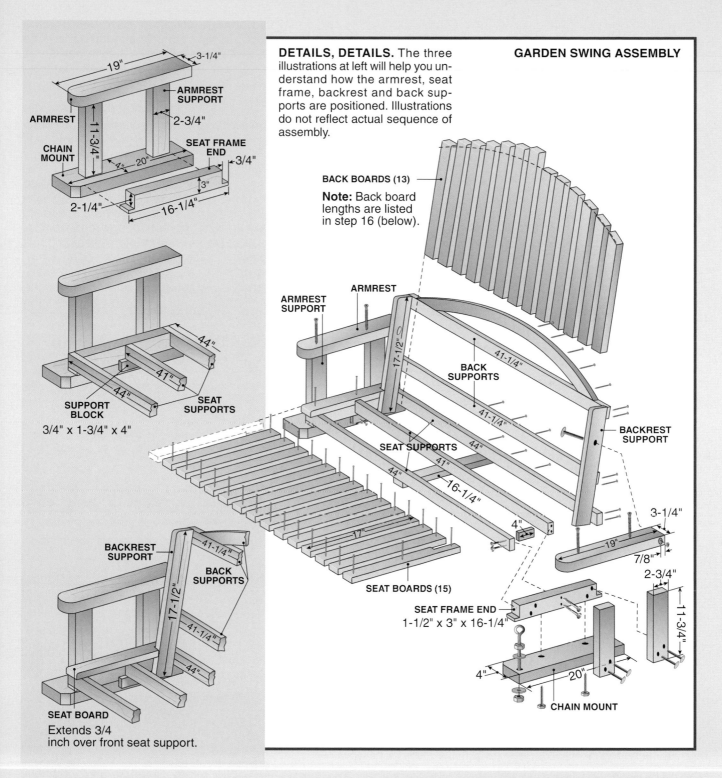

DETAILS, DETAILS. The three illustrations at left will help you understand how the armrest, seat frame, backrest and back supports are positioned. Illustrations do not reflect actual sequence of assembly.

GARDEN SWING ASSEMBLY

ARMREST
ARMREST SUPPORT
CHAIN MOUNT
SEAT FRAME END
19"
3-1/4"
2-3/4"
3/4"
11-3/4"
4" 20"
3"
2-1/4"
16-1/4"

44"
41"
44"
SUPPORT BLOCK
3/4" x 1-3/4" x 4"
SEAT SUPPORTS

BACKREST SUPPORT
BACK SUPPORTS
41-1/4"
41-1/4"
17-1/2"
44"

SEAT BOARD
Extends 3/4 inch over front seat support.

BACK BOARDS (13)
Note: Back board lengths are listed in step 16 (below).

ARMREST SUPPORT
ARMREST
BACK SUPPORTS
17-1/2"
41-1/4"
41-1/4"
SEAT SUPPORTS
44"
41"
44"
16-1/4"
17"
4"
BACKREST SUPPORT
3-1/4"
19"
7/8"
2-3/4"
11-3/4"
SEAT BOARDS (15)
SEAT FRAME END
1-1/2" x 3" x 16-1/4"
CHAIN MOUNT
4" 20"

inch nut and washer will neatly rest inside the 7/8-inch hole (see bottom left photo).

15. Select two pieces of 2-1/4-inch stock for the horizontal back supports. *It's important that these pieces be free of large knots.* Cut them to 41-1/4 inches long.

Position the lower back support 2 inches above the seat boards and the upper support flush with the top of the backrest supports. (See plan above and photo at bottom of page 178.) Drill and countersink two holes at both ends of each board and attach them with 2-inch deck screws.

16. Cut thirteen back boards from 2-1/4-inch stock, eliminating knots wherever possible. Cut *two pieces each* at 16-1/2 inches, 19 inches, 20-1/2 inches, 21-1/2 inches, 22-1/4 inches and 22-1/2 inches. Cut *one* piece at 22-3/4 inches for the center board.

17. Lay the swing on the floor, resting it on its back. Position the back boards 3/4 inch above the seat boards. Start by laying out the shortest pieces at the ends and work toward the middle. Space the pieces 3/4 inch apart (again use a piece of 3/4-inch stock for spacing),

(Continued on next page)

squaring them to the horizontal back supports as you go. Each back board should line up with a seat board. Do not attach until step 20.

Step 18

18. Assemble a string-and-pencil "compass" for drawing the arc on the back boards. Attach the string (use string without a lot of elasticity) with a nail or small screw eye so it's centered on the middle seat board just below the back boards (see photo at left).

Place your pencil point at the outside edge of an outermost back board so it is 3/4 inch above the upper horizontal back support (mark this spot for step 19). Wrap the string around the pencil a few times, pulling it tight while keeping the pencil in place. Tape the pencil to the string when it is taut.

Now that the pencil is attached, swing it to the same position on the other outside back board. The pencil should again line up 3/4 inch above the horizontal support (again, mark here for step 19). If it's not, make sure the string is tacked in the *center* of the middle seat board and that all the "stretch" is out of the string before attaching the pencil.

No Porch? No Problem

With this sturdy base, your swing can stand (or glide) on its own... wherever you like.

IN YEARS PAST, it was a rare front porch that didn't have a swing. Today, it's the porch itself that's a rarity.

This stand, designed for use with the garden swing plan that starts on page 173, allows you to glide in comfort wherever you like. Set up the swing in sun or shade, on the patio or the deck, near your garden or bird feeders. All you need is a level surface...and a spot with a beautiful view.

Let's Start Building

1. Cut the pieces listed in the cutting list at bottom right.

2. Make a 3-1/2-inch dado, 1/2 inch deep, on each upright. The dadoes start 3 inches below the top of each upright. The 2 x 4 arms should fit tightly into each dado.

3. Round the tops of the uprights. Draw an arc with a 2-5/8-inch radius and cut with a saber saw. Smooth with sandpaper.

4. Center a 5-1/4-inch dado, 3/4 inch deep, on each base running across the 7-1/4-inch width. The 2 x 6's should fit tightly into these dadoes.

5. Round the top corners of the arms. Draw a cutting line with a 1-3/8-inch radius, or trace a half-pint paint can. Cut and sand.

6. Center one upright into a dado on one base piece. Line up the bottoms so they're flush and clamp in place. Drill four holes through the two pieces and fasten together with 3/8-inch x 3-inch carriage bolts, washers and nuts. Assemble the other upright and base piece the same way.

7. Fasten the base connectors to each base. Position the connectors on end, one on each side of the uprights. Bore 3/8-inch holes

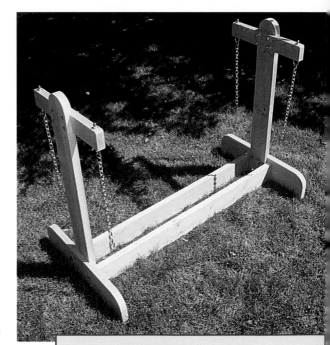

Swing Stand: Here's What You'll Need...

- ❏ One 6-foot 2-inch x 8-inch board
- ❏ One 8-foot 2-inch x 6-inch board
- ❏ Two 6-foot 2-inch x 6-inch boards
- ❏ One 6-foot 2 x 4 (as free of knots as possible)
- ❏ Sixteen 3/8-inch x 3-inch carriage bolts
- ❏ Eight 3/8-inch x 4-inch lag bolts
- ❏ Four 4-inch eyebolts
- ❏ Twenty-eight 3/8-inch washers
- ❏ Twenty 3/8-inch nuts
- ❏ Twelve 3/8-inch acorn nuts

Step 20

SPACER

19. Draw the arc, starting from either of the points that are marked on an outside back board in step 18. Make a sweeping arc that ends at the other point on the other side of the seat back. *Be very careful* not to move any of the back pieces as you draw since they're not attached!

20. Using a saber saw, cut the top of each back board along the line you just drew. Sand the cut edges and attach the pieces from the back with 1-1/4-inch deck screws. Spring clamps work well for holding

the pieces in place as you square and align them with the seat boards. (Remember they're 3/4 inch above the seat boards.) A scrap piece of 3/4-inch lumber can be used as a spacer at the bottom of each board to set them in position (see photo at left).

21. Make the chain mounts by cutting two 20-inch pieces from the 2-inch x 6-inch board. These pieces support the entire swing.

Drill two 3/8-inch perpendicular holes for 3/8-inch x 2-1/2-inch eyebolts. Locate these holes as indicated on the illustration at the bottom of page 178. Then locate and drill the two 5/16-inch holes for 4-inch lag bolts as shown in the illustration.

22. Attach the chain mount pieces to the swing. These pieces should be centered (front to back) on the ends of the frame. The inside edges of each

(Continued on next page)

---

into each base board, and 5/16-inch pilot holes 3 inches deep into the ends of the base connectors. Make sure these holes line up by drilling the 5/16-inch hole through both pieces first. Then enlarge the hole in the base to 3/8 inch. Attach with 3/8-inch x 4-inch lag bolts and washers from the outside of the base pieces.

8. Attach base pads to the underside of the bases with 1-1/4-inch deck screws. Drill pilot holes first.

9. Connect the arms to the uprights. Center the 2 x 4's in the dadoes cut in step 2. Bore four 3/8-inch holes through both pieces. Attach each arm with four 3/8-inch x 3-inch carriage bolts, washers and nuts. Add acorn nuts on the ends.

10. Drill vertical holes for eyebolts through each arm. Locate these

holes 1-1/2 inches in from each end. Insert 4-inch eyebolts from the underside. Tighten with 3/8-inch nuts and washers. Top with acorn nuts.

11. Attach chains to the eyebolts with S hooks. You'll need 15-1/2 inches of chain for the front eyebolts and 18 inches for the back. After you've suspended the swing and made sure it's level, close the upper S hooks with a grip-type pliers. Leave the bottom hooks open so the swing can be removed from the stand when moving it or for storage. Now have a seat...and start swinging!

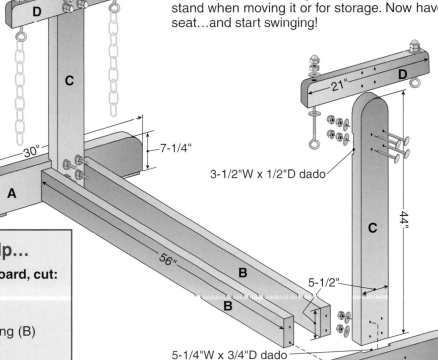

3"
1-1/2"
D
C
30"
7-1/4"
A
56"
B
B
21"
D
3-1/2"W x 1/2"D dado
44"
C
5-1/2"
5-1/4"W x 3/4"D dado
A
E
E
3/4" x 1-1/2" x 3-1/2"

Here's a Cutting List to Help...

From one 6-foot 2-inch x 8-inch board, cut:
• Two bases, 30 inches long (A)

From 2-inch x 6-inch boards, cut:
• Two base connectors, 56 inches long (B)
• Two uprights, 44 inches long (C)

From one 6-foot 2 x 4, cut:
• Two arms, 21 inches long (D)
• Rip four 3/4-inch x 1-1/2-inch x 3-1/2-inch base pads (E)

chain mount should be flush with the inside edge of the seat frame ends.

Mark the location of the holes for the lag bolts and drill 5/16-inch holes 2-1/4 inches deep. Fasten each mount to the swing with two 3/8-inch x 4-inch lag bolts and washers.

23. Attach 2-1/2-inch eyebolts through the chain mount holes. Use 3/8-inch nuts and washers on top of the chain mount and another set below the mounts. Tighten the nuts toward each other using two wrenches.

24. Cut a center seat support 41 inches long from knot-free 2-1/4-inch stock. Fasten with two 2-1/2-inch deck screws through each end. Be sure to drill perpendicular pilot holes.

25. Cut two 3/4-inch x 1-3/4-inch x 4-inch blocks and place below and against the center seat support. Drill pilot holes and fasten with 1-5/8-inch deck screws.

26. From 2-1/4-inch stock, cut a 16-1/4-inch-long seat support. Fasten this piece centered to the underside of the front and back seat supports with 1-5/8-inch deck screws (see photo at bottom right).

27. Clamp a 39-1/2-inch piece of 1-inch x 10-inch pine board at the top of the back boards. Mark the position of the outermost boards on this piece. Remove the board and use your string-and-pencil "compass" to draw two arcs between these marks—one with a 25-3/8-inch radius and one with a 23-1/8-inch radius. Cut out the support with a saber saw and sand.

Center the arc on the back of the swing so each end

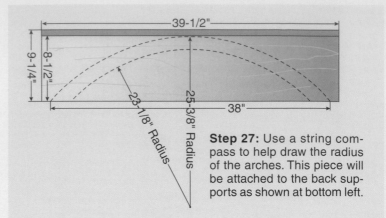

Step 27: Use a string compass to help draw the radius of the arches. This piece will be attached to the back supports as shown at bottom left.

sits on top of the upper horizontal back support and at the outside edges of the outermost back boards (see photo at bottom left). Clamp it in place and fasten to each back board with one 1-1/4-inch deck screw from the back side. Predrill and countersink the holes first.

28. Before you take a seat, you'll need to mount the swing to a *sturdy support* with chain. The rear chain should be 2-1/2 inches longer than the front chains. Use heavy-duty S hooks to attach the chain to the eyebolts. Crimp the hook ends closed with a grip-type pliers. Fasten the other end of the chain to anchors in porch rafters with S hooks, leaving them open so the swing can be removed if needed. If you don't have a porch, no need to worry—just make the sturdy freestanding frame by following the plan on page 176.

Swing the night away—you've earned it!

Step 21: Chain mounts (make two).

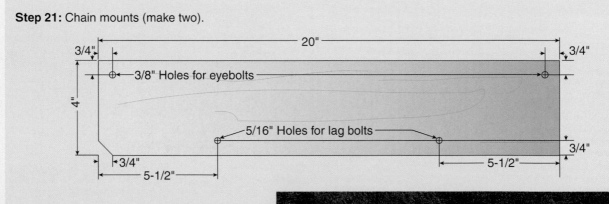

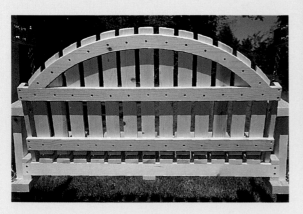

BACK AND BOTTOM. Plenty of support is given to the backrest and seat of this garden swing. These detailed photos of the finished project will help as you assemble your swing.